AF323033

# POLITICAL CORRUPTION AND CORPORATE FINANCE

# Transformations in Banking, Finance and Regulation

Print ISSN: 2752-5821
Online ISSN: 2752-583X

Series Editors:  Sabri Boubaker
*(EM Normandie Business School, France)*
Duc Khuong Nguyen
*(EMLV Business School, France)*

---

Presently, the banking and finance sectors evolve within a globalized and highly uncertain environment. Each business and financial decision requires careful consideration of country-specific and international factors due to high levels of shock transmission and volatility spillovers. Furthermore, it would be remiss to omit the COVID-19 health crisis, which caused harmful effects to all areas of the real economy and made profound changes in the way our firms, economies, and markets used to function.

Many other already well-known aspects, including the repercussions of quantitative easing policies, disruptive technologies in finance (e.g., FinTech, Big Data, Data Analytics, Artificial Intelligence, and Blockchains), as well as innovative financing instruments for startups (e.g., ICOs and crowdfunding) are currently revolutionizing banking and finance and posing numerous challenges to regulatory bodies and policymakers. Climate change emergencies also put pressure on governments and firms worldwide to improve policy on governance, corporate social responsibility, and sustainability practices.

This book series "Transformations in Banking, Finance and Regulation" attempts to address these issues by focusing on transformative perspectives in banking and finance. Accordingly, it provides evidence-based guidance, recommendations, and pathways to assist businesses and policy decision-makers through an interdisciplinary and in-depth understanding of ongoing changes in the behavior of economic agents.

*Published*

Vol. 8    *Political Corruption and Corporate Finance*
by Quoc Trung Tran and Duc Khuong Nguyen

Vol. 7    *Corporate Risk Management after the COVID-19 Crisis*
edited by Suman Lodh and Monomita Nandy

Vol. 6    *Islamic Accounting and Finance: A Handbook*
edited by Khaled Hussainey and Hidaya Al Lawati

Vol. 5    *FinTech Research and Applications: Challenges and Opportunities*
edited by Daisy Chou, Conall O'Sullivan and Vassilios G Papavassiliou

For the complete list of volumes in this series, please visit
www.worldscientific.com/series/tbfr

Transformations in Banking, Finance and Regulation
Volume 8

# POLITICAL CORRUPTION AND CORPORATE FINANCE

**Quoc Trung Tran**
*Foreign Trade University, Vietnam*

**Duc Khuong Nguyen**
*EMLV Business School, France*

**World Scientific**

NEW JERSEY · LONDON · SINGAPORE · BEIJING · SHANGHAI · HONG KONG · TAIPEI · CHENNAI · TOKYO

*Published by*

World Scientific Publishing Europe Ltd.

57 Shelton Street, Covent Garden, London WC2H 9HE

*Head office:* 5 Toh Tuck Link, Singapore 596224

*USA office:* 27 Warren Street, Suite 401-402, Hackensack, NJ 07601


**Library of Congress Cataloging-in-Publication Data**

Names: Trần, Quốc Trung, author.

Title: Political corruption and corporate finance / Quoc Trung Tran, Foreign Trade University,
  Vietnam, Duc Khuong Nguyen, EMLV Business School, France.

Description: Hackensack, NJ : World Scientific, [2024] | Series: Transformations in banking,
  finance and regulation, 2752-5821 ; vol. 8 | Includes bibliographical references and index.

Identifiers: LCCN 2023016732 | ISBN 9781800614253 (hardcover) |
  ISBN 9781800614260 (ebook for institutions) | ISBN 9781800614277 (ebook for individuals)

Subjects: LCSH: Corporations--Finance. | Political corruption.

Classification: LCC HG4026 .T7177 2024 | DDC 658.15--dc23/eng/20230524

LC record available at https://lccn.loc.gov/2023016732


**British Library Cataloguing-in-Publication Data**

A catalogue record for this book is available from the British Library.


Copyright © 2024 by World Scientific Publishing Europe Ltd.

*All rights reserved. This book, or parts thereof, may not be reproduced in any form or by any means,
electronic or mechanical, including photocopying, recording or any information storage and retrieval
system now known or to be invented, without written permission from the Publisher.*


For photocopying of material in this volume, please pay a copying fee through the Copyright Clearance
Center, Inc., 222 Rosewood Drive, Danvers, MA 01923, USA. In this case permission to photocopy
is not required from the publisher.


For any available supplementary material, please visit
https://www.worldscientific.com/worldscibooks/10.1142/Q0420#t=suppl


Desk Editors: Soundararajan Raghuraman/Rosie Williamson/Shi Ying Koe

Typeset by Stallion Press
Email: enquiries@stallionpress.com

# Preface

Political corruption is public servants' exploitation of public power to serve their personal benefits. It is considered "public enemy number one" since it erodes people's trust in the government, squanders public resources and deepens social injustice. According to the World Economic Forum (2018), the world economy incurs a cost of US$3.6 trillion (equivalent to 5% of the world GDP) due to corruption. Especially, political corruption is more severe in developing and transition countries where the political, legal and economic environment lacks transparency and accountability.

From a taboo topic in the early 1990s, corruption has become an intriguing issue in economics and has attracted much attention from academics and practitioners. In their pioneering macro-economic research, Mauro (1995) typically finds that political corruption reduces investment, thereby deteriorating economic growth. Subsequent studies have shown the negative effects of corruption on many macro-economic variables such as foreign direct investment, wages and export revenues as well as the positive effect of corruption on inflation growth (Al-Marhubi, 2000; Jain, 2001; Lambsdorff, 1999; Lambsdorff & Cornelius, 2000). After documenting consistent evidence of the relationship between political corruption and macro-economic factors, scholars have started to investigate how political corruption, as an institutional factor, affects corporate decisions in recent years. This book tells a story about corporate finance decisions in a corrupt environment.

The field of corporate finance involves a whole set of decisions made by corporate managers to maximize shareholders' wealth. These decisions are often classified into three groups, namely, investment decisions (to invest corporate resources that firms have mobilized either internally or externally), financing decisions (to raise and allocate funds for these investment projects) and dividend decisions (to disgorge cash to shareholders). According to Modigliani and Miller (1958), corporate financial decisions are irrelevant in a perfect capital market. For example, corporate investment only relies on investment opportunities; firms are indifferent to all sources of funds, and dividend payment is not related to firm value. However, market frictions make corporate finance relevant in the real world. As an essential factor in the institutional environment, political corruption affects corporate financial decisions through these market frictions.

This book aims at providing readers with a comprehensive overview of corruption-related issues and theoretical and empirical studies in corporate finance. Especially, it analyzes how political corruption at both country and local levels determines corporate financial decisions. This is the first book tackling the effect of political corruption on corporate finance by summarizing and analyzing this new line of research to help readers understand how a corrupt environment affects firm-level financial behavior. The first three chapters introduce political corruption, the status of political corruption and anti-corruption campaigns around the world. The last three chapters focus on how firms make financial decisions and the role of political corruption in corporate finance.

# About the Authors

 **Quoc Trung Tran** is an Associate Professor at the Foreign Trade University (Vietnam). He is also the Vice Director of Ho Chi Minh City Campus of Foreign Trade University. He holds a Ph.D. in Management Science from University of Lille (France). His research focus is on corporate finance, corporate governance and international business. He has published many papers in *Economic Modelling, Research in International Business and Finance, The North American Journal of Economics and Finance, Economic Analysis and Policy, The Quarterly Review of Economics and Finance, Journal of Multinational Financial Management, International Journal of Emerging Markets, Australian Journal of Management* and *Multinational Business Review*, etc. Most of his works are about the effect of the business environment on corporate finance and corporate finance in emerging markets. He has served as a reviewer of many high-quality journals in finance and business.

**Duc Khuong Nguyen** is a Professor of Finance and Associate Dean of EMLV Business School (France). He holds a Ph.D. in Finance from the University of Grenoble Alpes (France), obtained an HDR (Habilitation for Supervising Scientific Research) in Management Science from the CY Cergy Paris University (France), and completed an executive education program in "Leadership in Development" at Harvard Kennedy School (United States). He is also a Visiting Professor at the International School, Vietnam National University (Hanoi, Vietnam), and Prague University of Economics and Business (Czech Republic). His research works focusing on asset pricing, climate finance, risk management, and corporate sustainability have been published in, among others, *European Journal of Operational Research, Journal of Economic Behavior and Organization, Journal of Economic Dynamics and Control, Journal of Banking and Finance, Journal of International Money and Finance, Technological Forecasting and Social Change*, and *Social Sciences & Medicine*. Professor Nguyen has edited many books on corporate finance and financial markets issues and serves as an editor and associate editor of several leading economics and finance journals.

# Acknowledgments

First and foremost, we would like to sincerely thank Foreign Trade University for supporting us in publishing this monograph. This research is funded by Foreign Trade University under the research program number FTURP01-2020-07. We would like to express our sincere gratitude to our colleagues for their valuable comments on our work.

# Contents

# List of Figures

# List of Tables

# Chapter 1

# Introduction to Political Corruption

*This chapter presents an overview of political corruption. Corruption is the abuse of entrusted power for private benefits. Corruption may exist in both public and private sectors. Political corruption is defined as dishonest behavior by public servants, to use their political power for their personal interest. The main causes of political corruption include political factors (government size, political instability, political centralization, weak democracy, limited press freedom and ineffective legal system); demographic factors (country size, gender and education); cultural factors (national culture, public sector culture and religion) and economic factors (economic development, economic freedom and international economic integration). Moreover, there have been many measures of political corruption such as Corruption Perceptions Index (CPI) of Transparency International (TI), the Index of Public Integrity (IPI), the Control of Corruption Indicator of the World Bank Governance Indicators, the Bertelsmann Stiftung Sustainable Government Indicators and the PRS Group's International Country Risk Guide. Besides, local corruption measures in some countries are also presented.*

# 1.1.   What Is Political Corruption?

## 1.1.1.   *Definition of political corruption*

Corrupt behavior is as old as human beings. The term "corruption" comes from a Latin word *corruptus* — the past participle of *corrumpere*. The prefix "cor" means completely and the stem "rumpere" means destroy. These imply that corruption may destroy the society. Moreover, in China and many Asian countries, corruption (貪冗) means greedy (貪) with many trivial things (冗). Eastern culture shows that greed is the root of corruption and corrupt behavior is diverse.

According to Transparency International (TI), corruption is defined as "the abuse of entrusted power for private gain". With this broad definition, corruption may exist across all economic sectors and organizations in society. Wherever there is an entrustment, the entrusted party tends to exploit its power to serve its own benefits. Corruption may be present in both private and public organizations. However, the effect of corruption in private organizations is limited to their shareholders or even stakeholders. In addition, private organizations are more dynamic and proactively adapt corruption control mechanisms. Meanwhile, corruption in the public sector or political corruption has a wide range of effects on political, economic and socio-cultural environments in a local area or a country. Therefore, political corruption attracts much attention from both academics and practitioners all over the world. Political corruption is a narrower definition of corruption.

The World Bank (1997) proposes a straightforward definition of political corruption as "the abuse of public office for private gain". A public office is a public trust. Public officers including appointed civil servants and elected politicians are obliged to exercise public power in order to serve the people. Public power consists of the judiciary, government procurement, public administrative procedures, privatization, trade policy, financial integration, tax policy, subsidies, police, public goods and services (Lambsdorff, 2007a). However, due to their greed, public officers may abuse their office to serve their own interests instead of the people's. What public officers receive from their corrupt behavior may be money, valuable assets or non-financial benefits in the form of nepotism and favoritism. From an ethical perspective, Gould (2001) posits that corruption is a moral problem. Accordingly, corruption is defined as an immoral and unethical situation in which there are aberrations from ethical principles of a society. These moral aberrations make people lose their respect for and trust in duly constituted authority.

## 1.1.2. *Supply side of political corruption*

Rose-Ackerman (1999) posits that the World Bank's definition reflects one side of corrupt behavior. Public officials are not the only party in a corruption case. It often has a receiver and a donator. Individuals or organizations make bribery payments to corrupt officials in order to obtain favorable benefits. Corruption is present when both parties can satisfy their own needs. Even individuals or organizations may actively offer bribes to public officials. Therefore, Rose-Ackerman (1999) concentrates on the supply side to define political corruption. Accordingly, political corruption is making illegal payment to public agents with the aim of gaining specific benefits or avoiding particular expenses.

According to Elliott (1997), the demand for corrupt services has three determinants, including government benefits, cost avoidance and official positions. First, firms may pay bribes to government officials to exploit benefits from government procurement, credit supply, subsidies, privatization of state-owned enterprises and concessions. When the government intends to buy goods and services, firms have high incentives to pay bribes in all phases of government procurement to become the winning contractor. Even when they have won, they continue to pay in order to have inflated prices or reduce the quality of goods and services. According to a survey of 3000 business executives across 30 countries conducted by TI (2012), 27% think that their companies fail to win a government contract or get new business since their competitors pay bribes. Moreover, when the government controls the financial system strictly, firms are willing to pay bribes in order to have better access to credit and lower interest rates for their loans. Besides, firms may pay bribes to receive subsidies or support from the government when public officials have the right to judge which firms are qualified and what levels of subsidies or support are appropriate. Furthermore, political corruption also exists in the process of privatizing state-owned enterprises. Firms pay bribes to government officials to buy the government's assets at lower prices or gather insider information. In addition, businesspeople may bribe corrupt officials to extract government concessions that grant them the right to exploit natural resources. In Vietnam, these corruption cases constitute over 55% of total land-related violations.

Second, firms have high incentives to pay bribes in order to avoid costs. Regardless of the parties on which the government levies a tax, both sellers and buyers share the tax burden. Therefore, firms always try to lower their tax payment. They may collude with tax collectors who have the right to judge their tax payment in order to reduce the tax payable. Then, firms and tax collectors share the reduced amount. Alm *et al.* (2016) use the data from the World Enterprise Survey and the Business Environment and Enterprise Performance Survey to investigate how corruption affects tax evasion across 32 countries. They find that the existence of corrupt tax inspectors makes sales reported for tax payment decrease by 4–10%. The magnitude of bribery payment is positively related to levels of evasion. Amoh and Ali-Nakyea (2019) also find that corrupting activities lead to tax evasion in Ghana. In addition, firms bribe government officials to speed up public administrative procedures including customs formalities, business registration, business licensing, etc. in order to save time. For example, a survey conducted by the United Nations Office on Drugs and Crime and the Institute of Statistics of Albania in 2011 shows that Albanian people have to pay bribes for better treatment (71% of respondents), administrative procedures (9%) and avoidance of fines (9% of respondents) (Shehu, 2016).

Finally, people pay bribes to be recruited by a government agency and government officials pay bribes to be promoted or rotated to a better position or government agency. Some government agencies or positions are attractive to both normal citizens and government officials due to their high income, corruption opportunities or good reputation. Therefore, bribery payment is considered an initial investment that generates future cash flows.

### 1.1.3.  *Types of political corruption*

There are two common types of political corruption, namely, petty and grand corruption. Petty corruption or bureaucratic corruption is the abuse of public power by civil servants when they provide ordinary citizens with public administrative procedures and basic public goods or services. Petty corruption is common in police stations, hospitals, schools and local government agencies. People pay bribes to public officials to speed up administrative procedures or have better access to healthcare, education and other public services. Grand corruption is the abuse of public power by high-ranking public officers or politicians to strengthen their power, positions and wealth. This type of corruption involves manipulation of legal regulations, public policies, rules and procedures in public resource allocation. For example, public officials often receive bribes to grant one or some companies preferences in large government projects. Grand corruption benefits a small group of individuals at the expense of many people or society.

Political corruption has parallels to a tax, lobbying and rent-seeking, but they are not perfectly interchangeable (Svensson, 2005). Both corruption and a tax increase marginal production cost. However, corruption fails to create government revenue and its transaction costs are higher. Taxation is legal, transparent and predictable while a corrupt agreement is illegal and bribery payment may be different for the same service. Moreover, corruption and lobbying are similar in the way they are conducted, but their effects are different (Harstad & Svensson, 2011). Corruption benefits a specific firm while lobbying increases the wealth of a group of firms or an industry. Corruption focuses on rule enforcers while lobbying focuses on rule makers. A corrupt contract is unofficial and relies on the relationship between corrupt officials and individuals/organizations while lobbying tends to change a policy or a legal regulation. Therefore, the effect of lobbying is more sustainable. Furthermore, rent-seeking uses public resources to benefit individuals/organizations without increasing the government's wealth. Corruption is present when public officials receive benefits from rent-seeking activities (Zúñiga, 2017).

## 1.1.4.  *Theories to explain corruption*

### 1.1.4.1.  *Principal–agent theory*

According to Klitgaard (1988), corruption is caused by information asymmetry in a three-party relationship, principal–agent–client. In this relationship, elected politicians are the principal, government officials are the agent and citizens are the client. Citizens elect politicians and entrust to them power to provide the citizens with public goods and services. However, elected politicians cannot execute this duty by themselves. As a result, they employ government officials to work on their behalf. Among the three parties, government officials have more information on the administration than both elected politicians and citizens. The agents may exploit this advantage to serve their own interests through corrupt activities (Lio *et al.*, 2011). Therefore, the principal tends to have monitoring and bonding mechanisms to prevent the agents from adopting corrupt behaviors (UNODC, 2021).

### 1.1.4.2.  *Collective action theory*

Based on the principal–agent theory, many countries improve their legal systems and design various anti-corruption mechanisms; however, corruption is still widespread in some countries as a systemic phenomenon. Therefore, Persson *et al.* (2013) argue that corruption is not only explained by the traditional agency problem but also government officials' collective action. According to collective action theory, people tend to rationalize their actions based on their perceptions of how others behave in the same situation (UNODC, 2021).

When corruption is perceived as a common practice or norm in society, people still engage in corrupt activities although they recognize anti-corruption punishment. People think that an honest person fails to reduce corruption while it works as a system (Marquette & Peiffer, 2015). In an environment of systemic corruption, traditional agency problems are less likely to exist and thus anti-corruption efforts to reduce it are not effective. Collective and coordinated solutions to change institutional or organizational culture should be used instead (Appolloni & Nshombo, 2014).

### 1.1.4.3.  *Institutional theory*

Institutional theory posits that corruption is determined by a country's institutional environment such as rule of law, anti-corruption practices and institutions. This theory investigates how the procedures and mechanisms work as authoritative guidelines to govern people's behavior in society (Amenta & Ramsey, 2010). From the institutionalist perspective, the causes of corruption lie in the "bad barrel" (distorting institutional norms and mechanisms) instead of the "bad apples" (individual misbehavior). Therefore, the government should focus on improving the institutional environment to control corruption.

### 1.1.4.4.  *Game theory*

Macrae (1982) is a pioneer in applying game theory to explain corrupt behavior. Particularly, government officials also face a "prisoner's dilemma" described by Tucker (1950) and corruption is a game in which there is a conflict of interest between a government official and his/her group. A government official has to make a decision to engage or not to engage in corruption while he/she fails to have information on other officials' decisions. He/she is afraid of a negative consequence if he/she refuses to adopt corrupt behavior while his/her colleagues do not. Therefore, all government officials tend to engage in corruption and receive a benefit that is smaller than that they may receive if they refuse (UNODC, 2021).

# 1.2.   Causes of Political Corruption

## 1.2.1.   *Political factors*

### 1.2.1.1.   *Government size*

According to Goel and Nelson (1998), a large government inevitably implies much red tape and bureaucratic delay. Therefore, government officials have many opportunities to adopt corrupt behavior and firms also have high incentives to pay bribes in order to eliminate these obstacles. This argument is consistent with the "crime and punishment" model proposed by Becker (2000). Illegal behavior has higher expected payoff in a large government and thus government officials are more likely to undertake illegal activities. Similarly, Alesina and Angeletos (2005) develop a theoretical model that supports a positive effect of government size on corruption. They posit that a large government leads to high corruption, which in turn increases income inequality. The poor advocate redistributive policies to improve equality and justice in society, and the rich also endorse these policies since they exploit rents from the large government. Consequently, the redistributive policies are less effective and corruption is still high. Using a panel data of 244 observations across 50 states in the US from 1983 to 1987, Goel and Nelson (1998) find that government size, state government expenditure in particular, positively affects corruption. Ali and Isse (2002) and Rose-Ackerman (1999) also show that when a government becomes larger, the possibility of corruption opportunities increases. Corrado and Rossetti (2018) find a positive effect of local government expenditure on corruption in Italy from 2000 to 2011. Besides, Zhao and Xu (2015) investigate how e-government determines political corruption in 80 countries from 2003 to 2010 and find that government size is positively associated with perceived corruption while the development of e-government reduces perceived corruption.

However, some prominent studies show that government size may have a negative impact on corruption. They argue that a large government has a strong mechanism to monitor public officials and promote their accountability; therefore, public officials have fewer opportunities to engage in corrupt behavior and firms also have fewer opportunities to pay bribes. A large government has a large budget to ensure the enforceability of anti-corruption legislation. This viewpoint is supported by the fact that developed countries have bigger governments than developing countries and they face lower levels of corruption. Countries with high government expenditure commonly have lower corruption scores (Kotera *et al.*, 2012). Elliott (2017) examines how government expenditure affects corruption in 83 countries and documents that the average government expenditure ratio of the 16 highest corruption countries is 11% lower than the full sample average. La Porta *et al.* (1999) investigate potential determinants of government quality in 152 countries in the 1990s and find that a larger government has a lower corruption score. In their study, government size is measured by government transfers and subsidies, government expenditure, the size of state-owned firms and the size of government employment. Adserà *et al.* (2003) investigate the role of governments in creating accountability in their officials' behavior in 131 countries between 1982 and 1998 and show supporting evidence for the negative relationship between government size and corruption. In addition, Goel and Budak (2006) argue that governments in transition economies especially concentrate on building their nations; therefore, they have strict constraints and enforcement measures to ensure the efficiency of their spending. They employ a sample of annual data from 25 Eastern European and Asian transition countries over the period 1998–2002 to investigate determinants of corruption. Their findings show that government size tends to decrease corruption and comprehensive transition reforms are effective in reducing corruption. Billger and Goel (2009) use a data of cross-sectional observations over the period 2001–2003 to investigate determinants of corruption across 99 countries and find that when government size is larger, the Corruption Perceptions Index (CPI) published by the TI is lower. Goel and Nelson (2010) find that an increase in government size results in higher corruption.

Furthermore, Gerring and Thacker (2005) investigate the effect of neoliberal economic policies on political corruption with cross-national data collected from 181 countries from 1997 to 1998. They find that there is no consistent effect of government size on political corruption. Lambsdorff (2007a) shows that there may be a reverse causality between corruption and government expenditure. Governments in high corruption countries may be ineffective in financial management. Recognizing mixed results in the relationship between government size and corruption, Kotera *et al.* (2012) attempt to examine the role of democracy in this relationship. With annual data of 82 countries over the period 1995–2008, they document that the effect of government size on corruption relies on levels of democracy. Particularly, when democracy is adequately strong, a larger government entails lower corruption. In contrast, this effect is the opposite when democracy is too weak.

### 1.2.1.2. *Political instability*

Political instability may lead to high political corruption due to two reasons. On the one hand, political instability reduces government officials' job safety. When government officials recognize that the probability to remain in their offices is lower, they are more likely to conduct illegal behavior such as corruption in order to serve their personal interests as much as possible by the end of their tenures (Adem, 2021). Shleifer and Vishny (1993) also posit that sociopolitical instability increases the ephemerality of government official tenure; as a result, they become more irresponsible and have several illicit rent-seeking behaviors. Corruption gives them a strong financial status after their tenure ends. On the other hand, political instability increases uncertainty, anxiety and civil unrest in the society and the "status strain" mechanism starts working (Lipset & Raab, 1973). In countries with high political instability, the government becomes less effective at taking care of citizens and protecting their property rights. Socially well-established citizens feel anxious and threatened by this uncertain and unpredictable environment; therefore, they tend to do anything in order to maintain their status and properties. People are willing to initiate bribe payment or struggle to pay bribes provided that they can achieve their goals (Park, 2003). Alesina and Perotti (1996) show that sociopolitical instability increases corruption through higher social uncertainty across 72 nations from 1960 to 1985. Brunetti and Weder (2003) and Leite and Weidmann (1999) also find a positive relationship between political instability and political corruption. Serra (2006) examines determinants of corruption with a sensitivity analysis and shows that political instability increased political corruption in 62 countries from 1990 to 1998.

Moreover, political stability is a guarantee for public servants' job safety; therefore, they are less likely to conduct illegal behavior and sacrifice their promising future. According to Lederman *et al.* (2005), political stability under a democratic regime significantly improves checks and balances. Using over 2,000 observations all over the world over the period 1984–1999, Lederman *et al.* (2005) find that political stability decreases corruption. Park (2003) also shows that socio-political stability negatively affects corruption across countries all over the world. Ghaniy and Hastiadi (2017) investigate how political, social and economic factors determine perceived political corruption in 92 observed countries in 2014. They document that political stability has a positive effect on perceived political corruption. MacDonald and Majeed (2011) show that political stability is an important cause of political corruption in European countries. Furthermore, Adem (2021) examines determinants of political corruption in Sub-Saharan Africa where political corruption is considered a social epidemic. They also find supporting evidence for the positive relationship between political stability and political corruption. However, political stability may create opportunities for government officials to engage in corrupt behavior. When they maintain their positions for a long period, they tend to build long-lasting relationships with those who are willing to pay bribes (Adem, 2021; Elbahnasawy & Revier, 2012).

### 1.2.1.3. *Political centralization*

When investigating corruption under various market conditions, Shleifer and Vishny (1993) find that if there are many government agencies supplying the same administrative service, bribery payment made to speed up that service may be reduced to zero. Consistently, Tanzi (1994) posits that a centralized government leads to high corruption since the connection between citizens and public officials is weak. However, when government officials are close to their citizens or government agencies compete for mobile resources, governments can improve their accountability and discipline. Therefore, their officials are less likely to conduct corrupt behavior (Fan *et al.*, 2009). Political decentralization is the process in which the central government distributes political power to local governments. This distribution improves power control since the local government is accountable to the central government for all authorized activities. Besides, bringing the government to every citizen or organization also reduces corruption since local officials are effectively controlled by social pressure. When local officials and citizens know each other well in decentralized settings, local officials find it difficult to offer under-the-table deals to their neighbors. Several prior studies show that political decentralization reduces corruption. In addition, a government monopoly in natural resources may also create many corrupt opportunities since government officials have the right to distribute and allocate them.

Huther and Shah (1998) investigate the correlation between decentralization in government expenditure and the quality of governance across 80 countries. They find that the Pearson correlation coefficient between fiscal decentralization and the absence of corruption is positive and statistically significant. This finding implies that fiscal decentralization may reduce corruption. Further, Fisman and Gatti (2000) conduct a pioneering empirical study on how decentralization in government spending affects political corruption across countries. They find that increased decentralization leads to lower corruption. In addition, looking within the US, they document that when a state relies more on federal transfers, its public servants are more likely to abuse public power. When investigating determinants of corruption, Treisman (2000) uses a dummy variable assigned 1 if a country follows federalism and 0 otherwise to measure political decentralization. His findings show that corruption is higher in federalist countries. Similarly, Kunicova and Rose-Ackerman (2005) employ a dummy variable to compare whether corruption in centralized and federal states is different. They document that federal states are more corrupt than centralized states. Barenstein and Fund (2001) also find supporting evidence for the negative relationship between fiscal decentralization and political corruption.

In addition, Arikan (2004) uses a tax competition framework with rent-seeking activities to analyze how fiscal decentralization influences political corruption in 40 countries. He also finds that fiscal decentralization reduces political corruption. With a data of 9000 firms from the World Business Environment Survey over the period 1999–2000, Fan *et al.* (2009) investigate the effect of political decentralization on bribery payment's frequency and costliness across 80 countries. They document that countries with a greater number of government or administrative levels and more local government officials have higher frequency of bribery payment. Besides, Ivanyna and Shah (2011) try to provide more insights into the relationship between political decentralization and corruption all over the world by measuring political decentralization with various dimensions such as empowering local governments and decentralized local governance. They find that all dimensions of political decentralization are effective in reducing corruption in 158 countries. Andersen (2009) analyzes how e-government controls political corruption across 149 countries in two years, including 1996 and 2006. Their findings show that when the e-government distribution slides from the 10th to the 90th percentile, the corruption control distribution moves from the 10th to the 23rd percentile. Bhatnagar (2003) and Elbahnasawy (2014) also find that e-government plays an important role in controlling corruption.

On the other hand, political decentralization may create opportunities for corrupt activities. A strong and close relationship between government agencies and citizens is a promising environment in which corrupt officials collaborate with those who are willing to pay bribes (Fan *et al.*, 2009). In addition, political decentralization leads to smaller jurisdictions and fewer means to threaten corrupt officials (Arikan, 2004). Consistently, Neudorfer and Neudorfer (2014) posit that government officials in countries of strong regional self-rule have higher incentives and more chances to establish their collusion networks. With a dataset on regional authority in 36 countries during the period 1984–2006, they find that self-rule countries are more corrupt than shared rule countries. Remarkably, Albornoz and Cabrales (2013) develop a political agency model to investigate how decentralization in government expenditure influences political corruption. Using data from 110 countries over the period 1996–2007, they document that the relationship between decentralization and corruption relies on political competition. Particularly, fiscal decentralization decreases (increases) corruption if political competition is high (low).

### 1.2.1.4.  *Weak democracy*

Shabbir and Anwar (2007) posit that government officials in democratic countries utilize their entrusted state power to benefit citizens, while government officials in non-democratic countries try to exploit public power to serve their personal interests. Democracy is a political system granting people political rights to vote in competitive elections and monitor rulers (Cheibub & Przeworski, 1999; Trantidis, 2016). Myerson (1993) developed a theoretical model to examine how various electoral systems decrease political corruption. In the model, parties with given corruption levels and given positions on a main policy question struggle to have legislative seats. In competitive electoral systems, the opposition attempts to look for corrupt behavior of the incumbent; therefore, corrupt officials are more likely to be exposed and punished. Voters will not select the party with many corrupt officials. Their findings show that approval voting and proportional representation have full effectiveness in eliminating corrupt parties from the voting game, while plurality voting has partial effectiveness. Moreover, Hollyer *et al.* (2011) find that democratization leads to higher transparency in policy making. De Tocqueville (1988) also posits that political democratization entails press freedom, enfranchisement, separation of powers and representation. They provide several checks and balances to reduce the probability of government officials' adopting corrupt behaviors

(Lederman *et al.*, 2005). Besides, corrupt behavior is less attractive in democratic countries as it is greatly stigmatized (Kolstad & Wiig, 2016). Therefore, democratization tends to restrict government officials' misconduct. Goldsmith (1999) documents a negative effect of political democracy on corruption in 34 emerging markets. Sandholtz and Koetzle (2000) also find that democracy decreases political corruption in 54 countries. Treisman (2000) shows that democracy has a negative impact on political corruption in a country if it has a long history.

Furthermore, Persson *et al.* (2003) investigate how various characteristics of the electoral system influenced corruption in eight democratic areas in the 1990s. They find that districts with larger voting populations are less corrupt. With a sample of 496 observations from 131 countries between 1982 and 1998, Adserà *et al.* (2003) document that the existence of a transparent electorate in a democratic environment explains from 1/2 to 2/3 of the variance in government performance and corruption. Schopf (2011) shows that when corruption is measured by corruption perception, a young democracy like South Korea identifies as having a high level of corruption. However, when he uses an objective measurement of elite corruption, democratization still results in lower corruption in many fields such as industrial restructuring activities, bank financing and government procurement. Elbahnasawy and Revier (2012) show that free expression and accountability perceived by citizens significantly reduces political corruption. Kalenborn and Lessmann (2013) use a cross-sectional data of 170 countries over the period 2005–2010 and a panel data of 175 countries over the period 1996–2010 to examine the joint effect of democratization and press freedom on political corruption. They document that democratic elections are only effective in reducing corruption. Jetter *et al.* (2015) examine the role of income in the relationship between democracy and corruption in 155 countries over the period 1998–2012. They document that democracy only leads to lower corruption when GDP/capita measured by 2005 US\$ is over US\$2,000. Kolstad and Wiig (2016) argue that the negative impact of democracy on corruption may be biased due to the endogeneity of democracy. However, after controlling this econometric problem, he still finds that democracy plays an important role in decreasing corruption. Dominik and Heldman (2017) plot a graph to investigate the effect of voice and accountability on corruption control across 192 countries in 2014. The graph shows that there is a strong negative relationship between democracy and corruption.

However, the extant literature also shows that the relationship between democratization and corruption is positive or nonlinear. According to Rose-Ackerman (1999), politicians need to raise funds from individuals and firms for their election campaigns. When an electoral system is more competitive, politicians are more likely to collaborate with funders in order to have enough financial resources. Examining the effects of democracy, economic freedom and government strength on political corruption across 91 countries, Shen and Williamson (2005) find that countries with high levels of democracy are more corrupt. In addition, Mohtadi and Roe (2003) propose an endogenous growth model to explain how democratization affects political corruption. They argue that young democracies fail to control rent-seeking activities; therefore, democracy increases corruption at first. Nevertheless, when democracy is mature, competition among rent seekers increases and thus this relationship turns to be negative. Their empirical study also shows an inverted-U relationship between democratization and political corruption. Rock (2009) also finds an inverted U pattern for the effect of democratic maturity on corruption all over the world. In the early stages of a democracy, higher levels of democracy lead to higher political corruption. However, this relationship turns out to be negative when democracy reaches a certain level. Dong and Torgler (2011) show that the effect of democracy on political corruption relies on income equality and property rights protection. Democratization is more effective in reducing corruption when property rights are strongly protected and income equality is low. However, democracy leads to high levels of corruption in countries with poor property rights protection and high-income equality. Moreover, Sung (2004) argues that the relationship between democracy and corruption may not be just linear. With a sample of observations from 103 countries between 1995 and 2000, he finds that the best pattern to describe the effect of democracy on corruption is a cubic function. Besides, some studies show that there is no significant relationship between democracy and corruption across countries (Brunetti & Weder, 2003; Chowdhury, 2004).

### 1.2.1.5.  *Low press freedom*

Historically, journalism is expected to demand accountability of government agencies for people and, most significantly, the ideals of the democratic polity (Ettema, 2007). Journalism gives voice to the voiceless and holds government officials accountable (Rao, 2008). Especially when a government is autocratic and centralized, journalism is more important to protect citizens from the abuse of authority by government officials. Journalists even challenge the government when they implement their mission and duty (Newton *et al.*, 2004). According to Norris (2009), investigative journalism may have three effects on government institutions and officials such as deliberative effect, individualistic effect and substantive effect. First, it raises problems to create public discussions about these problems and their solutions. Second, it makes individuals conducting illegal behavior face sanctions. Finally, it creates tangible changes in legislation. Therefore, investigative journalism increases the cost of corruption and improves anti-corruption mechanisms.

Early definitions of press freedom were coined after the Second World War. They concentrate on freedom from government control in the context of geopolitical constructions (Färdigh *et al.*, 2011). This classical viewpoint states that the role of media is preventing the state from abusing citizens (Hachten, 1989; Hagen, 1992; Lowenstein, 1970; Picard, 1985; Weaver, 1977). Then, the definition of press freedom is broadened with the development of democracy. From a more radical democratic perspective, press freedom includes two components: (1) the freedom and independence of the media; (2) the freedom of citizens to access media contents (McQuail, 2010). According to Klitgaard (1988), government officials are more likely to adopt corrupt behavior since they have information advantage and the opportunity to engage in discretionary activities in the administration with low accountability. Press freedom gives the media opportunities to shed light on corrupt activities and monitor government officials more effectively. TI (2013) considers an independent media to be an important factor of a country's integrity and strong governance. Macdonell and Pesic (2006) show that the media is vital in curbing corruption.

Investigating how a free press influences corruption control across 128 countries between 1994 and 1998, Brunetti and Weder (2003) find a negative effect of press freedom on political corruption. Freille *et al.* (2007) also show that aggregate press freedom measured by the average of press freedom scores during the period 1995–2004 is negatively related to corruption. Although Lederman *et al.* (2005) and Pellegrini and Gerlagh (2004) measure press freedom by various calculation methods, they still find that a free press leads to lower political corruption. Moreover, Kalenborn and Lessmann (2013) examine the joint effect of democratization and press freedom with cross-sectional data from 170 countries over the period 2005–2010 and panel data from 175 countries over the period 1996–2010. They document that press freedom is only effective in reducing political corruption when democracy reaches a certain level in a country, and vice versa. Investigating the role of press freedom and democracy in corruption control in 111 countries over the period 2004–2015, Hamada *et al.* (2019) find that press freedom tends to deter political corruption. Besides, press freedom and democratization are complements in reducing corruption.

In addition, when the Internet became widespread all over the world, traditional media became less important in society and thus in the control of corruption. Print and broadcast media are mainly one-way communication modes and this gives an opportunity to autocratic governments to censor and eliminate what they consider as bad news (Jha and Sarangi, 2017). When the public fail to have full information about government officials, they are more likely to indulge in illegal behavior. However, the proliferation of the Internet has changed the way people communicate significantly. Modern and social media create multi-way communication and a wider range of information. Social media has significantly contributed information about cases of corruption and government agencies can be monitored more effectively in many countries due to its advantages. First, each victim of any corruption-related case can spread information quickly to a large number of users. Second, interaction between friends and users may provide people with knowledge, experience and understanding when they face corruption-related problems. Therefore, government officials have fewer opportunities to expropriate citizens. Andersen *et al.* (2011) attempt to examine how changes in Internet adoption affect changes in political corruption. They find that Internet diffusion reduces political corruption in 48 contiguous US states from 1991 to 2006. With a panel data from 70 countries during the period 1998–2005, Lio *et al.* (2011) show that internet use is able to reduce political corruption, but the effect is not substantial. Goel *et al.* (2012) argue that when people are more aware of corruption thanks to the internet, political corruption is lower. Their research data include searches of corruption-related key words on two common search engines, namely, Google and Yahoo! from 150 countries. Internet corruption awareness is measured by the number of searches per capita. They find that high Internet awareness about corruption leads to lower political corruption. Elbahnasawy (2014) also shows that Internet adoption and e-government are complements in controlling corruption in 160 countries during the period 1995–2009. Jha and Sarangi (2017) investigate how social media affects political corruption across 150 countries. They document that Facebook penetration has a negative impact on political corruption. Besides, this impact is strongest in countries with low press freedom. Charron (2009) finds that press freedom plays an important role in the negative effect of political on social corruption. The effect is negligible in countries with low press freedom.

### 1.2.1.6. *Ineffective legal system*

With a two-period model to analyze the behavior of government officials, Andvig and Moene (1990) posit that the appeal of corruption toward government officials in a country relies on the effectiveness of its legislation. In an effective legal system, the probability of corrupt activities being detected and punished is high. When a corrupt official is caught by a colleague, there are two scenarios. First, the corrupt official is punished if the colleague is not corrupt. Second, the corrupt official bribes the colleague to avoid punishment if the colleague is also corrupt. Therefore, government officials are less likely to conduct corrupt behavior. Besides an effective legal framework provides strong checks and balances, reduces information asymmetry and thus corrupt opportunities are less available (Lederman *et al.*, 2005). However, when the legal system is ineffective, people fail to respect government authority and legislation and thus government officials have more opportunities to exploit their power (Sanjian, 1994). Similarly, Becker (2000) argues that criminal behavior can be explained by the general economic theory of rational choice. Rational people commit crimes if their expected utility is higher than the utility of other activities. The probability that perpetrators are apprehended is an important factor determining the extent of illegal behavior in a country. An ineffective legal system encourages public servants to engage in corrupt activities since they realize that corruption is rarely caught and/or convicted. According to Berman (1977), legal violations and corruption are commonplace in a country when people think that a criminal is an unfortunate victim of society. Rose-Ackerman (1997) shows that corrupt government officials have high incentives to apply or interpret the law arbitrarily and give discretionary judgment in order to expropriate their citizens.

Shah (2006) shows that weak governance in the public sector leads to corruption. An ineffective legal framework is a cause of weak governance. Leite and Weidmann (1999), Sanjian (1994), Tanzi and Davoodi (1998), and Treisman (2000) also attribute an ineffective legal system as the cause for high corruption. Damania *et al.* (2004) investigate why corruption and policy distortions are highly persistent in some countries from the late 1990s. They find that countries with more inefficient judicial systems are more corrupt. Consistently, Broadman and Recanatini (2001) document that clear and transparent rules can mitigate rent-seeking opportunities. Dong and Torgler (2011) find that property rights protection strongly reduces corruption. Ali and Isse (2002) find a negative impact of judicial efficiency and corruption across countries in the 1980s and 1990s. Brunetti and Weder (2003) show that an effective rule of law index lowers political corruption in 125 countries over the period 1994–1998. Park (2003) also documents that countries with an effective rule of law index are less corrupt. Moreover, Bhattacharyya and Jha (2013) examine how the legal system affects political corruption in 20 Indian states from 2005 to 2008. They show that the "Right to Information Act (RTI) 2005" was able to reduce both the experience and the perception of corruption. Mohamed *et al.* (2015) document that the rule of law is highly effective in controlling corruption across 42 Sub-Saharan countries between 2000 and 2010. Examining the inter-relationship between the (in)effectiveness of legal regulations and different corruption measures in up to 130 countries during the period 1982–1997, Herzfeld and Weiss (2003) find that an effective legal framework was a major factor in controlling corruption.

## 1.2.2. *Demographic factors*

### 1.2.2.1. *Country size*

Thousands of years ago, political philosophy tried to answer the question: What is the optimal size of a nation? According to Plato, the optimal population of a state is 5040 citizens, and the government should control the population at this exact number (Pangle, 1988). Aristotle (1932) also posited that governing a populous state by laws is difficult if not impossible. The population should be large enough so that the state can be self-sufficient, but it should be small enough so that the government can manage and survey citizens easily (Knack & Azfar, 2003). Consistent with this classical viewpoint, Jalan (1982) argues that governments in small countries can adapt their policies to new chances and threats more efficiently since these countries have stronger social cohesion and fewer vested interests. However, small countries also face many problems. They have no economies of scale, high vulnerability, limited access to capital markets, high macro-economic policy dependence and overstated real income (Srinivasan, 1986). Especially, they face more difficulties to survive and develop in a hostile environment (Sardar, 1995; Sheila, 1985).

According to Root (1999), large countries experience economies of scale, but economies of scale may lead to political corruption. He argues that in large countries, government officials have more available resources and thus they can exploit them to maintain their political power. Moreover, when the number of public servants per capita is lower in large countries due to economies of scale, people have higher incentives to pay bribes in order to avoid queuing (Fisman & Gatti, 2002a). Seldadyo and De Haan (2005) also posit that if large countries exploit economies of scale by maintaining a low rate of public administrative outlets per capita, their citizens are more likely to pay bribes. Besides, in large countries, people are less likely to have family relationship or other intimate ties with officials; therefore, government officials harass their citizens to collect bribes (Knack & Azfar, 2003). Investigating the effect of country size on political corruption across 60 countries, Root (1999) finds that countries with a larger population are more corrupt. Mocan (2008) also shows a positive effect of population on political corruption in 49 countries. When the population increases by one million, the propensity of being requested a bribe increases by 0.01%. Furthermore, Goel and Budak (2006) document that the geographic size of a nation has a positive effect on political corruption. This implies that governments are less effective in reducing corruption in dispersed locations. Goel and Nelson (2010) also show that countries with a large geographic size and low population density are more corrupt. With a survey data collected from 47,952 firms across 135 countries over the period 2006–2018, Amin and Soh (2019) find that country size measured by both population and surface area is positively related to petty corruption.

However, there are some prior studies that fail to show a significant relationship between country size and political corruption. Knack and Azfar (2003) find that the effect of country size on corruption becomes weaker and disappears when the sample selection bias is reduced. Goel and Nelson (2011) show that the relationship between population size and corruption varies with different measures of corruption. Zheng (2016) also documents that population size fails to explain corruption variances.

## 1.2.2.2.  *Gender*

According to the differential association theory proposed by Sutherland (1939), people commit crime since they learn from those who engage in criminal behavior and they have opportunities to conduct illegal activities (Sutherland *et al.*, 1992). In other words, interactions and opportunities are two key determinants of people's criminal actions. In line with this argument, government officials conduct corrupt behavior if they frequently interact with corrupt colleagues and have more opportunities for being corrupt regardless of their gender (Alhassan-Alolo, 2007; Matsueda, 1988). Therefore, the presence of male or female officials fails to make the government control political corruption more or less effectively. However, the social role theory developed by Eagly (1987) argues that gender may matter in people's behavior since men and women have different roles in society. The behavior of an individual is determined by three factors: (1) his/her cognition of proper behavior for his/her position; (2) his/her perception of others' expectations for his/her position; (3) his/her perception of the pressure that may arise when he/she fails to satisfy others' expectations. In other words, people's behavior is the consequence of social pressures from their socialization. Through socialization men and women realize their gender roles in the division of labor. Dividing social roles as suitable for males or females is not fixed; however, their inherent attributes and socio-economic environment significantly affects this division (Eagly & Wood, 2016). Based on this theory, male and female officials may have different roles in government agencies and thus their presence affects corruption levels.

Analyzing results of overt integrity tests conducted by 724,806 job applicants, Ones and Viswesvaran (1998) find that women have higher integrity scores than men. Glover *et al.* (1997) investigate the effect of personal values on ethical choices and document that women take stronger stances on ethical decisions. Beltramini *et al.* (1984), Chonko and Hunt (1985), Jones and Gautschi (1988), Reiss and Mitra (1998) and Ruegger and King (1992) also show that women are more ethical in activities undertaken outside of the work place than men. Moreover, several studies on political representation show that elected female politicians are more effective in improving public service provision than male politicians. Investigating how gender affects social expenditure in 12 industrialized countries across 20 years, Bolzendahl (2009) find that the presence of women in legislative bodies has the strongest impact on social spending. Bratton and Ray (2002) show that female representation improves public childcare service in Norwegian municipals. Holman (2014) finds that the presence of a female mayor increases the probability of a city engaging in financing social welfare projects and the magnitude of its funding. Schwindt-Bayer and Mishler (2005) document that women's descriptive representation results in higher responsiveness of legislatures to women's policy concerns. These findings imply that women tend to be less individual-oriented than men, they are less willing to abandon the common good in order to obtain private gain (Dollar *et al.*, 2001). Therefore, the presence of female officials may help governments control corruption more effectively and the presence of female managers or employees in firms may reduce firms' propensity to pay bribes.

Swamy *et al.* (2001) conduct a pioneering empirical study to examine how gender influences political corruption in both developed and developing nations. They argue that the presence of female officials may reduce corruption due to four reasons. It is therefore important for us to clarify that we do not claim to have discovered some essential, permanent, or biologically determined differences between men and women. Indeed, the gender differences we observe may be attributable to socialization, or to differences in access to networks of corruption, or in knowledge of how to engage in corrupt practices, or to other factors. Their research data include 18 surveys conducted in 1981 and 43 surveys conducted from 1990 to 1991. They find that political corruption is lower in countries where women have more seats in parliament, high positions in the government administration and constitute a larger percentage in the labor force. Dollar *et al.* (2001) also find that countries with greater female representation in their parliaments are less corrupt. Seldadyo and De Haan (2005) use factor analysis to investigate 70 economic and non-economic factors that may determine corruption. They find that the participation of women in labor force results in lower corruption. According to Barnes *et al.* (2018), people believe that women are more effective in controlling corruption than men and people's beliefs become stronger when they have information about women's outsider position and risk aversion. Esarey and Schwindt-Bayer (2018) find that female representation has a negative effect on corruption and this effect is stronger when corrupt behavior is more likely to be apprehended and punished by voters. They explain the relationship between female representation and corruption by two major mechanisms: (1) females are more risk-averse than males and (2) voters tend to assign females higher criteria in elections. Donfouet *et al.* (2018) show that the presence of women in parliaments has a long-term negative impact on perceived corruption. With data from a survey of 85,000 people across 182 European regions, Bauhr *et al.* (2019) find that the percentage of female representatives in local councils is negatively related to the prevalence of petty and grand corruption. Furthermore, Stensöta *et al.* (2015) investigate the effect of gender differences on corruption in institutional logic and find that the asymmetry experience causes gender differences instead of basic properties. Women are more able to control corruption in an electoral system than a bureaucracy.

Moreover, prior research shows that firms with more female managers or employees are less likely to pay bribes. Using data from the surveys conducted by the World Values Survey Association and the European Values Study Foundation over the period 1981–1999, Torgler and Valev (2006) show that women consider corruption as an unjustifiable behavior. Examining how men and women participate in corrupt cases as bribers or bribe receivers (government officials), Rivas (2013) documents that men have a higher frequency of accepting bribes than women and men tend to offer larger bribes than women. Jagger and Shively (2015) investigate how supply chain participants pay bribes and how government officials collect taxes with a sample of 433 firms in the supply chains of charcoal and timber in Uganda. They find that men are more willing to pay bribes than women. Further, Breen *et al.* (2017) use firm-level data to investigate whether female owners and managers can help firms reduce corruption across 105 countries. They document that firms with female owners have lower propensity to pay bribes and smaller levels of bribery. Firms with female top managers are less likely to suffer corruption.

However, some prior studies show that gender differences are insignificant in the context of corruption-related activities. Sung (2003) find that the effect of gender on corruption is spurious. The effect is present since the political system encourages gender equality and maintains strong governance.

Alhassan-Alolo (2007) uses data from a survey of Ghanaian male and female government officials to examine their attitudes toward corruption. They document that the presence of female officials may not lead to lower corruption if corrupt opportunities and connections are not controlled. Examining the relationship between female population and corruption across 29 Chinese provinces from 1995 to 2012, Hao *et al.* (2018) find that the effect of gender on corruption is relatively ambiguous. The differences in socio-economic environments across provinces may strongly determine the relationship between female population and corruption. Debski *et al.* (2018) show that the presence of women in politics and labor markets fails to reduce corruption directly in 177 countries over the period 1998–2014. Besides, Nguyen *et al.* (2021) investigate how differences between men and women in entrepreneurship affect firm-level bribery in 16,560 firms across 32 emerging economies. Remarkably, they find that female-led firms pay higher levels of bribery than male-led firms and the positive effect of female entrepreneurs on firm-level bribery tends to be stronger in corruption-prone countries. These findings clarify that female-led firms are more likely to pay bribes in order to survive in emerging markets.

### 1.2.2.3. *Education*

Education improves citizens' legal knowledge and social responsibility and enhances social cohesion (Heyneman, 2002). Poorly educated citizens fail to have enough knowledge and information to recognize corrupt activities and monitor government officials effectively. Corrupt officials have high incentives to create red tape and bureaucratic procedures in order to collect bribes from uneducated citizens. Educated citizens are capable of overseeing their government, identifying corruption risks and disciplining corrupt officials (Koyuncu, Ozturkler, & Yilmaz, 2010; Elbahnasawy & Revier, 2012). Ades and Di Tella (1999) and Svensson (2005) conduct empirical studies across countries and document that education decreases corruption. When investigating the relationship between privatization and corruption in 27 transition economies over the period 1995–2008, Koyuncu *et al.* (2010) also find that countries with higher gross tertiary enrollment rates are less corrupt. Truex (2011) conducted a survey of 853 individuals in Kathmandu to investigate determinants of their attitudes toward corruption. He finds that education is the strongest determinant of Kathmandu residents' attitudes toward corrupt behavior. Particularly, highly educated respondents are less likely to accept corrupt activities and more likely to denounce them. Analyzing bribery's costs and benefits across households in Peru and Uganda, Hunt and Laszlo (2012) find that improving literacy and publishing costs of public services are effective ways to decrease the extent to which poor citizens are exposed to corruption. Dong and Torgler (2013) investigate the causes of corruption across China's provinces and find that provinces with higher educational attainment are less corrupt. Uslaner and Rothstein (2016) develop a model to describe the causal relationship between universal education and corruption control across 78 countries. Their findings show that introduction of mass education in 1870 strongly reduced corruption levels in 2010 despite the ensuing the changes in education levels, GDP per capita and democratization of governments.

However, education may also increase corruption. Highly educated people have more opportunities to develop relationships with government officials. Besides, they tend to have higher income, which makes them more willing to pay bribes in order to speed up their administrative procedures (Kaffenberger, 2012). Hakhverdian and Mayne (2012) use a multilevel model to examine how education affects trust in government agencies and corruption across 21 European democracies. They document that the negative relationship between corruption and trust in government agencies is lower in countries with higher education. Ali and Isse (2002) find that education negatively influences corruption. Maria *et al.* (2021) control macroeconomic variables to investigate how education affects corruption in the G20 member countries. They find no significant effects of primary school enrollment and the lifelong learning score on corruption for the full sample and the sub-samples of developed and developing countries. Secondary school enrollment has a significantly negative relationship with corruption in all categories of countries. Tertiary school enrollment decreases corruption in developing member countries but increases corruption in developed countries.

## 1.2.3.  *Cultural factors*

According to Hofstede (1984), culture is defined as a collection of shared beliefs, attitudes, rules, values and expected behaviors governing people in a society. Culture works as a coordination device leading a society to a particular equilibrium while multiple equilibria are present (Greif, 1994). Culture distinguishes people in a community from those from another (Hofstede, 2011). From the institutional-based view, cultural values determine a wide range of social activities and human behaviors (House *et al.*, 2002; Scott, 1995). Culture affects people's perception of ethical issues, norms for their behaviors and ethical judgement; therefore, national culture may influence corruption (Vitell *et al.*, 1993). Fisman and Miguel (2007) investigate the effect of national culture on corruption through the parking behavior of United Nations diplomats from 149 countries. They find that diplomats from countries with high corruption tend to have more unpaid parking violations than those from countries with low corruption. This finding implies that cultural norms are effective in explaining corrupt behaviors. Barr and Serra (2010) conducted two bribery experiments in 2005 and 2007 to examine people's choice of corruption over honesty and the role of culture in their decisions. Participants of these experiments were Oxford University students. In the 2005 experiment, students are from 34 countries with various levels of corruption. They find that the undergraduates' corrupt actions are related to their home countries' corruption levels.

In the 2007 experiment, they use a sample including students from 22 countries and find a consistent result. Besides, they document that students living in the UK for longer periods are less likely to bribe. However, Cameron *et al.* (2009) fail to find a correlation between corruption and cultural differences. They conduct experiments in four countries (e.g., Australia, India, Indonesia, and Singapore) to investigate the propensity to pay bribes across cultures. They find that students' propensities to pay bribes fail to vary significantly across countries including Australia, Singapore and Indonesia although they have different levels of corruption. Furthermore, students' propensities to pay bribes in Indonesia are lower than in Singapore while the former is more corrupt than the latter.

### 1.2.3.1.  *Hofstede's cultural dimensions*

Hofstede is a pioneer in identifying cultural values and proposing cultural indices to measure national culture. His cultural dimensions are the most influential measures of national culture in the academic world. Hofstede (1984) conducts a survey of IBM employees across 40 countries and finds that people in different countries are different in work-associated cultural values represented by 4 cultural dimensions: power distance representing attitude toward human inequality, uncertainty avoidance representing attitude toward an unknown future, individualism representing attitude toward integration into a community and masculinity representing attitude toward success. In addition, Hofstede (1990) further develops the fifth dimension based on a survey on Chinese cultural values conducted by the Chinese Culture Connection (1987). Respondents who are university students from 22 countries express their opinions on traditional Chinese cultural values through 40 scale items. Factor analysis shows that 3 out of 4 factors have strong correlations with Hofstede's original dimensions. The only factor that is not correlated with them is the Confucian work dynamic represented by 4 items: ordering relationship, thrift, persistence and having a sense of shame. Therefore, Hofstede (1990) adopted this factor as the fifth dimension. Then, Hofstede (2001) renamed it as long-term orientation representing attitude toward the passage of time. Moreover, after analyzing data from the World Values Survey, Hofstede *et al.* (2010) propose the sixth cultural dimension called indulgence representing attitude toward control of human desires. Each cultural dimension is measured by an index ranging from 0 to 100.

First, power distance is defined as the degree to which less powerful individuals in a community expect and accept that the distribution of power is not equal (Hofstede, 1984). Hierarchical culture is a compatible environment for corruption (Licht *et al.*, 2007). According to Cohen and Nelson (1992), unequal power distribution prevents non-power holders from challenging authority. If a subordinate whistle-blows against his/her superior, he/she is criticized for his/her disloyalty. People in a society with high power distance are less likely to sympathize with whistle blowers for their betrayals (Park, 2003). Moreover, subordinates have low propensities to blow the whistle since they are afraid of retaliation from power holders (Victor & Cullen, 1988). In countries with a high power distance, people are less likely to question authority and rules; therefore, government officials have more opportunities to adopt corrupt behaviors. Besides, government officials at higher levels tend to grant favors and preferences to their subordinates so that their subordinates are loyal to them. This provides government officials at lower levels with more opportunities to be corrupt (Achim, 2016).

Second, individualism is defined as the extent to which people are expected to care for themselves and their immediate families only (Hofstede, 1984). People in individualistic societies tend to pursue their own interests more than their groups' interests. Their behaviors are motivated by their own views and opinions instead of their groups' norms and rules (Hofstede *et al.*, 2010). Individualistic societies emphasize personal rights, achievements and autonomy. In countries with high individualism, such as the US, Australia and Great Britain, people respect legal regulations and highly appreciate initiative, competition and democracy (Achim, 2016; Davis & Ruhe, 2003). Therefore, government officials in countries supporting high individualism are more likely to recognize their own accountability and responsibility in their behaviors and they have lower incentives to engage in corruption (Park, 2003). Besides, cooperation and conspiracy that lead to widespread corruption are not compatible with individualism. Government officials in individualistic cultures tend to be more vocal against corrupt behaviors conducted by their colleagues and even superiors in order to protect their own rights and benefits and avoid legal violations (Jha & Panda, 2017).

Third, masculinity is defined as the concern of people for material success, heroism, independence, assertiveness and achievement in power, wealth and status (Hofstede, 1984). A masculine society tends to prefer fast and substantial success to legitimacy and social justice. Therefore, it encourages people, especially men, to achieve material goals with a "now or never" attitude (Park, 2003). When both sides, including individuals/firms and government officials, are driven by big and fast achievement motives, many corrupt opportunities are created. On the one hand, individuals are more likely to pay bribes in order to speed up administrative procedures or obtain more competitive advantages than their competitors (Brademas & Heimann, 1998). On the other hand, government officials also have high incentives to conduct corrupt activities in order to achieve material success and higher positions in the political system. Therefore, masculinity leads to widespread corruption.

Fourth, uncertainty avoidance is defined as the concern of people for an unknown future. People in societies with high uncertainty avoidance are uncomfortable when they face uncertainty and ambiguity (Hofstede, 1984). Therefore, they tend to prevent anxiety and uncertainty in their lives by avoiding illegal activities and high-risk behaviors. Political corruption is a risky behavior since corrupt officials may be exposed to punishment and lose their reputation, status and wealth. In order to avoid the fear and anxiety that may arise from corrupt activities, government officials in high uncertainty avoidance cultures are less likely to engage in corruption affairs. Tong (2014) also shows that corruption is more popular in a country with low-risk avoidance like China since people are more likely to fit into situations due to high ambiguity and adaptability in legislation and rules.

Fifth, long-term orientation is defined as the extent to which people have connections with the past when they handle the challenges and obstacles of the present and future (Hofstede, 1984). Societies with long-term orientation govern people's behaviors with a sense of shame while societies with short-term orientation focus more on reciprocation of greetings and gifts (Achim, 2016). Both government officials and firms in long-term orientation cultures are more ashamed of their illegal activities and more likely to maintain their good reputation; therefore, they have lower incentives to adopt corrupt behaviors.

Finally, indulgence is defined as the extent to which a society allows people to gratify their basic and natural desires to enjoy their lives (Hofstede *et al.*, 2010). Societies given to high indulgence respect leisure time and emotional expression as well as happiness. Government officials in these societies tend to pursue enjoyment of life such as recreation, consumption and money spending; therefore, they have high incentives to offer and receive bribes.

Husted (1999) finds that countries with high scores of power distance, masculinity and uncertainty avoidance are more corrupt. Davis and Ruhe (2003) conduct a survey to investigate how Hofstede's cultural dimensions determine perceived corruption across 42 countries. They find that power distance, individualism and masculinity can explain a considerable portion of the variance in corruption. Power distance and masculinity are positively related to corruption while individualism is negatively associated with corruption. Park (2003) examines determinants of corruption across countries and documents that countries with power distance and masculinity are more corrupt. Robertson and Watson (2004) show that uncertainty avoidance and masculinity increase perceived corruption across 99 countries. Murdoch (2009) investigates the effects of cultural values on economic behavior and finds that power distance increases corruption but individualism decreases corruption. Halkos and Tzeremes (2011) also show that high power distance and low individualism lead to lower corruption across 77 countries. Besides, Jha and Panda (2017) find that individualistic countries are less corrupt. Moreover, Kittova and Stienhauser (2018) investigate how cultural features including individualism, long-term orientation and indulgence determine corruption across the Organization of Economic Co-operation and Development (OECD) members. They document that individualism increases corruption while they fail to find statistical evidence for the effects of long-term orientation and indulgence. Remarkably, Achim (2016) uses all of Hofstede's cultural dimensions to examine the relationship between national culture and corruption with a survey of 98 countries. She finds that the three dimensions of power distance, individualism and long-term orientation have a significant impact on corruption while masculinity, uncertainty avoidance and indulgence are not significantly related to corruption. Power distance, individualism and long-term orientation explain 35%, 37% and 10.8% of variance in corruption, respectively. In addition, Getz and Volkema (2001) find that uncertainty avoidance is the only dimension moderating the relationship between economic adversity and corruption across 50 countries.

### 1.2.3.2.  *The GLOBE project's cultural dimensions*

Although Hofstede's cultural dimensions are the most popular measures of national culture, they are criticized for their outdated data and lack of distinguishing societal values and practices. Based on the idea of charismatic leadership, Robert J. House established the Global Leadership and Organizational Behavior Effectiveness (GLOBE) project in 1991 to examine leaders' rules, values and beliefs across countries. This project was funded by the US Department of Education in 1993 and research started in 1994 (House *et al.*, 2004). A long-standing project, it involves 170 researchers collecting data on 17,000 corporate managers from 62 countries. Initial results show that there are 9 independent variables representing cultural values. However, seven out of nine dimensions are strongly related to Hofstede's dimensions since the cultural framework is based on Hofstede's model. Particularly, uncertainty avoidance and power distance are taken directly from Hofstede (1984). Future orientation is similar to Hofstede's long-term orientation. Gender egalitarianism and assertiveness are developed from Hofstede's masculinity. Institutional collectivism and societal collectivism are strongly related to Hofstede's individualism. Only two dimensions, performance orientation and humane orientation, are different.

First, human orientation is defined as the extent to which people encourage, respect and reward those who are friendly, helpful, courteous, caring and fair to others. Societies with high human orientation are more tolerant of mistakes, focus more on personal relations and show less respect for material success (Javidan & House, 2001). The GLOBE project also finds that societies are less human-oriented when they are economically developed and urbanized. However, societies are more human-oriented when they are poor due to difficulties in physical conditions and climate (Kabasakal & Bodur, 2004). A human-oriented culture appreciates sympathy and tolerance; therefore, government officials understand that people are more likely to sympathize with them for their misconducts. This leads to widespread corruption.

Second, performance orientation is defined as the degree to which people encourage and honor creativity, innovation and advancement (Mansour Javidan, 2004). Performance-oriented societies focus on the ability to overcome challenges and accomplish results. The GLOBE project shows that countries with high-performance orientation have higher national competitive advantages and well-being. People in these societies believe that education and training are critical for achievements and thus people should work hard for success. These cultural values imply that unethical and dishonest behaviors are not supported. Government officials should focus on improving their abilities and performance rather than adopting corrupt behaviors. Seleim and Bontis (2009) investigate how the GLOBE cultural dimensions of values and practices influence corruption across 62 countries. They find that human orientation practices and individualism practices increase corruption while uncertainty avoidance values decrease corruption.

### 1.2.3.3. *Schwartz's cultural dimensions*

Schwartz (1992) developed an alternative cultural model based on individual differences in value priorities and their impacts on people's beliefs and behaviors. This model has seven cultural dimensions including conservatism, intellectual autonomy, affective autonomy, egalitarianism, hierarchy, harmony and mastery. Then, Schwartz

(1994) renames the dimension conservatism as embeddedness. These seven dimensions are grouped into three pairs: embeddedness versus autonomy (i.e., intellectual autonomy and affective autonomy), hierarchy versus egalitarianism and mastery versus harmony.

First, embeddedness/autonomy is defined as the degree to which individuals are embedded/autonomous in their groups. Like Hofstede's collectivism, embeddedness represents respect for collectivity, tradition, family and social relationships. Intellectual autonomy emphasizes intellectual encouragement including innovation and creativity while affective autonomy represents affective encouragement including pleasure and happiness (Tekeş *et al.*, 2019). Second, hierarchy/egalitarianism refers to people's attitude toward social orderings. Like power distance, hierarchy respects authority, paternalism and social class while egalitarianism focuses on equality and social justice. Third, mastery/harmony represents the extent to which people concentrate on controlling/living in harmony with the natural and social world. Mastery societies tend to value achievement, success and material reward while societies tuned to harmony respect peace, adaptability and quality of life (Tekeş *et al.*, 2019). Therefore, the cultural value of mastery may lead to widespread corruption, and that of harmony is able to reduce corruption. Using Schwartz's data released in 2005, Yeganeh (2014) investigates the effect of Schwartz's cultural dimensions on corruption across 55 countries. He finds that conservatism (embeddedness) and harmony increase corruption while autonomy and mastery decrease corruption.

### 1.2.3.4. *Inglehart's cultural dimensions*

According to modernization theory, continued economic development may change shared beliefs, norms and practices in a society While industrial economy makes organizations become more rational and hierarchical, a post-industrial economy focuses on information processing and communication. Therefore, people prefer self-expression and autonomy to self-restraint and obedience (Inglehart, 1997; Inglehart & Baker, 2000). Inglehart's cultural framework includes two dimensions: traditional/secular–rational and survival/self-expression. The former represents the importance of tradition and religion in a society. The latter reflects people's attitude toward materialistic values and quality of life. Traditional societies tend to respect social relations, family ties and religious beliefs; therefore, they have low levels of democracy and accountability. These characteristics lead to widespread corruption. Moreover, countries with high survival focus on materialistic values more than interpersonal trust and subjective well-being. As a result, governments have high incentives to adopt corrupt behaviors and individuals/organizations are more likely to pay bribes. Sandholtz and Taagepera (2005) show that Inglehart's cultural dimensions can explain corruption to a large extent in non-communist countries. The extent to which a strong survival culture increases corruption is twice as much as the extent to which a traditional culture increases corruption. Besides, Yeganeh (2014) also shows that traditional and survival dimensions are positively related to corruption. By contrast, rational-secular and self-expression dimensions reduce corruption.

### 1.2.3.5.  *Public sector culture*

Sulitzeanu-Kenan *et al.* (2021) develop a theoretical framework in which corruption is determined by both public sector honesty and culture, based on the Becker–Stigler model of corruption. According to Becker and Stigler (1974), corruption has two major determinants, namely, government officials' intrinsic honesty and the incentives that they face. Sulitzeanu-Kenan *et al.* (2021) argue that public sector honesty is not only determined by societal culture but also public sector culture. Public organizations may have a unique system of values, informal rules and beliefs that respect or understate honesty. As a result, government officials' propensity to conduct honest behaviors is different from that of people from other groups. Public sector culture can nurture the norm of honesty through many activities such as recruitment, training and work socialization (Belle & Cantarelli, 2017). Furthermore, values and norms of the public sector culture are also present in institutional incentive structures and other anti-corruption policies. Therefore, public sector culture also directly affects corruption. Sulitzeanu-Kenan *et al.* (2021) use data about honest behavior from Cohn *et al.* (2019) to investigate the relationship between public sector honesty and corruption across 40 countries. They find that the public sector culture determines public sector honesty and public sector honesty reduces corruption. These effects are independent from the channel of incentive structures.

### 1.2.3.6. *Religion*

Religion is another channel through which culture determines corruption (Tunali & Weill, 2020). Religion is defined as human communication with what people regard as holy, sacred and spiritual. Religious doctrines provide people with definitions of good and bad behaviors and their consequences. The followers believe that those who do good will be welcomed in heaven and "evildoers" will be punished in hell (Xu *et al.*, 2017). According to La Porta *et al.* (1999), religion affects work ethic, tolerance and trust, which determine government practices. Religion may affect corruption in different ways (Tunali & Weill, 2020). First, most religions teach and expect their followers to be honest in their behavior. North *et al.* (2013) show that religion is an important force maintaining a social order through creating standards and rules for individuals' behavior. According to Rose-Ackerman (1997), corruption is partly a function of government officials' honesty and integrity; therefore, corruption is rapidly widespread in the whole society if government officials lose their honesty and integrity. Guiso *et al.* (2003) use data from the World Values Survey to investigate the effects of religiosity and different religions on many fundamental societal attitudes across 66 countries over the period 1981–1997. They find that religious people have higher trust in others, the government and legal regulations. Therefore, religion helps government officials avoid corrupt activities. Tunali and Weill (2020) also use the World Values Survey data to analyze the effects of religiosity and religious denominations on attitudes toward corruption in 59 countries from 2010 to 2014. Their findings also show that religious people have negative attitudes toward corruption.

Second, how religious denominations may affect corruption through two opposite channels including hierarchical or individualistic religions. According to Putnam and Leonardi (1993), hierarchical religions including Catholicism, Orthodox Christianity and Islam establish a vertical system of bonds in the society and respect authority. Moreover, followers of hierarchical religions have lower trust in others (La Porter *et al.*, 1997). They are also more tolerant of mistakes and evils (Lipset & Lenz, 2000). Therefore, countries with hierarchical religions tend to be more corrupt. However, individualistic religions like Protestantism tend to create horizontal bonds and focus on avoiding committing errors and sins (Lipset & Lenz, 2000). As a result, countries with individualistic religions are more corrupt.

Examining many measures of perceived corruption compiled from various surveys on business risk in the 1980s and 1990s, Treisman (2000) finds that Protestant traditions have reduced corruption across countries. Sandholtz and Koetzle (2000) investigate the effect of religion on corruption by developing a theoretical model in which both political-economic structures of incentives and cultural values determine corruption. They also document that predominantly Protestant countries are less corrupt. Gokcekus (2008) shows that the proportion of Protestants is negatively related to corruption, but his results in 2000 are weaker than that in 1990 and 1970. Furthermore, Paldam (2001) posits that religion is one of the key components of culture; therefore, he uses religion as a proxy of culture to analyze how culture influences corruption across 100 countries in 1999. He finds that Reformed Christianity (i.e., Protestantism and Anglicanism) and Tribal Religions have negative effects on corruption while Pre-Reform Christianity (i.e., Old Christianity, Catholicism, and Orthodoxy) leads to widespread corruption. North *et al.* (2013) examine how a dominant religious culture affects corruption and rule of law across 203 countries. They find that countries were least corrupt in 2004 if their largest religion was Protestantism in 1900. By contrast, countries were most corrupt in 2004 if their dominant religion was Orthodox Christianity in 1990. Mensah (2014) shows that Protestantism is not the only religion reducing corruption;

Buddhism and to a limited degree Hinduism also have a negative effect on corruption. Non-Protestant Christianity and Islam have a lesser deterrent effect on corruption compared to Protestantism, Buddhism and Hinduism. Xu *et al.* (2017) use provincial-level data to examine how religious beliefs affect bureaucratic corruption across provinces in China over the period 1998–2009. They find that local religious heritage is negatively related to local corruption. This result implies that China's traditional religions such as Taoism and Buddhism are more effective in controlling corruption. Moreover, the negative effect of religion on local corruption is weaker when law enforcement is stronger. Tunali and Weill (2020) show that hierarchical religions including Protestantism and Hinduism decrease corruption more than atheism. However, using data from the fourth wave of the World Values Survey across 64 countries, Ko and Moon (2014) fail to find strong evidence to support the positive effect of hierarchical religions including Islam, Catholicism and Orthodox Christianity on political corruption.

Moreover, many studies show that religious freedom is also a determinant of corruption. Douglas Beets (2007) utilizes Kruskal-Wallis's non-parametric statistical measure to analyze the relationship between religion and corruption across 133 countries and finds that a country is more corrupt when its citizens are poorer, have a low level of religious freedom and consider religion as a critical factor in their lives. Sommer *et al.* (2013) argue that the relationship between religion and political corruption relies on the institutional framework. They find that religious freedom can reduce corruption in democratic countries, but this effect fails to exist in non-democratic countries. Gokcekus and Ekici (2020) investigate whether religiosity (i.e., attachment to religion) is more effective than religious affiliation in corruption. Their findings show that the former increases corruption. Dincer (2008) investigates the relationship between religious diversity and political corruption in 48 US states over two periods: 1980–1989 and 1990–1999. Their findings show that the relationship between religious polarization and corruption is linear and positive while religious fractionalization and corruption have an inverse-U shaped relationship.

## 1.2.4.  *Economic factors*

### 1.2.4.1.  *Economic development*

Economic development brings a sustainable improvement in people's living standards. Before making corrupt decisions, government officials consider both its expected costs and benefits. The expected costs rely on the benefits that government officials may obtain from their jobs (e.g., salary and reputation) and the punishment that they may face (Saha & Gounder, 2013). Economic development may affect political corruption as follows. First, rich countries have more resources to prevent and detect corrupt activities while poor countries fail to have effective systems to control corruption (Bajada & Shashnov, 2019). Therefore, costs of corruption in poor countries are lower (Elbahnasawy & Revier, 2012). Second, poor countries have lower legal enforceability and thus government officials are more likely to adopt corrupt behaviors (Park, 2003). Finally, in poor countries, government officials have low salaries (Seldadyo & De Haan, 2005) while the marginal value of money is high (Shabbir & Anwar, 2007). When the material well-being gained from corrupt acts tends to exceed their expected costs, public servants have high incentives to engage in corruption (Adem, 2021).

Rijckeghem and Weder (1997) propose two efficiency wage models of corruption to investigate the role of civil service wages in corruption. Their findings show that wages are negatively related to corruption across developing countries. Shabbir and Anwar (2007) examine how economic and non-economic factors affect corruption across 41 developing countries and also find that there is a negative relationship between average income and corruption. Zakaria (2009) shows that economic development has a significantly negative impact on corruption, but its economic magnitude is small. When per capita income increases by 0.11, corruption decreases by only 0.01 points. Saha and Ben Ali (2017) investigate how economic development can control corruption in Middle Eastern and North African (MENA) countries from 1984 to 2013. They document that increases in income lead to higher corruption in countries that are rich in natural resources. Bajada and Shashnov (2019) argue that economic development improves government budget since tax revenue tends to increase. When the government has more money to develop and finance institutions adequately, they are more capable of detecting and preventing corrupt activities. Their findings show that economic development leads to lower corruption. This relationship is also present in various clusters of countries by geographical region. Several studies find that economic development measured by GDP per capita negatively influences corruption (Alt & Lassen, 2003; Bonaglia *et al.*, 2009; Brunetti & Weder, 2003; Chang & Golden, 2007; Damania *et al.*, 2004; Donfouet *et al.*, 2018; Fisman & Gatti, 2002a; Graeff & Mehlkop, 2003; Knack & Azfar, 2003; Kunicova & Rose-Ackerman, 2005; Lederman *et al.*, 2005; Persson & Tabellini, 2005; Rauch & Evans, 2000; Serra, 2006; Swamy *et al.*, 2001; Tavares, 2003, 2000).

In addition, Paldam (2002) finds that corruption is lower when an economy is in transition from being poor to rich, and inflation tends to increase corruption. Braun and Di tella (2004) also document a positive effect of inflation on corruption in 75 countries. In particular, corruption increases by 12% of a standard deviation when inflation increases by a standard deviation. Bhattacharyya and Jha (2013) investigate the effect of economic growth on corruption across 20 Indian states over the period 2005–2008. They find that GDP growth the value of bribes, but its impact on corruption perception is limited. Moreover, Saha and Gounder (2013) show that a quadratic function is the best description for the relationship between economic development and corruption. Countries with low and medium income experience an upsurge of corruption, but corruption tends to decline with advanced stages of economic development. Ali and Krammer (2016) document a nonlinear relationship between economic development and corruption in MENA countries. When economic development is low, an increase in per capita income leads to higher corruption; however, this effect is reversed after income reaches a threshold. Examining the effect of the macro-economic environment on corruption in G20 member countries, Maria *et al.* (2021) also find that GDP per capita has a positive and significant impact on corruption in developing countries, but the impact is opposite in developed countries.

### 1.2.4.2. *Economic freedom*

Economic freedom is defined as the protection of personal property and the freedom to choose, use and exchange property (Gwartney *et al.*, 1996). People have economic freedom when the property that they acquire legally is protected safely from physical invasion by others and when they can use and exchange their property freely without violating the identical rights of other people. In a society with high economic freedom, the main functions of the government include protecting property rights, enforcing contracts and supplying public goods (Graeff & Mehlkop, 2003). Therefore, government officials have fewer opportunities to engage in corruption. According to Goldsmith (1999), economic liberalization plays an important role in controlling corruption. Economic liberalization leads to privatization and deregulation. Privatization reduces opportunities for corrupt officials to exploit their power for their own interests. Privatized firms are controlled by the public more effectively. Deregulation restricts opportunities for government officials to give exceptions to rules and thus corruption is lower. When economic freedom is suppressed, citizens' economic achievements considerably rely on their abilities to influence government officials' decisions. However, when economic freedom is at a high level, political control over economic resources is limited (Shabbir & Anwar, 2007).

Goldsmith (1999) investigates correlates of political corruption across 34 low-income and middle-income economies and finds that economic liberalization can reduce corruption. Using various measures of economic freedom published by the Heritage Foundation, Fraser Institute and Freedom House, Chafuen and Guzman (2000) also show that countries with high economic freedom are less corrupt. Broadman and Recanatini (2002) also show that corruption is higher in countries where firms face more obstacles to entry and exit. Saha *et al.* (2009) examine the role of economic freedom and democracy and their interaction in corruption control across 100 countries over the period 1995–2004. They document that economic freedom is a deterrent to corruption regardless of the political environment whereas democracy only reduces corruption in countries with low economic liberalization. Apergis *et al.* (2012) investigate the relationship between economic freedom and political corruption in 50 US. states during the period 1981–2004. Their findings show that economic freedom is positively related to political corruption in the long run. Furthermore, Ali and Isse (2002), Kunicova and Rose-Ackerman (2005), Park (2003), Shabbir and Anwar (2007) and Treisman (2000) also find empirical evidence for the negative impact of economic freedom on political corruption.

Moreover, Saha and Su (2012) show that the interactive effect of economic freedom and democracy leads to lower corruption in 100 countries, especially in the most corrupt ones. Saha and Ben Ali (2017) also analyze the effects of both political freedom and economic freedom on corruption in the MENA economies from 1984 to 2013. They find that the interactive relationship between economic freedom, political freedom and government size can control corruption. Investigating how different components of economic freedom determine political corruption, Graeff and Mehlkop (2003) show that across 78 countries some components negatively affect corruption and these effects rely on economic development. Consistently, Pieroni and d'Agostino (2013) also find that a country's economic development plays an important role in the relationship between components of economic freedom and corrupt practices in Africa.

Although several studies show a negative effect of economic freedom on political corruption, Das and DiRienzo (2009), Paldam (2002) and Shen and Williamson (2005) document that economic freedom leads to higher corruption across countries. These opposite results clarify that individuals and firms in a free economy face more aggressive competition and market pressure; therefore, they are more likely to pay bribes in order to be a step ahead of their competitors (Graeff & Mehlkop, 2003).

### 1.2.4.3. *International economic integration*

International economic integration is defined as the process of eliminating barriers to trade, investment, labor mobility and technology transfer between countries. According to Sandholtz and Gray (2003), international economic integration may affect political corruption through two main channels. First, economic openness means that domestic firms face higher competitive pressures, while bribery or speed money increases their costs. If they are willing to pay bribes, they cannot compete with foreign competitors and may even go bankrupt. Besides, local firms calling for foreign investment may face difficulties in securing it or may have to pay a premium. Consequently, public officials have fewer corrupt opportunities and their corruption-related income tends to decline. Second, economic integration includes international social exchange. One locus of this exchange is international organizations. Most international organizations are dominated by developed countries that have effective anti-corruption legislation and thus international organizations become forums to diffuse and promote anti-corruption norms and rules. In addition, international organizations also have their own anti-corruption norms. When a country participates in an international organization, it has to adopt these norms and thus suffers less corruption. On the other hand, restrictions on international economic integration increase rent-related corruption. Government officials have more opportunities to engage in corruption when they have the rights to grant quota licenses, import/export licenses or permissions for firms to enter or exit a market (Elbahnasawy & Revier, 2012; Seldadyo & De Haan, 2005). Gurgur and Shah (2005) find that a lack of economic openness leads to high corruption across 30 countries.

Ades and Di tella (1999) argue that firms can obtain some of the rents by paying bribes for control rights. With two samples of 52 countries and 31 countries over the periods 1980–1983 and 1989–1990, respectively, they find that import intensity and proximity to large exporters in the world may enable reduction of corruption while export revenues from fuel and mineral tend to increase corruption. Leite and Weidmann (1999) also find that trade openness was negatively related to political corruption across 72 countries in 1995. According to Wei (2000b), trade intensity includes natural openness and residual openness. The former is explained by population and many geographic factors while the latter is explained by government policy. A country having a natural propensity to participate in international trade due to its small size and geographic advantages tends to invest more resources to develop strong institutions and thus it can control corruption more effectively. Wei (2000b) documents that natural openness leads to lower corruption, but residual openness has no significant impact on corruption. Herzfeld and Weiss (2003) show that economic openness reduces corruption across 72 countries. Zakaria (2009) investigates the effect of trade openness on political corruption in Pakistan and finds that trade openness led to lower corruption over the period 1984–2007. In addition, Brunetti and Weder (2003), Fisman and Gatti (2002a), Gurgur and Shah (2005) and Persson *et al.* (2003) also show supporting evidence for the negative relationship between trade openness and political corruption.

Furthermore, Shabbir and Anwar (2007) find that globalization measured by net exports to GDP ratio reduces political corruption across 41 developing countries. Using data from 102 countries from 1995 to 2005, Badinger and Nindl (2012) document that globalization, including trade and financial liberalization, negatively impacts political corruption in developing countries. Asongu (2014) shows that globalization can control corruption in middle- and high-income countries in Africa, but this relationship is not significant in low-income countries. Using data from 127 countries from 2006, Lalountas *et al.* (2011) also find that globalization is effective in corruption control only in middle and high-income countries. Besides, Tavares (2003) shows that foreign aid can reduce political corruption. Particularly, when foreign aid inflows increase by 1% of GDP, political corruption decreases by 0.2 points out of 10. Mohamed *et al.* (2015) also find that foreign aid leads to lower corruption in 42 Sub-Saharan African countries over the period 2000–2010. However, Maria *et al.* (2021) show that economic openness is positively related to political corruption in developing countries in G20. The policy implication of this study is the prioritization of secondary education to tackle corruption problems. Das and DiRienzo (2009) find that the relationship between globalization and corruption is nonlinear.

# 1.3.  Measures of Political Corruption

In principle, administrative data are a direct source of information to measure political corruption. However, the reliability of self-reported data from government agencies is a big concern since political corruption is practiced by government officials. Therefore, researchers commonly use data from other parties to measure corruption. According to Neudorfer and Neudorfer (2014), there are two groups of political corruption measures: perception-based and experience-based.

Perception-based corruption measures rest on opinions of citizens, corporate managers or experts. Perception-based data are usually collected through surveys. Academics show that perceived corruption measures have two main weaknesses: First, perception of political corruption is not corruption itself. Respondents (mainly experts) may have available mechanisms in their minds to describe a country's corruption level (Razafindrakoto & Roubaud, 2010). For example, when an expert has information on democracy or economic development, he/she tends to evaluate the level of corruption without considering whether his/her perception is consistent with the real world. Donchev and Ujhelyi (2014) show that the gap between corruption perception and corruption experience is caused by political, economic and cultural factors. Second, when the calculation method is changed, researchers cannot compare political corruption over time. Three common perception-based corruption measures include the aforementioned Corruption Perception Index (CPI) published by TI, Control of Corruption Index (CCI) published by the World Bank (WB) and Corruption Index (CI) published by the International Country Risk Guide (ICRG) (Judge *et al.*, 2011).

Experience-based corruption measures rest on experiences and knowledge of citizens, businesspeople or experts. Their experiences include but are not limited to bribery amount, bribery frequency, reasons to pay bribes and corrupt government agencies/officials. Their knowledge is about citizens'/firms' rights and obligations, and anti-corruption legislation, policies and practices. Experience data is also collected through surveys. Like perceived corruption, experienced corruption also has weaknesses. First, experience-based corruption measures are effective in measuring petty corruption but not effective in measuring grand corruption. Citizens and businesspeople only pay bribes to government officials at low levels such as local public servants and police officers. They fail to have the experience of corrupt behaviors adopted by top government officials. Second, respondents may not be willing to participate in the survey or may provide biased information since they do not want to reveal their illegal actions (Neudorfer & Neudorfer, 2014). Common experience-based corruption measures include the *Global Corruption Barometer* (GCB) and the *Bribe Payers Index* (BPI) published by TI, corruption information from the *World Business Environment Survey* (WBES) conducted by the World Bank, corruption information from the Interregional Crime and Victimization Survey (ICVS) conducted by the United Nations Inter-regional Crime and the Justice Research Institute (UNICRI), and corruption pillar from the European Quality of Government Index (EQI).

In addition to country-level corruption measures, there are local corruption measures. Most local corruption measures are experience-based. In the US, researchers usually use the administrative data from the Report to Congress on the Activities and Operations of the Public Integrity Section issued by the Department of Justice to construct the Corruption Convictions Index (Alt & Lassen, 2014; Dincer, 2019; Fisman & Gatti, 2002b; Fredriksson *et al.*, 2003; Glaeser & Saks, 2006). Besides, Dincer (2019) and Dincer and Johnston (2014) also use the corrupt cases presented in The Associated Press news wires to construct the Corruption Reflections Index (CRI). These political corruption measures are available across 50 US states. In China, researchers measure political corruption based on the number of corruption cases per 10,000 residents or government officials from the China Procuratorial Yearbooks (Dong & Torgler, 2013; Xu & Li, 2018). This political corruption measure is available for 22 provinces, 4 municipalities and 5 autonomous administrative regions except Hong Kong and Macao. In Vietnam, local corruption is measured by an informal payment score — a component of the Provincial Competitiveness Index (PCI) published by the Vietnam Chamber of Commerce and Industry (VCCI) and the US Agency for International Development (USAID) (Jie Bai *et al.*, 2019; Nam *et al.*, 2020; Nguyen & Van Dijk, 2012; Tran, 2019, 2021b). This experience-based corruption indicator is calculated from the data of business surveys conducted annually across the 63 provincial territories in Vietnam. Moreover, local corruption may also be measured by a corruption control score — a component of the Provincial Governance and the Public Administration Performance Index (PAPI). The data of PAPI are from face-to-face survey-based interviews with citizens across the 63 provinces and cities in Vietnam.

# Chapter 2

# Political Corruption — A Worldwide Problem

*This chapter describes political corruption as a severe problem that many countries in the world are facing. It summarizes corruption in some regions and countries. Then, it analyzes the possible effects of political corruption on countries' political issues (political trust, political stability and government budget), macro-economic issues (domestic investment, foreign investment, inflation, economic growth, international trade and the shadow economy) and the socio-cultural environment (income inequality, public services, environment and emigration).*

## 2.1. Political Corruption Around the World

"The world has enough for everyone's need, but not enough for everyone's greed" — Mahatma Gandhi. Corrupt opportunities may be more available when the world's economy develops. The database of Corruption Perception Index (CPI) published by Transparency International (TI) in 2020 shows that political corruption is a severe problem faced by most countries in the world. Nordic countries have

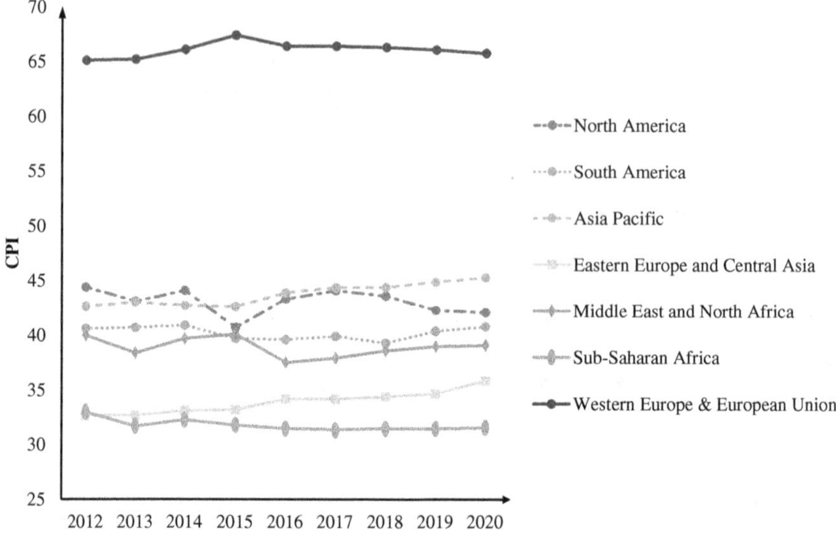


**Figure 2.1. Political corruption across regions over the period 2012–2020**

*Source*: The Transparency International.

the lowest levels of corruption while some countries in Africa, South America and Asia have the highest levels of corruption.

Figure 2.1 presents CPI of different regions from 2012 to 2020. The score for each region in a year is measured by the average of all the countries' indices. Overall, there have been no significant changes in corruption across regions over the past 9 years. Western Europe and the European Union (EU) form the least corrupt region. Its annual CPI ranges from 65 to 67, much higher than those of the two following regions, namely, Asia Pacific and North America. Sub-Saharan Africa is the most corrupt region with a CPI ranging from 31 to 33. In addition, Asia Pacific, Eastern Europe and Central Asia tend to face less corruption gradually with slight increases in CPI while Sub-Saharan Africa experiences a downward trend.

Table 2.1 presents the least and the most corrupt countries in the world with different measures of political corruption published in 2020. Ranking based on CPI from TI, Control of Corruption Index

**Table 2.1.  The least and the most corrupt countries in the world in 2020**

| Country rank | | CPI from the Transparency International | | CCI from the World Bank | | CI from the International Country Risk Guide | |
|---|---|---|---|---|---|---|---|
| | | Country | CPI | Country | CCI | Country | CI |
| The least corrupt countries | 1 | Denmark | 88 | Denmark | 100.0 | Denmark | 1.00 |
| | 2 | New Zealand | 88 | Finland | 99.5 | Finland | 0.92 |
| | 3 | Finland | 85 | Singapore | 99.0 | New Zealand | 0.92 |
| | 4 | Singapore | 85 | New Zealand | 98.6 | Sweden | 0.92 |
| | 5 | Sweden | 85 | Sweden | 98.1 | Germany | 0.83 |
| | 6 | Switzerland | 85 | Norway | 97.6 | Luxembourg | 0.83 |
| | 7 | Norway | 84 | Switzerland | 97.1 | Netherlands | 0.83 |
| | 8 | Netherlands | 82 | Luxembourg | 96.6 | Norway | 0.83 |
| | 9 | Germany | 80 | Netherlands | 96.2 | Singapore | 0.83 |
| | 10 | Luxembourg | 80 | Liechtenstein | 95.7 | Switzerland | 0.83 |
| | 11 | | | | | United Kingdom | 0.83 |
| The most corrupt countries | 1 | Somalia | 12 | South Sudan | −1.91 | Somalia | 0.08 |
| | 2 | South Sudan | 12 | Syria | −1.71 | South Sudan | 0.08 |
| | 3 | Syria | 14 | Equatorial Guinea | −1.69 | Congo, Rep. | 0.17 |
| | 4 | Venezuela | 15 | North Korea | −1.68 | Congo, Dem. Rep. | 0.17 |
| | 5 | Yemen | 15 | Yemen | −1.68 | North Korea | 0.17 |
| | 6 | Equatorial Guinea | 16 | Somalia | −1.67 | Libya | 0.17 |
| | 7 | Sudan | 16 | Libya | −1.62 | Syria | 0.17 |
| | 8 | Libya | 17 | Congo | −1.57 | Venezuela | 0.17 |
| | 9 | Congo, Dem. Rep. | 18 | Venezuela | −1.56 | Yemen | 0.17 |
| | 10 | Haiti | 18 | Turkmenistan | −1.54 | Zimbabwe | 0.17 |
| | 11 | North Korea | 18 | | | | |

*Source*: The Transparency International, the World Bank and the International Country Risk Guide.

(CCI) from the World Bank and Corruption Index (CI) of the International Country Risk Guide consistently show the same group of least corrupt countries despite some small differences in their orders. Denmark is the least corrupt country in the world with the maximum values of CCI and CI. Moreover, the majority of highly corrupt countries are from Africa. Corruption is most widespread in Somalia and South Sudan. The differences in the three corruption measures between the least and the most corrupt groups are large.

Figure 2.2 illustrates the distribution of CPI in 2020 by economic development. Overall, developed economies are far less corrupt than economies in transition and developing economies. The most corrupt

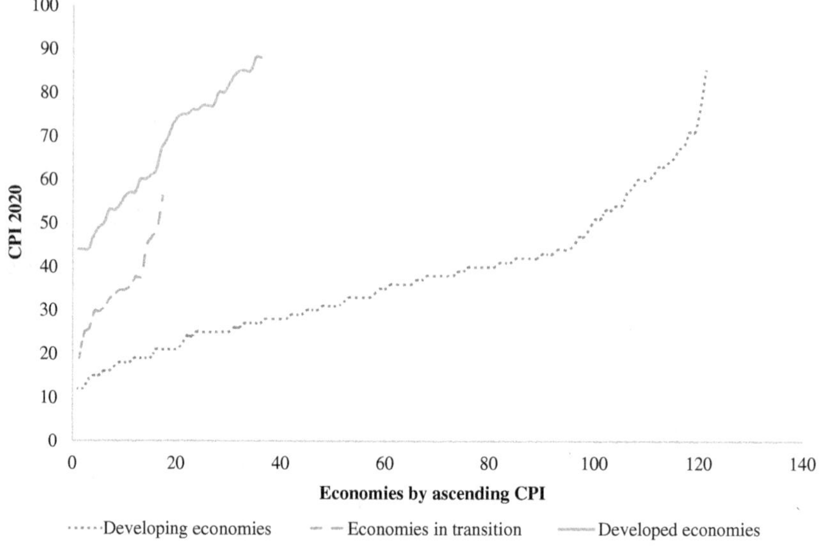


**Figure 2.2.  Political corruption across economies**
*Source*: The Transparency International.

developed country has a CPI of 44. This corruption level is higher
than CPIs of over 75% of the transition economies and developing
economies. About 50% of developed countries have CPIs higher than
70 while this number is only 3.3% for developing countries. The maximum CPI of transition economies is only 56. In developing and transition economies, governments often have excessive interventions and
non-state institutions' monitoring is ineffective. Besides, their legal
enforcement is poor (Fisman & Gatti, 2002a). These factors make
corruption become widespread.

Figure 2.3 shows bribery incidence in 79 countries from the World
Bank's Enterprise Surveys over the period 2016–2020. Bribery incidence is measured by the proportion of firms experiencing at least
one bribe payment request. There are 40 countries in which over
10% of firms requested to pay bribes and 9 countries in which over
70% of firms received at least one bribe payment request. Estonia,
Luxembourg and Sweden are the most transparent countries with 0%

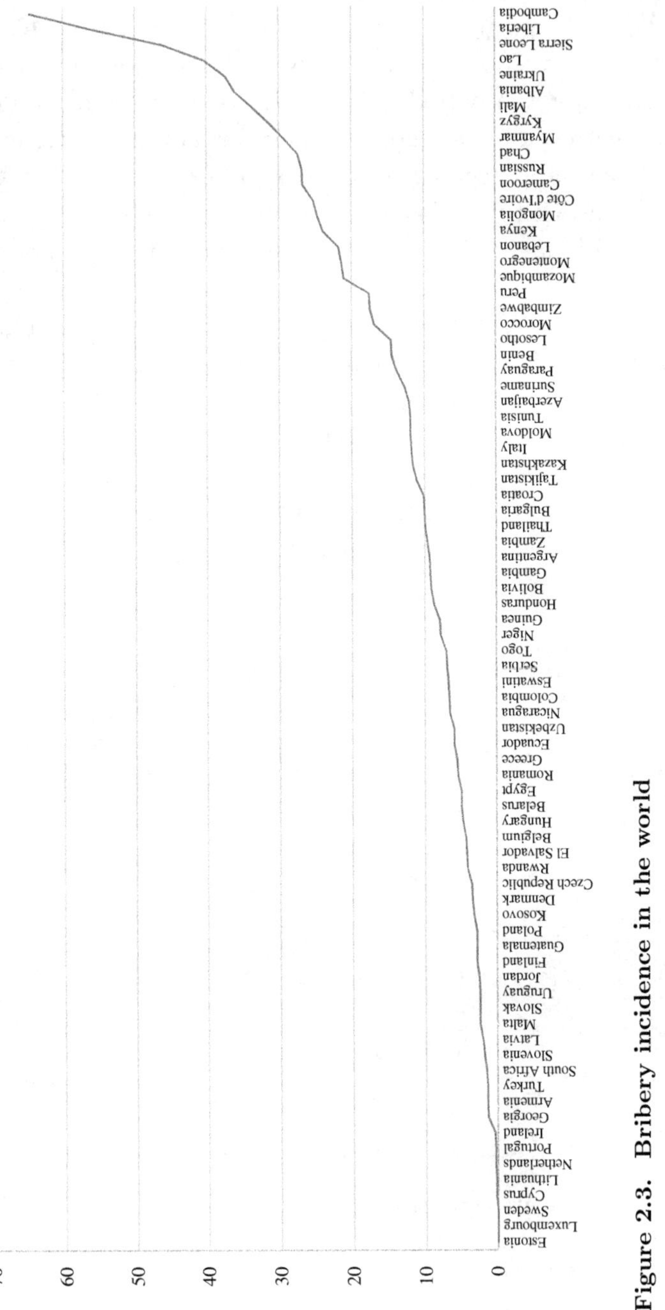

**Figure 2.3.   Bribery incidence in the world**

*Source:* The World Bank's Enterprise Surveys from 2016 to 2020.

corruption while Cambodia has the highest corruption percentage with 64.7%, followed by Liberia (56%) and Sierra Leone (46.1%).

Figure 2.4 shows political corruption by institutions across regions in the world over the period 2015–2017. Its data are from TI's surveys in which respondents indicate their perception of corrupt institutions. The total percentage of two responses including "Most" and "All" for each institution is presented in Figure 2.4. Religious leaders and traditional leaders are the least corrupt while police, legislature, government officials and local government councilors are the most corrupt. About 38% respondents in the world think that most policemen are corrupt. Legislature also has 38%. Government officials and local government councilors received 32% and 31% of responses, respectively. In addition, the most corrupt institution in Africa is the police. People in Europe and Central Asia consider legislature as the most corrupt institution. Legislature, government

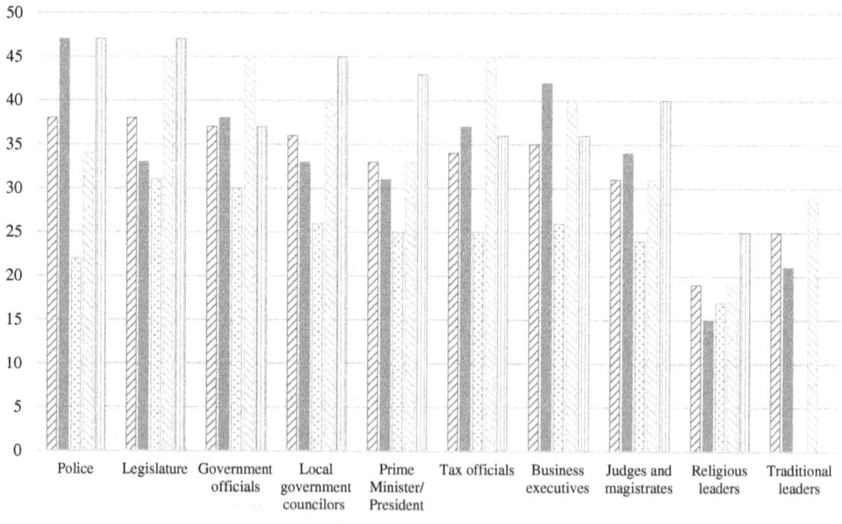



**Figure 2.4.   Political corruption by institutions over the period 2015–2017**

*Source*: The Transparency International.

officials and tax officials are the most corrupt institutions in Middle East and North Africa (MENA) with 45% of responses. Besides, police and legislature are also the most corrupt in Latin America and the Caribbean.

## 2.2.  Political Effects

### 2.2.1.  *The effect on political trust*

Political trust or system support is a fundamental evaluative orientation toward a political system based on how well political authorities and institutions perform to satisfy citizens' normative expectations (Hetherington, 1998; Miller & Listhaug, 1990; Stoke, 1962). In a democratic political system, the government is held accountable to execute laws equitably and fairly, conduct transparent policies and ensure people's rights to participate in the political process (Anderson & Tverdova, 2003). When government officials abuse public power to serve their own interests, the procedures to hold the government accountable are less effective (Bardhan, 1997). Consequently, democratic principles become weaker and citizens are more likely to receive unfair treatment. According to Miller and Listhaug (1999), political corruption erodes people's belief in institutional effectiveness and fairness, which represent the performance of a political system. Disaffected people become disappointed with the existing political system and thus they seek radical changes to have a better one (Solé-Ollé & Sorribas-Navarro, 2014).

Seligson (2002) employs a data of 9,000 observations from national surveys across four Latin American countries to investigate how political corruption affects regime legitimacy. They find that corruption dampens citizens' trust in the political system. Anderson and Tverdova (2003) use data from the International Social Survey Program to examine the impact of political corruption on people's attitude toward democratic political institutions across 16 countries. These countries include both developed countries (Australia, Canada, Germany, Great Britain, Ireland, Italy, Japan, New

Zealand, Norway, Sweden and the US) and developing countries (the Czech Republic, Hungary, Latvia, Russia and Slovenia). Their study shows that people in highly corrupt countries tend to have a more negative attitude toward the government and lower trust in government officials. In addition, using data of political scandals collected from the US and the UK, Bowler and Karp (2004) find that scandals involving lawmakers negatively affect citizens' evaluation of the political system. This implies that political scandals erode not only the reputation of individual politicians but also political institutions. Chang and Chu (2006) continue to examine the relationship between political corruption and institutional trust across five developed and newly established democracies (Japan, the Philippines, South Korea, Taiwan and Thailand). Using the East Asia Barometer database, they document that political corruption strongly erodes institutional trust in Asian democracies. This trust-eroding effect is stable across all countries and is not affected by contextual factors. Morris and Klesner (2010) also show a negative relationship between political corruption and trust in political institutions in Mexico. Linde and Erlingsson (2013) find that political corruption reduces support for the democratic system in Sweden. Furthermore, Obydenkova and Arpino (2018) investigate the effect of political corruption on political trust in the European Union before and after the outbreak of the Great Recession. With data from the European Social Survey, they document that the negative relationship between political corruption and trust in the national parliament was stronger after the outbreak in 2008. However, political corruption increased trust in the EU before 2008. These findings imply that in countries with high corruption, citizens have lower levels of trust in national institutions, but they have positive attitudes toward and expectations from international organizations.

After investigating the changes in political trust across developed and newly founded democracies over 25 years, Catterberg and Moreno (2006) find that there is an observable decrease in political trust. They posit that this trend indicates the post-honeymoon dis-illusionment instead of an increase in critical citizenry. When people live in peace for many years, they no longer expect the government to just ensure their survival. They tend to evaluate the government based on its ability to improve economic growth and reduce social problems. These more demanding evaluation standards make political trust decline. Extracting data from the World Values Survey and the European Values Survey, Catterberg and Moreno (2006) examine determinants of political trust and find that corruption permissiveness reduces political trust. Moreover, Villoria *et al.* (2013) examine the effect of political corruption on people's attitudes and behaviors toward the government in Spain after the country faced a severe outbreak of corruption during a booming period of urban development. Many corrupt cases anger people and provoke calls for political reform. Based on data from a survey conducted in 2009, Villoria *et al.* (2013) show that political corruption has negative effects on citizen satisfaction and social and institutional trust. Solé-Ollé and Sorribas-Navarro (2014) also investigate how corruption scandals affect citizens' belief in local governments in Spain. With data of local corruption scandals from 1999 to 2009, they find that corruption scandals reduce citizens' trust in local politicians. This effect is stronger when citizens fail to have ideological connection with the corrupt party. Besides, examining the role of education in institutional trust across countries, Hakhverdian and Mayne (2012) show that education reduces the negative effect of political corruption on institutional trust.

However, Manzetti and Wilson (2007) argue that citizens in countries with high corruption may support their governments. When corruption is widespread, government institutions are less effective and government resources are more at the discretion of corrupt politicians. Therefore, they can intentionally allocate these resources to their clientelistic networks. Despite their bad reputation, corrupt politicians maintain their positions since people expect to receive benefits from this patron–client relationship. Using data from the World Values Survey and country-specific data across 14 countries around the world, Manzetti and Wilson (2007) find that when citizens are more permissive about corruption, they support the government more. This support is still strong even if they perceive that the government is highly corrupt.

## 2.2.2.  *The effect on political stability*

Classical theorists in political science define political stability based on the change in political regime. According to Lipset and Man (1960), a country is stable if its political regime (a democracy or a dictatorship) stands in power for over 25 years. Sanders (1981) claims that political stability should be relatively defined. This relative definition is based on comparative time or other political regimes. Then, Siermann (1998) broadens this definition with social tensions. Miljkovic and Rimal (2008) define political stability as no change of government. Recently, scholars presented a broad definition of political instability, which is considered a sum of negative political events (e.g., strikes, riots, assassinations and revolutions) (Aurore, 2013). Accordingly, a country without these negative events is considered stable. When political corruption becomes popular in a country, it destroys formal and fundamental functions of the government (Neudorfer & Theuerkauf, 2014). Therefore, corruption increases both economic and social inequalities among various groups of people. These conflicts are common causes of negative political events. Moreover, the United Nations recognizes the negative effect of corruption on political stability. The preamble to the Convention against Corruption (Convention 58/4) issued in 2003 stipulates that corrupt activities have a strong relationship with organized criminal groups and economic crimes; therefore, they are a severe threat to political stability and social security.

Moidfar and Ahmadi (2011) investigate the role of income equality in the relationship between political corruption and political stability in 208 countries from 1996 to 2009. They find that corruption erodes political stability. However, the mediating role of income in this effect is mixed for the full sample. It is only significant in Asian countries. Examining how political corruption influences economic growth in Vietnam over the period 2000–2012, Anh *et al.* (2016) find that the negative effect of political corruption on economic growth is mainly transmitted through political stability. The effect of political corruption on political stability explains 53% of the relationship between political corruption and economic growth. Farzanegan and Witthuhn (2017) use data from over 100 countries during the period 1984–2012 to investigate how the youth bulge affects the relationship between corruption and political stability. They document that this relationship is negative if the youth population constitutes more than 20% of the adult population. Moreover, analyzing the impact of political corruption on the instability of a dictatorship receiving foreign aid in 164 countries during the period 1970–2006, Aurore (2013) also shows that if political corruption increases political instability in a dictatorial country, foreign aid is able to help it consolidate internal stability. In addition, using data from two surveys on 644 and 848 Ethiopian firms conducted by the World Bank in 2011 and 2015, respectively, Shumetie and Watabaji (2019) examine how political corruption and political instability affect firms' innovativeness. Their findings show that political corruption increases political stability, which in turn reduces firms' innovativeness.

On the other hand, some scholars posit that patronage politics makes political corruption support political stability since corrupt politicians and officials can use state resources to buy their opponents. According to Fjelde and Hegre (2014), political corruption is considered an informal institution in which corrupt leaders illegitimately grant special preferences and private gains to selected groups of people in the population to build political loyalty. These preferences and gains include financial support (tax exemptions or reductions, subsidies, better access to credit or foreign currency and low-cost financing), favorable administrative procedures, land allocations and discriminatory legal enforcements. Those who receive benefits from corrupt leaders are more loyal to the political regime. Examining how oil rents affect political stability, Fjelde (2009) shows that political corruption can moderate the negative impact of oil rents on political stability. This implies that a discriminatory distribution of private interests from political corruption may decrease the probability of armed conflicts in resource-rich countries. With data from 133 countries from the period 1985–2008, Fjelde and Hegre (2014) find that among autocratic and hybrid regimes, those that have higher levels of corruption are more stable. Corruption makes formal institutions control democratizations, and formal institutions also maintain political corruption in autocratic and hybrid regimes.

Consistently, corruption is less widespread in democratic countries and their political regimes are more stable.

### 2.2.3.    *The effect on government budget*

Taxes are the main source of government budget. However, most individuals and organizations in the economy have high incentives to reduce their tax obligations. Therefore, they are willing to pay bribes to public officials in tax administration agencies in order to pay less taxes. Bird *et al.* (2008) argue that countries that have more legitimate and active governments can easily have adequate tax revenues to spend on public services. Using data from both developing and high-income countries over the period 1990–1999, they find that when the corruption index of Kaufmann *et al.* (2003) increases by 1 unit, the percentage of tax revenue in GDP decreases by 0.24–0.38%. Ajaz and Ahmad (2010) investigate how institutional and structural factors influence total tax revenue across 25 developing countries from 1990 to 2005. They find that political corruption has a negative impact on tax collection while governance has a positive effect on tax revenue. Arif and Rawat (2018) also examine the effects of corruption and governance on tax revenue in 10 emerging and growth-leading economies (EAGLEs) over the period 2001–2015. Their findings show that countries with good governance and low corruption have higher tax revenue. Analyzing the effect of corruption on revenues across taxes in the Middle East, Imam and Jacobs (2014) show that corruption is a significant factor that makes the Middle East collect less taxes than other middle-income regions. However, the negative impact of corruption on tax revenue varies across different types of taxes. Taxes that require taxpayers to interact with tax authorities frequently (e.g., import and export tariffs) are more influenced by corruption. Huňady and Orviská (2015) and Hwang (2002) also find supporting evidence for the negative relationship between corruption and tax collection across countries.

In addition, many prior studies investigate the relationship between political corruption and tax evasion. Tax evasion is defined as the participation in illegal activities intentionally conducted by taxpayers to decrease their tax obligations. When political corruption is rampant in a country, individuals and firms may choose to pay bribes so that corrupt tax collectors support their tax-evading activities. Investigating the effect of corruption on tax evasion in 26 transition economies in two years, 2002 and 2005, Uslaner (2010) finds that firms in countries with high corruption are less likely to pay taxes. Alm *et al.* (2016) also examine how bribery affects corporate tax evasion with data from the World Enterprise Survey and the Business Environment and Enterprise Performance Survey. Their findings show that bribery of tax collectors increases firms' incentives to evade taxes through tax reporting procedures. When a tax inspector asks for a bribe, firms reduce 4–10 percentage points of taxable sales and the bribe magnitude is positively related to tax evasion. Ivanyna *et al.* (2010) show that the increase in the corruption culture drives the private sector to evade taxes and thus reduces tax revenue. Using data from international organizations and the Bank of Ghana during the period 2007–2016, Amoh and Ali-Nakyea (2019) also find that corruption leads to tax evasion. Besides, Khlif and Amara (2019) extend this line of research by investigating the role of corruption in the relationship between political connection and tax-evading activities. With data from 35 countries, they document that political connection has a positive impact on tax evasion and this impact is stronger in countries with high corruption. These findings imply that political connection and corruption are complements in creating tax-evading practices.

Further, Picur and Riahi-Belkaoui (2006) analyze the effects of bureaucracy and corruption control on tax compliance in 30 developed and developing countries. They find that bureaucracy negatively affects tax compliance while corruption control has a positive impact on tax compliance. Payne and Saunoris (2020) argue that the effect of bribery on tax evasion depends on the prevalence of tax evasion. With data from the Business Environment and Enterprise Performance Survey over two years, 2002 and 2005, they document that political corruption increases tax evasion and this relationship is stronger when tax-evading activities are rampant. However, Akdede (2006) shows that the effect of corruption on tax evasion is not always negative. When the bribe reaches a certain level, taxpayers choose to pay taxes rather than evade taxes.

## 2.3.  Economic Effects

### 2.3.1.  *The effect on domestic investment*

Corruption creates an inhospitable environment for investment activities. It leads to uncertain investment outcomes and decreases expected investment returns (Mauro, 1995). Bribes are considered to be taxes imposed on investment income (Bardhan, 1997). Therefore, investors are less likely to invest in places with high political corruption. In a pioneering study, Mauro (1995) examines how political corruption affected total and private investment across 67 countries during the period 1980–1983. He finds a strong negative relationship between corruption and country-level investment. When bureaucratic efficiency — a proxy of political corruption — increases by one standard deviation, investment rate increases by 4.75% of GDP. Edgardo Campos *et al.* (1999) argue that investment is determined by both the magnitude of political corruption and the nature of political corruption. With data from the World Bank for 1997, they document that the predictability of corruption mitigates the negative effect of corruption on investment. Investigating how political corruption influences economic growth and income distribution in African countries, Gyimah-Brempong (2002) shows there is a negative impact of corruption on investment in physical capital. Gyimah-Brempong and de Gyimah-Brempong (2006) also find a consistent result in OECD and Asian countries. Moreover, Rock and Bonnett (2004) document that political corruption dampens investment in most developing economies, specifically small developing economies. With a sample of 63 to 71 economies over the period 1970–1998, Méon and Sekkat (2005) find that the negative relationship between political corruption and investment depends on governance quality. Furthermore, Swaleheen (2007) analyzes how political corruption affects national investment efficiency across 90–140 countries from 1995 to 2004. His findings show that corruption is negatively related to the incremental capital output ratio (ICOR) and this relationship is stronger in countries with high corruption.

However, some studies show that countries with high corruption have higher levels of investment. According to Tanzi (1998), investors may take advantage of political corruption to simplify the investment process; therefore, their investments obtain benefits from corruption. Wedeman (2003) considers the positive relationship between corruption and investment in East Asia — a highly corrupt region — as a paradox. Examining the effects of political corruption on economic growth and investment around the world in four periods, 1980–1983, 1988–1992, 1984–1996 and 1994–1996, Rock and Bonnett (2004) find empirical evidence for the East Asian paradox. Besides, with a sample of 74 developing economies during the period 2000–2008, Das and Parry (2011) also document a positive relationship between political corruption and the rate of investment. This positive effect is significant in Sub-Saharan Africa, Latin America and the Caribbean while it is not significant in Asia.

## 2.3.2.  *The effect on foreign investment*

Political corruption hinders Foreign Direct Investment (FDI) not only by creating a negative macro-economic environment (high uncertainty, much red tape and high costs of investment) but also distorting competition. Corrupt officials may facilitate bribe payers to enter profitable markets and create obstacles for non-payers. Furthermore, the difference in the extent of political corruption between the home country and the host country also reduces investment incentives (Habib & Zurawicki, 2002). Firms prefer near and similar markets to distant and less similar ones (Davidson, 1980). In a pioneer study, Wei (2000a) use data of FDI from 12 home countries to 45 countries to examine the nexus between political corruption and FDI. They find that host countries where political corruption is widespread receive less FDI. Using data from 40 countries, Zhao *et al.* (2003) also find that countries with high corruption and low transparency have lower inward FDI. Voyer and Beamish (2004) argue that foreign investors tend to avoid countries with high corruption in order to decrease risk and uncertainty of their investment. They investigate the effect of political corruption on FDI from Japan to 59 industrialized and emerging countries with a data of 29,546 investments. Their findings show a negative relationship between corruption and inward FDI from Japan. Egger and Winner (2006) argue that political corruption can either play the role of a grabbing hand or a helping hand for FDI. Using data of 21 home countries and 59 host countries over the period 1983–1999, they find that the grabbing hand effect outweighs the helping hand effect. Besides, political corruption is a crucial deterrent of FDI to developed countries but not less developed countries. Castro and Nunes (2013) and Gründler and Potrafke (2019) also find that highly corrupt countries are less attractive to foreign investors.

Moreover, Habib and Zurawicki (2002) conduct an initial empirical study to investigate how the difference in political corruption levels between the home country and the host country affects FDI. They find that both political corruption in the host country and corruption distance reduce FDI. Wu (2006) shows that corruption distance is more likely to be an important deterrent of outward FDI from countries with low corruption. Using data from 45 countries during the period 1997–2007, Qian and Sandoval-Hernandez (2016) find that the home–host difference in political corruption negatively influences both the decision to invest in foreign countries and the magnitude of FDI. Brada *et al.* (2019) also show that the host country's corruption and corruption distance have negative impacts on FDI.

On the other hand, some studies show supporting evidence for the helping hand hypothesis. Foreign investors may pay bribes to speed up their administrative procedures and have information advantages. Corrupt officials may become their consultants who give them advice to have better access to resources and profitable markets. With data from 73 countries from 1995 to 1999, Egger and Winner (2005) find that political corruption positively affects FDI inflows. Investigating the relationship between corruption and FDI across transition economies from 1996 to 2013, Kizilkaya (2017) also finds that there is a positive effect of corruption on FDI in a certain period.

## 2.3.3.   *The effect on inflation*

According to Al-Marhubi (2000), political corruption may increase inflation in a country due to four main reasons. First, countries with high corruption have serious tax evasion and high tax collection costs. Therefore, inflation tax is a potential source of government revenue. Second, political corruption creates many obstacles for business individuals and organizations. Consequently, they are more likely to switch their business from official to unofficial economies. This makes the government rely more on inflation tax. Third, political corruption increases capital flight, which diminishes taxable assets and income. Le and Rishi (2006) and Osei-Assibey *et al.* (2018) find that political corruption results in capital flight across countries. When government revenue from taxation is lower, the government resorts to using inflation tax. Finally, political corruption also increases public spending that leads to larger budget deficit. During the election period, politicians tend to increase government expenditure to attract voters in order to be re-elected and retain their positions (Nordhaus, 1975). High budget deficit drives politicians to use monetary emission since increasing tax rates may hurt their voters. Catão and Terrones (2005) also show that seigniorage is the main source of government revenue in countries with high corruption.

Al-Marhubi (2000) conducts an empirical study to investigate how political corruption affects inflation across 41 countries. He finds that political corruption is positively related to inflation. Abed and Davoodi (2000) also show consistent empirical results with a cross-section data from 24 countries and a panel data from 82 countries. Samimi *et al.* (2012) document a positive relationship between political corruption and inflation tax in 25 developing countries over the period 2003–2008. Piplica (2011) finds that the positive effect of corruption on inflation is weak across transition economies in the EU. Based on the optimal government finance theory, Rahmani *et al.* (2012) argue that as a rational organization, the government should choose a combination of revenue sources to minimize the total distortion impact of its financing. Therefore, inflation tax and normal taxes (direct and indirect taxes) should have equal marginal costs. They hypothesize that the former has higher marginal cost than the latter in countries with high corruption. With data from 110 countries over the period 1996–2009, they find supporting evidence for their hypothesis. The positive relationship between political corruption and inflation is also found in other studies (Blackburn & Powell, 2011; Özşahin & Üçler, 2017; Samimi & Abedini, 2012).

Furthermore, Myles and Yousefi (2015) investigate whether the effect of political corruption on inflation is caused by seigniorage that the government exploits to finance the public deficit due to political corruption. They embed political corruption within an overlapping generations economy in which the only store of value is money and the government pursues optimal money growth rate. They find that political corruption increases inflation. This finding implies that the government uses seigniorage to compensate fiscal deficit created by political corruption and thus inflation increases. Ali and Sassi (2016) also examine how political corruption influences inflation across 100 developing and developed economies from five geographical regions including America, Asia-Pacific, Europe, Middle East, North Africa and Sub-Saharan Africa. After the money supply is controlled, they still find a positive effect of corruption on inflation. This indicates that political corruption increases inflation not only through seigniorage but also through other channels.

### 2.3.4.   *The effect on economic growth*

The extant literature shows that political corruption may affect economic growth in two opposite directions. On the one hand, political corruption has long been considered a deterrent to economic growth (Shleifer & Vishny, 1993). Corrupt officials "sand the wheel" by illegally extracting rents and developing bureaucratic frictions (Jain, 2001). The negative impact of political corruption on the macro-economic environment reduces investment incentives, which usually leads to lower economic growth (Mauro, 1995). On the other hand, political corruption has a positive impact on economic growth. This is a result of the so-called "grease the wheels" mechanism. Corrupt officials receiving bribes are more helpful and enthusiastic to facilitate payers and speed up administrative procedures (Dreher

& Gassebner, 2013; Leff, 1964). Besides, corrupt officials allocate resources to the right firms that can use these resources efficiently since most bribe payers are efficient firms. This improves economic efficiency, especially when countries have weak institutions (Méon & Weill, 2010).

Although estimating the full effect of political corruption on the world economy is not simple, some reputable organizations such as the International Monetary Fund, the World Economic Forum and the World Bank show that political corruption costs from 2% to 5% of the global GDP (Bajada & Shashnov, 2019). Furthermore, the TI's estimation shows that political corruption increases the cost of public procurement by 50%.[1] Investigating cost overruns in urban rail and other infrastructure across 20 countries during a 75-year period, Flyvbjerg (2007) shows that on average rail projects incur a cost overrun of 44.7%, followed by bridges and tunnels with 33.8% and road construction with 20.4%. The Sochi Olympic Games had historical costs that are at least four times the estimated amount. This made it the most expensive in Olympic history (Rose-Ackerman & Palifka, 2016).

With a sample of 67 countries over the period 1980–1983, Mauro (1995) shows that political corruption reduces economic growth mainly by lowering investment. Gyimah-Brempong (2002) investigates how political corruption affects economic growth across 21 African countries from 1993 to 1999. They find that political corruption directly and indirectly reduces both GDP growth and GDP per capita growth. When political corruption increases by one point, GDP growth rate decreases by 0.75–0.9% and GDP per capita growth declines by 0.39–0.41%. Gyimah-Brempong and de Gyimah-Brempong (2006) also show that a 10% increase in political corruption index makes the growth rate of GDP per capita decrease by 1.7–2.8% across geographical regions. Both Gyimah-Brempong (2002) and Gyimah-Brempong and de Gyimah-Brempong (2006) find that political corruption decreases GDP growth directly through lowering

---

[1]https://www.transparency.org/en/our-priorities/public-procurement.

productivity of resources and indirectly through reducing investment in physical capital. Moreover, their findings show a positive impact of political corruption on income inequality across countries. Pellegrini and Gerlagh (2004) use data from 48 countries to estimate both direct and indirect effects of political corruption on economic growth. They document that indirect transmission channels (investment, trade openness, education and political stability) can explain about 81% of the negative relationship between corruption and economic growth. Gründler and Potrafke (2019) show that the negative relationship between political corruption and economic growth is transmitted through FDI and inflation across 175 countries from 2012 to 2018 and it is stronger in countries with autocratic governments. With data from 71 countries over the period 1970–1998, Méon and Sekkat (2005) find that political corruption reduces both economic growth and investment. However, the negative effect of political corruption on economic growth is independent from the negative effect of political corruption on investment.

On the other hand, some earlier empirical studies show that political corruption stimulates economic growth. With a sample of all countries around the world over the period 1999–2004, Podobnik *et al.* (2008) find that when CPI increases by one unit, the growth rate of GDP per capita increases by 1.7%. For a sub-sample of the European transition economies only, GDP per capita growth rate rises by 2.4%. These findings imply that the "grease the wheels" mechanism is more pronounced in countries with weak governance. Méon and Weill (2010) investigate whether corruption is effective in "greasing the wheel" across 69 countries. They also find that political corruption increases economic efficiency in countries with poor institutions. In addition, with a sample of 60–80 countries from 1970 to 2000, Aidt (2009) shows that political corruption has a positive effect on GDP per capita growth rate, but this effect is weak.

### 2.3.5. *The effect on international trade*

According to Musila and Sigué (2010), there are three major channels through which political corruption influences international trade. First, political corruption may increase or decrease economic efficiency and thus stimulate or restrict international trade. If government officials consider bribes as a piece rate system, they tend to work harder to facilitate bribe payers. Therefore, importers and exporters paying bribes can bypass bureaucratic delays and improve their working process. However, if government officials intentionally develop red tape and complicate administrative procedures to collect more bribes, international traders paying bribes still have bureaucratic delays. Second, corruption may increase or decrease cross-border trade through price mark-up channels. When corrupt officials intend to steal government revenue, they impose bribes lower than the official tax. A shipment is cleared through customs if importers or exporters agree to pay bribes without paying the official tax. This "corruption with theft" mechanism benefits international traders and thus stimulates international trade. Nevertheless, when corrupt officials request importers or exporters pay the official tax plus bribes as a condition to clear through customs, transaction costs of international trade are much higher. High transaction costs are a considerable barrier to international trade. Third, political corruption in the importing country may increase or decrease international trade if exporters pay or do not pay to win competitive contracts. There are special contracts whose winners have exclusive rights to import or sell a particular commodity. Firms that pay bribes to corrupt officials can have these contracts.

Musila and Sigué (2010) investigate how political corruption affected international trade in African countries over the period 1998–2007. They find that corruption in African countries and their trading partners significantly reduces the value of trade flows. Particularly, if CPI decreases from 2.8 — the average level of African countries — to 5.9, exports increase by 15% and imports rise by 27%. Horsewood and Voicu (2012) also document that political corruption in both importing and exporting countries negatively affects cross-border transactions. De Jong and Bogmans (2011) show that corruption generally hinders cross-border trade, but paying bribes to customs officials promotes imports. Moreover, Charoensukmongkol and Sexton (2011) also document that local corruption strongly hampered exports in Latin American and Caribbean countries during the period 1980–2005. Zelekha and Sharabi (2012) examine the effect of political corruption on international trade in Israel, which has a sharp drop in CPI from 14th in 1995 to 33rd in 2008. They find that the effect is still negative and stable. With data from bilateral trade in goods between 139 economies during the period 1975–2021, Gil-Pareja, Llorca-Vivero and Martínez-Serrano (2019) show that political corruption has a negative impact on cross-border trade, but it is not comprehensive.

However, with a sample of Middle East and Latin American countries, Shirazi (2012) finds that the nexus between political corruption and international trade volume is an inverted U. This indicates that political corruption increases cross-border trade when political corruption is low; however, the relationship is opposite after political corruption reaches a certain level. Thede and Gustafson (2012) investigate how corruption characteristics (degree, prevalence, customs location, function and predictability) influence cross-border trade and find that imports range systematically with them. Besides, Dutt and Traca (2010) show that the relationship between political corruption and trade flows is unclear and dependent on tariffs.

## 2.3.6.  *The effect on the shadow economy*

The shadow economy includes all economic activities that create added value but are not recognized in the gross national product (Schneider *et al.*, 1989). It may be called by different names such as underground economy, informal sector, unofficial economy, black economy and hidden economy. In theory, political corruption and the shadow economy are intertwined (Goel & Saunoris, 2014). On the one hand, political corruption encourages the shadow economy. Shadow operators may pay bribes to corrupt officials in order to obtain official permits and mitigate potential punishment. Besides, when corruption is rampant, official economic activities tend to go underground to avoid corrupt officials' rent seeking. On the other hand, the shadow economy facilitates or restricts political corruption. The shadow economy is a good environment for corrupt officials to handle their corrupt earnings. Consequently, the existence and development of the shadow economy drives political corruption. However, when many firms and individuals go underground, rent-seeking opportunities are less available for corrupt officials and thus political corruption is lower (Choi & Thum, 2005).

With data from 69 countries, Friedman *et al.* (2000) show that firms go underground to lower the burden of political corruption and bureaucracy rather than avoid official taxes. Katsios (2006) investigates the nexus between political corruption and the shadow economy in Southeastern Europe. He finds that taxpayers participate in underground economic activities due to three reasons. First, they are not willing to pay bribes. Second, they fail to have enough financial resources for bribery. Finally, they cannot connect with corrupt officials. In addition, Dreher *et al.* (2008) document that political corruption and the underground economy were substitutes across 145 countries during the period 1999–2003. With data from 98 countries, Dreher and Schneider (2010) find that the nexus between political corruption and the size of the underground economy is not robust. However, their findings show that the relationship is complementary in low-income economies but not in high-income economies. Using a cross-section dataset of 106 countries from 1999 to 2008, Goel and Saunoris (2014) also find a complementary relationship between political corruption and the underground economy. Dell'Anno and Teobaldelli (2015) find a consistent relationship in centralized economies. However, some empirical studies show that the nexus between political corruption and the shadow economy is not robust or significant (Shahab *et al.*, 2015; Virta, 2010).

## 2.4.   Socio-Cultural Effects

### 2.4.1.   *The effect on income inequality*

Political corruption may affect income equality through several channels including biased tax systems, wrong targeting of social supports, concentration of asset ownership, inequality in public services and biased risk distribution (Gupta *et al.*, 2002). First, politically connected and wealthy people may bribe tax collectors for tax evasion, exemption or reduction while low-income people have to pay enough taxes. This decreases the progressivity of the tax system and results in higher income inequality. Second, corrupt officials have incentives to divert government social support to well-connected people instead of the truly needy. This mitigates the role of social support in reducing income inequality. Third, when a small group of people hold a large amount of assets, they tend to pay bribes to government officials for favorable policies. These policies help them increase their wealth faster than the average rate of society. Consequently, the social divide becomes larger. Four, political corruption decreases government revenue with a biased tax system and increases operating costs. This restricts government expenditure on public services such as education and healthcare. Besides, wealthy groups and urban citizens have more opportunities to lobby government officials to provide them better public services. Akhter (2004) shows that political corruption reduces human development across 85 countries. Finally, when political corruption creates more uncertainty, the less-well-connected people face more risks than the well connected. Therefore, the former are less likely to invest and their income is relatively lower.

Gupta *et al.* (2002) investigate how political corruption influences income inequality and poverty across countries from 1980 to 1997. They find that when political corruption increases by one standard deviation, the Gini coefficient increases by 11%. Gyimah-Brempong (2002) and Gyimah-Brempong and de Gyimah-Brempong (2006) also show a positive relationship between corruption and income inequality in African, OECD and Asian countries. Dincer and Gunalp (2005) posit that data from US are more comparable than data from different countries to investigate the effect of political corruption on income distribution. Measuring political corruption by the number of government officials arrested for corruption-related crimes, they find that political corruption positively affects the Gini Coefficient of income inequality. Besides, Ullah and Ahmad (2016) show that political corruption increases unequal income distribution in 71 developed and developing economies.

However, Andres and Ramlogan-Dobson (2011) provide new evidence on the nexus between political corruption and income distribution in Latin America. They show that political corruption has a negative impact on income inequality. These findings are contrary to many prior studies but consistent with the institutional environment of Latin America. Moreover, Ahlin (2001) shows that the relationship between corruption and income inequality is an inverted-U. Dwiputri *et al.* (2018) find a reciprocal association between political corruption and unequal income distribution in Asian countries. This nexus is called the corruption-inequality trap. High corruption increases income inequality and high income inequality raises corruption. With a panel data of 50 economies during the period 1995–2015, Policardo and Carrera (2018) document that there is no significant effect of political corruption on income distribution.

## 2.4.2.   *The effect on public services*

Corrupt officials tend to focus on using public resources to serve their own interests rather than the public interest. Therefore, political corruption leads to decreases in both the volume and the quality of public services (Menocal *et al.*, 2015). Reviewing economic costs of political corruption, Dreher and Herzfeld (2005) show that when corruption score increases by 1 point, government expenditure decreases by 1.3–3%. Delavallade (2006) investigates how political corruption affects the structure of government expenditure across 64 countries over the period 1996–2001. He finds that political corruption leads to lower government expenditure on education, health and social protection. Gupta and Tiongson (2000) and Lambsdorff (1999) also find that government expenditure on public services, including education and healthcare, is lower when corruption is spread. Dizaji *et al.* (2016) show that countries with autocratic and corrupt governments tend to have higher expenditure on militaries than education and healthcare services.

In addition, Davis (2004) examines corruption in government agencies supplying water and sanitation services in many South Asian localities. Using focus group discussions with 1,400 participants (employees, customers and key informants), he finds that service providers are more accountable when corruption is lower. With the aim of understanding corruption in delivering public services, Barr *et al.* (2009) conduct an experiment to investigate the behavior of public service suppliers and their monitors. Participants in their experiment are nursing students who are destined to work in public healthcare organizations in Ethiopia. Public servants in the healthcare sector also have incentives to adopt corrupt behaviors like in other public sectors. They document that service suppliers have better performance when service recipients are able to select monitors through election and when elected monitors exert more effort toward their monitoring activities. Besides, service suppliers perform better when they face higher observability. These findings imply that political corruption reduces the quality of public service. According to Vian (2020), common corrupt practices in public healthcare sector are "undue denial of coverage, overbilling or under-provision of care, embezzlement, informal payments, bid rigging, kickbacks and conflicts of interest affecting procurement and prescribing". Nikoloski and Mossialos (2013) employ the Eurobarometer survey to investigate determinants of public healthcare quality across European countries. They show that patients' perception of healthcare quality is lower when corruption is more spread. Examining how local corruption affects public service quality in Vietnam, a transition economy, Nguyen *et al.* (2017) find that local corruption has a negative impact on the quality of healthcare and primary education. Hsiao *et al.* (2019) use survey data over the period 2014–2015 to investigate how bribery influences access to medical care in 32 Sub-Saharan countries. They find that bribery restricts people's access to healthcare services and thus it may prevent these countries from achieving Universal Health Coverage — a Sustainable Development Goal. Using data from the 2010 Life in Transition survey, Habibov (2016) shows that corruption negatively affects people's satisfaction with public healthcare services across 12 transition countries. In addition, Suryadarma (2012) investigates the effectiveness of government expenditure in the education system in Indonesia. He finds that government expenditure is likely to have a negligible impact on school enrollment in locations with high corruption, while this effect is positive and strong in locations with low corruption.

Furthermore, Gordon (2017) investigates the effect of corruption on judicial service in judicial institutions of Ghana and finds that bribery erodes justice. Several judgments are made in favor of bribe payers rather than in order to protect justice; therefore, poor and vulnerable people who cannot pay bribes receive discriminatory treatment in court. Pathak *et al.* (2009) show that in Fiji adoption of e-governance can restrict corruption in public service delivery by improving transparency and control.

On the other hand, many scholars believe that political corruption may increase the quality of public services when a country fails to have an effective administrative system. According to the "grease the wheels" theory proposed by Leys (1965), bribery improves public services due to two reasons: First, bribes are considered as bonuses for government officials when they make more efforts to speed up administrative procedures. Second, bribes are additional income to improve public servants' living standards when their wages are still low (Méon & Sekkat, 2005). Dreher and Gassebner (2013) investigate the role of corruption in the effect of regulation on entrepreneurship across 43 highly regulated economies from 2003 to 2005 and find supporting evidence for the "grease the wheels" theory. Corruption speeds up firm entry.

## 2.4.3.  *The effect on the environment*

Waste and emission treatment considerably raises production costs. Therefore, firms have high incentives to lobby government officials to ensure environmental regulations are less strict and effective. Fredriksson *et al.* (2004) show that energy policy stringency is lower when policymakers are more corruptible across 12 OECD countries from 1982 to 1996. Moreover, they are also willing to pay bribes to corruption officials to avoid or reduce punishment for their pollution. Besides, political corruption affects environmental quality through economic growth and natural resources. A country with low economic growth hindered by political corruption fails to have resources to improve its environmental quality. Countries with high political corruption focus more on exploiting natural resources and thus cause more pollution (Habib *et al.*, 2020).

Following the Kuznets Curve theory, Cole (2007) examines how political corruption affected air pollution emissions in 94 countries over the period 1987–2000. He finds that political corruption directly increases per capita emission of both sulfur dioxide and carbon dioxide. With data from 21 MENA countries between 1996 and 2013, Hassaballa (2015) also finds a positive relationship between political corruption and carbon dioxide emission. In addition, Oliva (2015) investigates how bribery influences automobile carbon dioxide emission in Mexico City. He finds that 9.6% of car owners pay 20 US dollars to testing center technicians to circumvent vehicle emission regulations. When this cheating is eliminated and car owners have to pay higher costs to retest, emissions are expected to reduce by 3,708 tons. Investigating the nexus between political corruption and carbon dioxide emission in the APEC countries, Zhang *et al.* (2016) find that this relationship is negative in countries with low emissions but insignificant in countries with high emissions. Corruption also has a positive indirect effect on environmental quality and the overall effect is positive. Masron and Subramaniam (2018) posit that environmental deterioration is a serious problem in developing economies and they investigate the impact of political corruption on environmental degradation across 64 developing countries. Their findings show that countries with high corruption suffer more serious pollution. With data from 61 countries over the period 2003–2016, Akhbari and Nejati (2019) find political corruption has a positive effect on carbon emission in developing countries, but the relationship between political corruption and carbon emission is not significant in developed countries. Pei *et al.* (2021) examine how political corruption and energy efficiency affect carbon emission in China's industry during the period 2005–2015. They document that corruption increases carbon emission while energy efficiency reduces carbon emission. Besides, political corruption increases carbon emission by reducing energy efficiency. Liu *et al.* (2021) also find that political corruption makes a contribution to carbon dioxide emission across 33 Asian countries from 2000 to 2015. Biswas *et al.* (2012) show that when the shadow economy is larger, environmental pollution is higher since underground economic activities can avoid environmental regulations easily. The effect of the shadow economy on environmental pollution depends on the levels of political corruption.

However, Ivanova (2011) shows that effective regulation increased sulfur emission in 39 European countries over the period 1999–2003. Sulemana and Kpienbaareh (2020) investigate how political corruption influenced air pollution with a sample of 48 Sub-Saharan African countries and a sample of 34 OECD countries from 1996 to 2014. They find that political corruption has a negative impact on air pollution. Goel *et al.* (2013) show that both political corruption and the shadow economy have negative effects on environmental pollution in 100 MENA countries during the period 2004–2007. With data from Chinese provinces between 1998 and 2016, Ren *et al.* (2021) show that political corruption raises carbon emissions in the short run and decreases carbon emissions in the long run. Yang *et al.* (2020) also examine the relationship between local corruption and carbon emission across 30 provinces from 2002 to 2017. They find that this relationship is N-shaped. Particularly, local corruption initially increases carbon emission, then reduces it and finally enhances it.

### 2.4.4.  *The effect on emigration*

According to Cooray and Schneider (2016), as a push factor, political corruption has both direct and indirect impacts on emigration. Countries with high corruption are poor living and working environments. Highly qualified and skilled people have high incentives to move to other countries that provide them with better conditions. However, people of low and medium educational levels are less likely to emigrate since their demand in terms of living standards is lower. In addition, political corruption indirectly affects emigration through many channels. Political corruption hinders economic growth, increases income inequality and reduces the quality of public services such as education and healthcare. Therefore, people are more likely to move to other countries.

Dimant *et al.* (2013) examine the nexus between political corruption and migration across 111 countries from 1985 to 2000. They find that political corruption is a push factor of migration and the effect of political corruption is strongest on fueling skilled migration. Poprawe (2015) also documents that political corruption increases emigration and decreases immigration in 230 countries. Cooray and Schneider (2016) examine how political corruption influences emigration across various levels of skills. Their findings show that political corruption encourages emigration of high-skilled people. The effect of political corruption on the emigration rate of low and medium-skilled people is positive at low corruption levels and then it turns to be negative at higher corruption levels. Schneider (2015) also finds that the nexus between corruption and emigration depends on people's skills and education.

# Chapter 3
# Anti-Corruption

*This chapter presents an overview of anti-corruption. Anti-corruption includes all plans, actions and efforts by government agencies, non-governmental organizations and individuals to reduce corruption. Many countries have applied a wide range of anti-corruption mechanisms in order to control and monitor public servants' behavior. Key anti-corruption actors are government institutions, private firms, civic organizations, the media and international institutions. Moreover, anti-corruption has become a global concern since it can restrict international economic integration. Therefore, there are many international anti-corruption initiatives including global organizations, regional organizations and non-governmental organizations. In addition, political corruption is a severe problem in developing and transition countries. According to the World Economic Forum (2018), corruption costs them $3.6 trillion each year. Recently, developing and transition countries have conducted anti-corruption campaigns to eliminate corruption and strictly punished corrupt officials.*

## 3.1. What Is Anti-Corruption?

### 3.1.1. *The concept of anti-corruption*

*The Code of Hammurabi* (Babylon, 18th century BCE) — one of the oldest written legal codes — included stipulations to fight against political corruption. Particularly, bribing judges and misappropriation of public resources were prohibited. These crimes were regarded as capital offenses (Urch, 1929). Other ancient legal texts such as the *Great Edict of Horemheb* (Egypt, 13th century BCE) and the *Arthasastra* (India, 2nd century BCE) also show that political corruption, especially bribery, was regarded as a severe crime (Olivelle, 2012; Terracino, 2012). Athenian democracy produced a wide range of legal documents to prevent and punish corrupt activities. Besides a specific anti-bribery law, there were laws to control misappropriation of public funds, fight bribery in the judicial system, restrict the misconduct of ambassadors and monitor public officials at the end of their tenure. Penalties for corrupt behaviors were fines of ten times the bribery value or the capital punishment (Kroeze *et al.*, 2018). In addition, Kroeze *et al.* (2018) found that Athenian democracy's anti-corruption practices included (1) legal actions against corrupt behaviors, (2) political institutions intentionally established to prevent political corruption and (3) social pressures restricting corrupt activities and encouraging non-corrupt behaviors. The Roman Empire also developed anti-corruption mechanisms. For example, in 331 when the Emperor Constantine recognized the severity of political corruption in his empire, he issued a decree to control corruption (Noonan, 1984). Most dynasties in the Western and the Eastern countries in the Middle Ages realized the negative effects of corruption and thus they tried to restrict corruption in order to maintain their regimes and social stability.

Traditional anti-corruption mainly focuses on corruption control. It includes public policies issued to eliminate corrupt opportunities and punish corrupt behaviors. According to Klitgaard (1988) and Sousa (2010), corruption is controlled by implementing an integrated collection of preventive, repressive, educational, legislative, institutional and procedural measures with a holistic or incremental scope. These anti-corruption measures have effects on individual ethical values and organizational behavior and display a complicated combination of incentives and sanctions to restrict the trends in and effects of corruption. In recent decades, both academics and practitioners have considered corruption a socio-political disease. Without anti-corruption mechanisms, political corruption may become a practical rule in society if more people are tolerant and acceptant of it over time (Zhang & Kim, 2017). Therefore, anti-corruption has become a priority in the policy-making process of the development communities set up for the purpose and many anti-corruption reforms have been developed.[1] Most countries consider corruption a criminal offense and punish corrupt officials by imprisonment and even the death penalty. However, in the modern world, anti-corruption is not limited to public policies (Sousa, 2010). Other parties such as private firms, non-governmental organizations and the media are also able to monitor public officials and expose corrupt behaviors. Moreover, along with international economic integration, political corruption is not only a national but also an international problem. For example, political corruption is a barrier to international trade and investment. Therefore, anti-corruption includes both national and international solutions (World Bank, 1997). Overall, anti-corruption is defined as a set of efforts and actions made by national or international organizations to prevent or oppose an abuse of public power for personal benefits.

## 3.1.2.  *Key anti-corruption actors*

Before the early 1980s, scholars and policymakers rarely paid attention to the roles of private companies and other stakeholders in society in combating political corruption. They claimed that anti-corruption activities should be conducted by government authorities with a wide range of instruments and officials (inspectorates, state auditors, inquiry commissions, magistrates, etc.). The conclusion was that there is no connection and cooperation between the public sector and other parties in fighting political corruption, and that anti-corruption efforts are ineffective. However, from the late 1980s to the late 1990s, many corruption scandals broke out across most Western countries. Their governments launched anti-corruption reforms and participated in multilateral negotiations to

---

[1] https://www.worldbank.org/en/topic/anticorruption/overview#1.

establish international anti-corruption institutions (Sousa, 2010). Today, key anti-corruption actors include government institutions, private firms, civic organizations, the media and international institutions.

### 3.1.2.1.  *Government institutions*

A political system with effective legislative, executive and judicial rights is vital to prevent and control political corruption since government officials are adequately monitored and audited. A good anti-corruption chain includes four main stages: prevention, detection, investigation and prosecution. Government institutions are classified into three groups: public sector oversight bodies, anti-corruption agencies and law enforcement bodies (United Nations Pacific Regional Anti-Corruption, 2020).

Public sector oversight bodies include parliamentary oversight committees, public service commission, state audit office, ministry of finance, etc. These bodies do not get involved in day-to-day activities of government organizations and officials but monitor and examine their policies, plans and projects. Oversight activities ensure that the performances of government organizations and officials achieve expected goals and comply with applicable laws, policies and ethical values.

Anti-corruption agencies are specialized institutions established by the government to prevent, investigate and prosecute corruption cases. These agencies undertake a wide range of anti-corruption tasks such as educating and raising citizen awareness about public integrity and anti-corruption, giving advice to senior politicians and officials on anti-corruption policies, receiving corruption-related complaints and denouncements from both the public sector and from the public, cooperating with other government institutions and international anti-corruption institutions to investigate and prosecute corrupt officials.

Law enforcement bodies include the ministry of justice, the police, public prosecution office, the judiciary, etc. These bodies are specialized institutions investigating and punishing corrupt behaviors.

Moreover, in some countries, they play an important role as anti-corruption reform bodies (United Nations Pacific Regional Anti-Corruption, 2020).

### 3.1.2.2.  *Private firms*

Political corruption distorts business environments by creating a lack of transparency, unfair competition and high costs of doing business. Although firms are willing to pay bribes to speed up administrative procedures or obtain some favorable treatment from the government, these bribes are additional costs that they do not have to pay in a non-corrupt environment. In addition, political corruption makes firms face many difficulties in finding foreign partners since multi-national companies and international investors tend to avoid countries with high corruption.

Private firms may combat political corruption through the following activities: First, they could integrate anti-corruption into their corporate culture and ethical values. Second, they could educate and train their employees on how to avoid and fight against corrupt behaviors. Third, they could participate in associations and organizations which have collective anti-corruption activities. Today, business associations play an important role in creating policy reforms and providing support to their members. Finally, private firms may cooperate with government institutions and civic organizations in actions to fight against corruption.

### 3.1.2.3.  *Civic organizations and the media*

Civic organizations include non-governmental organizations, not-for-profit organizations, community groups, churches, labor unions, indigenous groups, philanthropic organizations, faith-based organizations and professional associations. Civic organizations and the media may fight against political corruption through their influences on citizens' attitude and behavior. First, civic organizations and the media function as independent watchdogs to hold government institutions more accountable and responsible for their policies and plans. Second, civic organizations and the media provide citizens information and raise their anti-corruption awareness. This reduces corruption opportunities and improves transparency. Third, civic organizations and the media uncover corrupt cases and cooperate with government institutions to take legal actions against them. Finally, civic organizations and the media pressure the government to implement anti-corruption reforms.

### 3.1.2.4.  *International institutions*

After the Cold War ended, international integration began to develop rapidly. Accordingly, international institutions started to play an important role in the world anti-corruption agenda in the mid-1990s (Rose-Ackerman, 2012). International institutions undertake the following activities to help member countries in their anti-corruption efforts:

- **Financial support:** International institutions finance programs to improve governance and enhance anti-corruption in their member countries. International financial institutions even require borrowing countries to conduct reforms, establish accountability institutions and improve anti-corruption law enforcement as a condition of receiving their loans or financial support. Moreover, international institutions also support their members in increasing economic growth and reducing poverty. Such support may have indirect effects on anti-corruption efforts.
- **Knowledge support:** International anti-corruption institutions are professionals in investigating and analyzing socio-economic issues. They can provide their members with reports on national anti-corruption regulations and enforcement. They conduct empirical studies to evaluate and compare the level of corruption across countries in the world and provide policy implications. They issue documents to educate citizens about corruption and anti-corruption. Furthermore, they also have training programs for government anti-corruption institutions to improve their efficiency.
- **International integration:** International anti-corruption institutions connect member countries and facilitate their cooperation.

Member countries may have international anti-corruption agreements to share information and take collective actions when corruption cases involve many countries.

## 3.2.   Anti-Corruption Mechanisms

### 3.2.1.   *Approaches to anti-corruption*

#### 3.2.1.1.   *Basic approaches*

According to McCusker (2007), there are three approaches to preventing and controlling political corruption, namely, interventionism, managerialism and organizational integrity. Basabose (2019) suggests another set of basic approaches including a punitive legal framework, a preventive anti-corruption approach and an ethical values-based approach. Despite their different names, their main contents are similar to those proposed by McCusker (2007).

First, interventionism or a punitive legal framework concentrates on reactive responses to punish corrupt behaviors. When identifying corrupt acts, anti-corruption authorities investigate, arrest, prosecute, adjudicate and penalize offenders. Offenders are responsible for their behaviors and receive their just desserts. Potential offenders are less likely to commit similar practices since they are aware of potential punishment. This approach is effective when legal regulations and administrative procedures are available and enforceable in all stages, from defining to penalizing corruption. Although this approach is used commonly in many countries, it still has the following weaknesses: (1) The government cannot prevent corruption. Anti-corruption authorities wait for cases of corruption to appear and take legal action. Therefore, the consequence has already happened and cannot be undone. (2) Many corrupt crimes may not be defined and punished. Many forms of corruption are unreported. When they are not criminalized by the legal framework, anti-corruption authorities cannot investigate, arrest, prosecute, adjudicate and punish offenders. Besides, police officers or other investigators tend to focus on visible crimes. As a result, corruption cases are identified less frequently. (3) There are not enough resources for a complicated process from defining to punishing corrupt acts. Government budget is limited while anti-corruption with interventionism is resource-intensive. The government not only has to pay operational costs but also several costs to make laws and ensure their enforcement (Basabose, 2019).

Second, managerialism or preventive anti-corruption approach focuses on prevention by reducing or eliminating corrupt opportunities. Particularly, there are systems, procedures and protocols in which national integrity is respected, corrupt opportunities are restricted and eliminated, and corrupt behaviors are exposed. According to Basabose (2019), corruption prevention includes the following: (1) independent preventive agencies; (2) political will; (3) codes of ethics for public servants; (4) institutional reforms controlling corruption; (5) trustworthy and accountable political parties; (6) effective and efficient whistle-blowing systems; (7) citizen empowerment and participation; (8) civil society; (9) an operational national integrity system and its periodical review process; (10) freedom of expression, access to information and responsible media; and (11) creative alternatives to bureaucracy and enhancing transparency. Although managerialism establishes a set of rules to prevent corruption, people are motivated by different factors and affected differently by preventive systems. Therefore, its consequences are not predictable. For example, when a firm is willing to pay a bribe in order to win a procurement contract, a risk-averse public official may reject that offer. However, some officials may think that corruption is a normal practice and thus they may accept the offer or ask for a larger bribe to accept it.

Third, organizational integrity approach or ethical values-based approach considers corruption as a moral problem and thus focuses on ethical values to fight against it. The former posits that a norm of ethical behavior can be established in an organization by integrating its operational systems, corruption control measures and ethical values. The latter encourages ethical values supporting anti-corruption and individuals' desire to do what is right, good and proper. Accordingly, anti-corruption measures not only improve national governance and increase transparency but also make people more honest and enhance their consciousness (Basabose, 2019). Although using ethical values is sustainable in fighting against corruption, it takes a long time for them to become effective in people's attitude and behavior.

### 3.2.1.2. *Holistic approach*

Political corruption is a complicated and dynamic issue and has several causes. It is related to all facets of society. Therefore, anti-corruption cannot be successful if it focuses on a single factor or area within a short period of time. Fighting against political corruption should be effective on many fronts over a long period instead. According to Basabose (2019), the holistic and dynamic approach involves reactive (discouragement), preventive (detection and prevention) and proactive (awareness and ethics) anti-corruption systems. Discouragement includes legal regulations, legal enforcement measures, punitive and/or incentive systems to restrict and reduce corrupt acts. Detection and prevention consist of activities to understand drivers, causes, effects and consequences of political corruption and then to prevent corrupt practices. Awareness and ethics concentrate on changing people's shared ethical values and attitude to make corrupt acts unacceptable and even unthinkable. Ethics education is important to change individuals' values and attitudes. A holistic approach to political corruption is effective if it can increase public awareness of corrupt acts and their consequences, change people's attitude and behavior and maintain ethical values supporting anti-corruption among the society across generations.

McCusker (2007) posits that Transparency International is the strongest supporter of the holistic approach to fighting against political corruption, and its national integrity system proposed by Pope (2000) is an effective anti-corruption model. The national integrity system is illustrated by a model of a Greek temple including a roof — which represents national integrity — and eleven pillars. There are seven pillars (legislature, executive, judiciary, auditor general, ombudsman, watchdog agencies and public service) dominated by the government and four non-governmental pillars (media, civil society, private sector and international actors). This indicates that government institutions are the key players to establish and develop the national integrity system. The foundations of the temple are public awareness and society's values. Both government institutions and non-governmental organizations need people's support when they fight against political corruption. Therefore, the pillars have strong foundations if people's corruption awareness is high and society's values are against corrupt acts. Moreover, the top of the temple has three round balls, which represent sustainable development, rule of law and quality of life. They are three goals of the national integrity system. The pillars should be strong enough to keep the three balls stable on the top. In addition, Pope (2000) also suggests core rules and practices as the "toolkits" for the pillars. Pillars without these core rules and practices are weak.

To evaluate the integrity system of a specific country comprehensively, Transparency International (2011) introduced a new version of the national integrity system. This new model focuses on particular government institutions (legislature, executive, judiciary, public sector, law enforcement agencies, electoral management bodies, ombudsmen, supreme audit institutions and anti-corruption agencies) and non-state actors (political parties, media, civil society and business) that make significant contributions to the national integrity system. It uses "business" instead of "private sector" since businesses are the main actors in the private sector. "International actors" are removed since their activities fail to affect the national integrity system directly; they influence the national integrity system through domestic actors.

### 3.2.2.　*Anti-corruption strategies*

An anti-corruption strategy is traditionally a nationwide framework designed to facilitate both state and non-state bodies and individuals to participate in planning and implementing activities in order to reduce corruption as well as to develop the quality of accountability in a country. After analyzing anti-corruption strategies across 41 randomly selected countries, Pyman *et al.* (2017) find that each country typically expects one or two beneficial effects of its anti-corruption strategy. The common beneficial effects include: Gaining the EU membership, enhancing national security, adapting to international standards to combat corruption, promoting national democracy, transparency and/or integrity, increasing economic development or improving competitiveness, improving government and public service delivery, and strengthening national reputation. The two most desired benefits are improving government and better public service delivery and strengthening national reputation.

Moreover, the analysis of anti-corruption strategies in the 41 countries shows that they consider corruption an independent problem and mainly focus on country-specific corrupt activities and anti-corruption solutions. Pyman *et al.* (2018) define them as first-generation strategies. Recently, some countries have developed second-generation strategies with broader scopes and cooperation. According to the UK Home Office (2017), the UK government designs its anti-corruption strategy based on its long-term vision — a safer, more prosperous and confident country. Specifically, the long-term objectives of anti-corruption include eliminating threats to national security (terrorism, serious and organized crime, instability overseas), increasing prosperity at home and abroad and improving public trust in domestic and international institutions. Based on these objectives, the UK government focuses on six priorities, as follows:

(1) Decrease the insider threat in high-risk sectors.
(2) Enhance the integrity of the country as an international financial center.
(3) Develop integrity in both public and private sectors.
(4) Control corrupt behaviors in public procurement and grants.
(5) Promote the business environment globally.
(6) Develop international cooperation in anti-corruption.

When implementing these priorities, the government will consider the four following approaches: protect against corruption, prevent people from engaging in corruption, pursue and punish the corrupt and reduce the impact of corruption.

In addition, the first United States strategy on countering corruption has a similar structure (The White House, 2021). Table 3.1 shows that the US government has established five strategic pillars from which strategic objectives are developed. Then, each strategic objective has key lines of effort. The government amplifies its efforts domestically and internationally and cooperates with both governmental and non-governmental partners in order to prevent, limit and respond to corrupt activities and related crimes.

Moreover, some countries have strategies to support their partners in combating corruption. For example, the French government has designed an anti-corruption strategy in its cooperation action to reduce corruption in its partner countries. To achieve this overall objective, the government concentrates on three action thrusts: (1) reinforcing the French approach to combating corruption, (2) promoting anti-corruption and better governance in international cooperation and (3) supporting the work of international organizations, non-state actors and local institutions. Each thrust has its specific objectives.

After investigating the approaches to fighting against corruption across the 26 least corrupt countries ranked by Transparency International's Corruption Perceptions Index 2016, Pyman *et al.* (2018) show that the second generation strategies should focus on broadening the objectives of anti-corruption, enhancing integration with multi-national anti-corruption initiatives, developing national anti-corruption actions in high-risk sectors, promoting multi-national actions in sectors, building or enhancing anti-corruption actions in local governments, recognizing and cooperating with the private sectors to combat corruption and promoting other national feedback and review mechanisms. They suggest that an anti-corruption strategy includes priorities and actions at sub-national, sector-specific and national levels.

### 3.2.3.  *Successful anti-corruption models*

According to Topchii *et al.* (2021), there are three successful anti-corruption models in the world from three regions including Northern

Table 3.1.  The US anti-corruption strategy

| Approach | Strategic pillars | Strategic objectives |
| --- | --- | --- |
| Prevent, limit and respond to corruption and related crimes domestically and internationally with governmental and non-governmental partners | 1. Modernizing, coordinating and resourcing US government efforts to fight corruption | 1.1. Enhance corruption-related research, data collection and analysis<br>1.2. Improve information sharing within the US government, with non-US-governmental entities and internationally<br>1.3. Increase focus on the transnational dimensions of corruption<br>1.4. Organize and resource the fight against corruption, at home and abroad<br>Integrate an anti-corruption focus into regional, thematic and sectoral priorities |
| | 2. Curbing illicit finance | 2.1. Address deficiencies in the anti-money laundering regime<br>2.2. Work with partners and allies to address deficiencies |
| | 3. Holding corrupt actors accountable | 3.1. Enhance enforcement efforts<br>3.2. Update tools available to hold corrupt actors accountable at home and abroad<br>3.3. Work with partner countries to bolster anti-corruption enforcement to amplify the use of tools<br>3.4. Strengthen the ability of foreign partner governments to pursue accountability in a just and equitable manner<br>3.5. Bolster the ability of civil society, media, and private sector actors to safely detect and expose corruption, increase public awareness and pursue accountability |
| | 4. Preserving and strengthening the multilateral anti-corruption architecture | 4.1. Bolster existing anti-corruption frameworks and institutions<br>4.2. Redouble efforts at multilateral fora |
| | 5. Improving diplomatic engagement and leveraging foreign assistance resources to advance policy goals | 5.1. Elevate and expand the scale of diplomatic engagement and foreign assistance that address corruption<br>5.2. Protect anti-corruption actors<br>5.3. Leverage innovation in the fight against corruption<br>5.4. Improve coordination and risk analysis across foreign assistance<br>5.5. Improve security assistance and integrate corruption considerations into military planning, analysis and operations |

*Source*: The White House (2021).

Table 3.2.  Successful anti-corruption models

| Models | Typical countries | Components |
| --- | --- | --- |
| Northern and Western Europe | *Norway, Sweden, Finland and Denmark* | • An active role of public authorities to redistribute funds in the state<br>• Maximum transparency and accountability<br>• Free competition in the economy<br>• A developed civil society<br>• An important role of the media |
| East Asia | *Singapore, Hong Kong, Taiwan, Malaysia, South Korea and Japan* | • Strict laws (equality of all before the law and severe punishment)<br>• Special anti-corruption agencies<br>• A verified personnel policy<br>• A decentralized economy |
| America | *The United States, Canada and partly Australia* | • Strict, restrictive laws (no immunities for officials)<br>• A system of incentives and rewards<br>• Standards of honor codes for public officials |

*Source*: Topchii *et al.* (2021).

and Western Europe, Eastern Asia and North America. Table 3.2 shows that the Northern and Western Europe model relies much on social pressure to prevent corruption. The media plays an important role in identifying and criticizing corrupt behaviors. In addition, public trust is high. Therefore, a corruption crime is considered immoral behavior and immediately becomes a national scandal. For example, there are approximately 20 acts that have regulations to control corruption. The government, the media and public activists are strongly integrated to combat corruption. People are willing to pay high taxes because they understand that the government uses its budget efficiently to serve the public. The government also commits to providing citizens with high-quality public services and social support systems.

The second model is from East Asian countries such as Singapore, Hong Kong, Taiwan, Malaysia, South Korea and Japan. These countries have strict legal systems that treat all people equally when they commit crimes and severely penalize corruption-related crimes. Besides, they also establish special anti-corruption agencies that monitor, investigate and even prosecute public officials who commit corrupt crimes. Furthermore, the governments follow a verified personnel policy to select highly qualified officials and pay them a high salary. For example, the Singaporean government is successful in fighting against corruption due to the following four initiatives:

(1) The public sector competes with the private sector in attracting high-quality human resources by paying competitive salaries to government officials.
(2) Government officials are required to report their assets and debts annually. When they are suspected of committing corruption crimes, the prosecutor is allowed to inspect their bank current and share accounts.
(3) When high-ranking officials commit corruption crimes, they receive harsher penalties.
(4) The administrative system is transparent, supportive and helpful. Excessive administrative procedures and obstacles to economic development are eliminated.

The third model is America. Typical countries following this model are the United States, Canada and partly Australia. They have strict and restrictive legislations to prevent and punish corrupt behaviors. Moreover, they also design many incentives and rewards in order to discourage government officials from adopting corrupt behaviors. In general, in order to be successful in combating corruption, the government should focus on developing a strict and restrictive legal system, encouraging the participation of social organizations and the media, promoting economic development and competition, improving transparency and accountability, conducting a verified personnel policy and developing moral standards for public servants.

## 3.2.4.   *Anti-corruption agencies*

### 3.2.4.1.   *Defining anti-corruption agencies*

An anti-corruption agency is an independent public body established to fight against corruption and eliminate corrupt opportunities with a set of preventive and/or repressive measures (Sousa, 2010). The Singaporean government is a pioneer in establishing an anti-corruption agency. The Singaporean Corrupt Practices Investigation Bureau was founded in 1952. Following Singapore, Malaysia and Hongkong also established their anti-corruption agencies in 1959 and 1974, respectively. In the early 1990s, there were about 20 anti-corruption agencies in the world. However, most countries in the world have established national anti-corruption agencies so far (Schöberlein, 2020).

### 3.2.4.2.   *Types of anti-corruption agencies*

According to Sousa (2010), in principle, an agency has to meet many requisites to be considered an anti-corruption agency. These requirements include the distinctiveness from other law enforcement bodies, the availability of preventive and/or repressive measures, the durability of the organization, the power to centralize informative resources, the coordination of initiatives conducted by other corruption controlling parties, the role of creating and disseminating knowledge, the rule of law and the accessibility of the public. However, anti-corruption agencies meeting these requisites are rare in the real world.

Quah (2017) classifies anti-corruption agencies into two groups, namely, A and B based on their functions. Type A anti-corruption agencies have a narrower scope of functions. They mainly focus on education on anti-corruption, awareness-raising on anti-corruption, prevention of corruption crimes and investigation and prosecution of corrupt officials. Since type A anti-corruption agencies are more specialized in combating corruption, they have lower operation costs, strong expertise and autonomy and much experience. Nevertheless, type B anti-corruption agencies have a broader scope of functions. They concentrate on both anti-corruption and non-corruption-related activities. The latter may be citizens' complaints about public services, administrative appeals, disciplinary control over government officials, etc.

In addition, Klemenčič and Stusek (2008) classify anti-corruption agencies into three groups by their most common manifestations. The first is multi-purpose agencies that have both preventive and investigative activities. This category is similar to type A of Quah (2017). The second is law enforcement agencies, which are generally a specialized department or division of the police force or the prosecution office. These agencies may have the right to investigate corrupt officials only or the right to investigate and prosecute them. They fail to participate in preventive activities. The third is agencies of prevention, policy development and coordination. They mainly concentrate on preventive measures such as education and raising awareness. Besides, they also participate in policy analysis, recommend amendments to legal regulations and suggest anti-corruption initiatives or action plans. However, they fail to have investigatory and law enforcement powers.

### 3.2.4.3. *Principles for effective anti-corruption agencies*

Although there are many anti-corruption agencies with various functions and tasks in the world, the effective ones have some features in common. According to Schöberlein (2020), there are six principles ensuring the effectiveness of an anti-corruption agency.

(1) **Political independence and no undue political interference:** Anti-corruption agencies should be independent in their political status and operation. Their performance should be consistent with their functions, rights and obligations stipulated in legal regulations. When corrupt officials are investigated or prosecuted, they tend to take all opportunities to avoid unfavorable consequences. Therefore, anti-corruption agencies may face much pressure from high-ranking officials or other government agencies that support them. When these undue political interferences are restricted and prohibited, anti-corruption agencies are

effective in controlling corruption. To maintain anti-corruption agencies' political independence, national leaders should be full of integrity and accountability and become good examples for officials at lower levels.

(2) **Clear yet broad mandates:** The mandate of an anti-corruption agency is determined by its functions. It should be presented in a law instead of a decree or an administrative order since a law is more stable and enforceable. In addition, a broad mandate helps an anti-corruption agency mobilize enough resources for its operation.

(3) **Transparent and independent appointment and dismissal of staff:** The process to appoint officials of anti-corruption agencies should be transparent and independent to ensure that the selected officers are competent, honest, neutral and full of integrity. Anti-corruption agencies become paper tigers if they have corrupt officials. Furthermore, leaders of anti-corruption agencies need stable and appropriate terms of tenure so that they have enough time to develop and implement their plans. They are not afraid of external pressure on their positions. The dismissal process should be clear so that anti-corruption officials feel safe and confident in their performance.

(4) **Financial independence and sufficient resources:** Anti-corruption agencies concentrate on their functions effectively when they have necessary resources such as budget, personnel and facilities. Other organizations and officials cannot pressure them or force them to compromise their integrity for budget or other resources.

(5) **Collaboration and coordination:** Anti-corruption agencies cannot perform effectively on their own since their activities are related to other organizations and individuals. They need information and support from both governmental and non-governmental organizations. Besides, they may receive financial aid, training courses and other support from international anti-corruption organizations.

(6) **Accountability and external reporting:** Accountability is necessary to restrict and mitigate the negative aspects of

independence. An independent agency may lead to abuse of power. Accountability ensures that anti-corruption agencies are obliged to perform within the legal framework and under the supervision of society.

### 3.2.4.4. *Mistakes in combating corruption with anti-corruption agencies*

According to Quah (2017), there are two mistakes leading to the failure of anti-corruption agencies. First, anti-corruption agencies are used as an attack dog. Instead of respecting and facilitating anti-corruption agencies' independence, neutrality and integrity, high-ranking politicians may take advantage of anti-corruption agencies to investigate and prosecute their political opponents. Therefore, anti-corruption activities turn out to be "witch hunts". In addition, anti-corruption agencies with undue performance may become a threat to most government bodies and officials. They only follow rigid principles to avoid unexpected problems and penalties caused by anti-corruption agencies. This reaction restricts creativity, flexibility and innovation in delivering public services.

Second, anti-corruption agencies are paper tigers. When leaders of a country do not have political commitment nor make efforts to fight against corruption, its anti-corruption agencies cannot have enough powers and resources to implement their functions. These paper tigers exist only because political leaders need to show their citizens that they support anti-corruption and respect integrity.

# 3.3.  International Anti-Corruption Initiatives

## 3.3.1.  *The Inter-American Convention Against Corruption (IACAC)*

Recognizing the negative effects of corruption and bribery, the Organization of American States started to develop a convention in 1994. Two years later, the organization's members ratified the

Inter-American Convention Against Corruption and it came into force on 6 March 1997. This is the first international convention to combat corruption. According to Article II, the convention focuses on two main objectives. First, it promotes and supports each member in their development of anti-corruption mechanisms including prevention, detection, punishment and eradication. Second, it strengthens and facilitates the cooperation of its members so that their anti-corruption measures and actions are effective.

### 3.3.2.  *The OECD Anti-Bribery Convention*

From the initiative of the US government, the Organization for Economic Co-operation and Development (OECD) started drafting a convention on international anti-bribery in 1989 (Khaghaghordyan, 2014) since there was a legal vacuum in international cooperation to combat corruption (Galtung & Pope, 1999). Eight years later, all of the OECD members and five non-member countries ratified the OECD convention on combating bribery of foreign public officials in international business transactions. The major requirement of the OECD Anti-Bribery Convention is criminalizing bribery of government officials in foreign countries. This controls and reduces political corruption from the supply side. Organizations and individuals bribing foreign public servants shall be punished in accordance with the criminal law. Jensen and Malesky (2018) investigate how the OECD Anti-Bribery Convention affects corruption across countries. They find that the convention is effective in reducing both the propensity to pay bribes and the willingness to admit to this crime.

### 3.3.3.  *Transparency International*

Transparency International is a non-governmental association established in 1993 by former experts of the World Bank. It has quickly become the most popular international anti-corruption organization in the world due to its great impact and contributions toward combating global corruption. Transparency International's mission is "to stop corruption and promote transparency, accountability and integrity at all levels and across all sectors of society". It has a system of local chapters. Each chapter is an independent organization located in a specific country. The chapters are in charge of addressing corruption, providing legal support and supporting policy reform in their countries. Besides, they also collaborate with each other to address regional and global corruption. The most important product of Transparency International is the Corruption Perceptions Index published annually since 1995. It also publishes other corruption-related products such as Global Corruption Report, Global Corruption Barometer and Bribe Payers Index.

### 3.3.4.  *The European Union's conventions on anti-corruption*

After ratifying the Convention on Protection of the European Communities' Financial Interests, European countries adopted a protocol to control corruption at both national and regional levels in 1996. However, since the scope of the first protocol is narrow, they continued to adopt the second one to stipulate detailed liability and punishment for serious corruption crimes such as fraud, active bribery and money laundering in May 1997. Moreover, the European Council adopted the Convention on the Fight against Corruption involving Officials of the European Communities or Officials of Member States of the European Union. This is an important milestone in the European Union's anti-corruption campaign. It focuses on controlling both passive and active bribery. From 1998 to 1999, the European Council ratified the Criminal Law Convention on Corruption and the Civil Law Convention on Corruption. These two conventions provided a sufficient and strong legal framework for anti-corruption in the region.

### 3.3.5.  *The Group of States against Corruption (GRECO)*

The Group of States against Corruption (GRECO) is a regional organization founded by the European Council in 1999. This organization is open to non-European countries like the United States of America. It does research to show weaknesses in anti-corruption policies of its members and promotes reforms in anti-corruption legislations, institutions and practices. GRECO evaluation reports provide evaluated members with practical suggestions so that their anti-corruption performance is consistent with EU standards.

## 3.3.6.  *The anti-corruption protocols in Africa*

African countries started to address corruption in early 2000s. The Southern African Development Community (SADC) and the Economic Community of West African States (ECOWAS) adopted protocols against corruption in 2001. These protocols focused on strengthening their members' commitment and actions to reducing corruption. In 2003, the African Union ratified the Convention on Preventing and Combating Corruption. This convention aimed at prevention, detection, punishment and eradication of corruption and related crimes in both public and private sectors.

## 3.3.7.  *The United Nations Convention against Corruption (UNCAC)*

The United Nations Convention against Corruption was the first worldwide anti-corruption agreement. It came into force in December 2005 and was ratified by most of the UN members. It focuses on the goal of enhancing and developing anti-corruption measures domestically and internationally. To achieve this goal, contracting parties follow four main groups of actions: preventive measures (Chapter 2), criminalization and law enforcement (Chapter 3), international cooperation (Chapter 4) and asset recovery (Chapter 5). This convention is a global and comprehensive framework to standardize and promote anti-corruption in each country or territory and strengthen their cooperation in controlling corruption at the international level.

### 3.3.8.  *G20 Anti-Corruption Working Group*

Addressing the negative effects of corruption on economic environments at the Toronto Summit in 2010, G20 leaders decided to establish the Anti-Corruption Working Group. Its performance is based on the St. Petersburg Strategic Framework and multi-year action plans. The group provides countries with key principles, good practices and guidance in anti-corruption. Additionally, it publishes annual reports on accountability or corruption control across countries. The 2022–2024 action plan has three overarching goals:

(1) Strengthening the current commitments and obligations in order to improve the effect of the international anti-corruption agenda.
(2) Developing actions whereby the group can add highest value and improve the role of G20 in the international community.
(3) Solving new problems in corruption and developing preventive measures in related areas.

## 3.4.  Anti-Corruption in Developing Countries

According to Hart (2009), the causes and solutions of corruption form a simple equation: Corruption = (Monopoly + Discretion) – (Accountability + Integrity + Transparency). The equation implies that the government can control political corruption by increasing accountability, integrity and transparency. However, several academics posit that reducing political corruption in developing countries is more difficult than in developed countries (Khan, 2006; Nguyen *et al.*, 2017). Developing countries face more severe corruption due to lower accountability and transparency; therefore, many politicians and officials have connections with corruption cases or corrupt officials. Fighting against corruption may pose a threat to their political positions. Moreover, legal regulations and human resources to control corruption are limited in developing countries.

Consequently, their anti-corruption agencies are less competent and effective. Besides, victims of political corruption are less likely to denounce corrupt officials since their denouncements may make them face more serious problems (Nguyen *et al.*, 2017).

China has become a typical anti-corruption model among developing countries in recent years. Since the 18th National Congress of the Chinese Communist Party (CCP) in November 2012, President Xi Jinping has been determined to combat corruption all over the country and an unprecedented anti-corruption campaign called "Attack tigers, kill flies" was launched. Tigers and flies represent corrupt officials at high and low levels, respectively (Guo & Li, 2015). Any official can be investigated and prosecuted regardless of their position, contribution or family background. In 2012, the Central Committee of the Chinese Communist Party approved increasing the intensity and severity of investigation and punishment in order to control widespread corruption in China. The Central Commission for Discipline Inspection (CCDI) and local Commissions for Discipline Inspection (CDI) are the key anti-corruption agencies. Although they fail to have judicial authority, they transfer corrupt cases to judicial bodies after investigation. At the beginning of the corruption crackdown campaign, the CCDI investigated four big tigers, namely, Xilai, a Politburo member and Party Secretary of Chongqing; Ling Jihua, Director of the General Office of the Central Committee of the Chinese Communist Party; Zhou Yongkang, a member of the Politburo Standing Committee and Secretary of the Central Committee's Politics and Law Committee; and Zhou Yongkang, a former Standing Committee member of the Political Bureau of the CPC Central Committee. They received severe punishment for their violations after effective processes of judgment.

In addition, the Chinese anti-corruption agencies have attracted public participation to combat corruption through social media. The slogan "Using the computer's mouse to connect the CCDI" shows the CCDI's efforts and enthusiasm to call for citizens' cooperation. In April 2013, many popular websites such as People.com.cn, Xinhuanet.com, Chinanews.com opened separate categories for people to denounce suspicious corruption cases. In September 2013, the

CCDI and the Ministry of Supervision introduced a joint website (www.ccdi.gov.cn) to provide news on anti-corruption and collect information from the public (Guo & Li, 2015).

However, the anti-corruption policy in China also faces some difficulties. First, the income of government officials is low and thus the demand side of corruption is still a serious threat to its success. Second, the policy mainly focuses on the investigation, prosecution and punishment of corrupt officials. These actions are necessary, but they cannot eliminate political corruption comprehensively. Therefore, the government should focus more on education and preventive measures. Corrupt officials may be competent ones. If the lack of preventive measures creates opportunities for them to be corrupt, then the government will lose competent officials.

# Chapter 4

# Political Corruption and Investment Decisions

*This chapter aims to analyze the effect of political corruption on investment decisions. First, it summarizes the main theories of corporate investment such as simple accelerator theory, flexible accelerator theory, Modigliani–Miller theorem, neo-classical theory, Tobin's Q theory, liquidity theory and agency theory. Second, it synthesizes empirical evidence to show key determinants of corporate investment from the three groups including financial characteristics, corporate governance and business environment. Then, it analyzes the effects of corruption on investment-related decisions such as risk-taking, capital expenditure and investment efficiency. Moreover, it also presents the role of anti-corruption in corporate investment.*

## 4.1. Theories of Corporate Investment

### 4.1.1. *Simple accelerator theory*

Clark (1917) proposes the initial principles of the simple accelerator theory. He posits that the demand for capital investment is determined by the acceleration of consumer demand instead of the volume of output. The simple accelerator theory assumes that excess capacity and financial constraint are not present and the desired capital–output ratio is unchanged (Junankar, 1972).

$$K_t^* = \alpha Y_t$$

where $K_t^*$ is the desired capital in $t$. $Y_t$ is the volume of output in $t$. $\alpha$ is the constant capital–output ratio.

Firms spend a certain amount of money during the period $t$ to increase their capital so that it reaches the desired level. For simplicity, depreciation is assumed to be negligible.

$$I_t = K_t^* - K_{t-1}$$

where $I_t$ is the capital investment in t. $K_{t-1}$ is the desired capital in $t-1$.

Since the capital in $t$-1 has reached the desired level in $t$-1 ($K_{t-1} = K_{t-1}^* = \alpha Y_{t-1}$), the equation to describe the relationship between the capital investment and the change in the volume of output is as follows:

$$I_t = \alpha Y_t - \alpha Y_{t-1} = \alpha(Y_t - Y_{t-1})$$

Accordingly, the simple accelerator model states that corporate investment expenditure has a linear relationship with the increase in production in the future. Increased sales imply that a firm may have a higher level of profit and a greater use of its production capacity in the next period. This makes the firm increase its capital investment. An increase in capital investment results in higher growth in sales and profits and thus it creates a multiplier effect (Meng, 2013).

## 4.1.2.   *Flexible accelerator theory*

Chenery (1952) and Koyck (1954) propose the flexible accelerator theory by loosening strict assumptions of the simple accelerator theory. They argue that the difference between the desired capital and the actual capital is not closed by capital expenditure in just one period. In each period, firms plan to reduce a fraction of this gap instead. Consequently, the equation of capital investment is presented as follows:

$$I_t = \varphi(K_t^* - K_{t-1})$$

where $\varphi$ is the partial adjustment speed. If the actual capital is lower than the optimal level, firms tend to increase their capital investment in installed productive capacity in order to close this gap by the fraction $\varphi$. Therefore, corporate investment in business equipment stock in period t is the sum of the partial investments from many prior periods.

$$I_t^n = \varphi \sum_{i=1}^{n}(K_{t-1}^* - K_{t-i-1}) = \varphi \sum_{i=1}^{n}(\alpha Y_{t-1} - \alpha Y_{t-i-1})$$

$$= \varphi \sum_{i=1}^{n}(Y_{t-1} - Y_{t-i-1})$$

where $I_t^n$ is the total capital investment from period 1 to period $n$.

### 4.1.3.  *Modigliani–Miller theorem*

When facing investment opportunities, firms need to choose funds in order to finance their investment projects. They may raise funds from three main sources including retained earnings, debt (bank loans and sales of debt securities) and new share issuance. Each of them leads to explicit and/or implicit costs and the cost of their investment is the total financing cost.

According to the Modigliani–Miller theorem, the capital market is perfect and people have full information about their choices. No firm can choose funding methods with lower costs. Therefore, firms incur the same level of financing cost regardless of their funding methods. In a perfect capital market, corporate investment expenditure is determined by only one factor — investment opportunities (Modigliani & Miller, 1958).

### 4.1.4.  *Neo-classical theory*

The neo-classical theory is developed by Jorgenson (1963). This theory emphasizes that firms tend to have an optimal level of capital investment that maximizes their value. Corporate investment expenditure is mainly determined by relative prices of production factors (capital and labor) and the production level. The theory is based on the following assumptions: (1) firms utilize fixed capital efficiently, (2) returns to production factors diminish, (3) adjustment costs are not present, (4) prices of production factors are perfectly flexible, (5) financial markets are perfect, (6) the price of capital investment equals the cost of capital and (7) putty-putty capital is present. The presence of putty-putty capital implies that technology is transferred freely across firms and thus corporate investment relies on the cost of capital rather than technology.

In the long run, a firm's production output depends on the amount of capital and labor, as follows. The flow of net cash flows from capital investment in period t is described as follows:

$$CF_t = p_t Y_t - w_t L t - r_t I_t$$

where $CF$ is the net cash flows. $Y$ is the level of output. $p$ is the unit price of products. $L$ is the amount of labor. $w$ is the wage rate. $I$ is the capital investment. $r$ is the price of capital. The present value of the firm is calculated by the following formula:

$$PV_t = \int_0^\infty e^{-ir_t} CF_t dt$$

where $PV$ is the present value, $e$ is the continuous discounting exponent, $ir$ is the constant interest rate. The firm has to choose paths for $I_t$ and $L_t$ so that $PV$ reaches its maximum, given the paths of $w$ and $p$.

Bischoff (1972) proposes the modified neoclassical theory by broadening the standard neoclassical theory. He argues that firms are highly flexible in their capital investment decisions at the planning stage. Therefore, the proportion of capital is soft-putty. However, when capital goods are installed, firms are less flexible in changing factor proportions. Consequently, the proportion of capital becomes clay-putty and thus reversing an investment decision is costly.

According to Bischoff (1972), changing factor proportions is easier when production factors cannot be substituted by the others. Hence, capital investment is more related to changes in the production output than the cost of capital. This implies that the distributed lag of capital expenditure on changes in the relative price of capital is not similar to that on changes in the level of production.

### 4.1.5.  *Tobin's Q theory*

Unlike prior theories in corporate investment behavior, Brainard and Tobin (1968) developed Tobin's $Q$ theory based on financial markets rather than the production output. They argue that corporate investment relies on the ratio of the market value of capital goods to their replacement cost. The replacement cost of capital goods is the actual amount that the firm has to pay if it buys them at their current prices. Consequently, firms tend to make their capital investment decisions based on their market value. This ratio is called Tobin's $Q$. A firm tends to increase its investment expenditure by one dollar if the market value of one dollar investment increase is greater than one dollar ($Q > 1$) and decreases its investment expenditure by one dollar if the market value of one dollar investment is lower than one dollar ($Q < 1$). In other words, firms are encouraged to invest in capital goods if the return on equity in the market is smaller than the real return on capital investment. It reflects the effects of all factors on corporate investment decisions and thus represents the market valuation of future investment opportunities.

According to Tobin (1969), the original Tobin's $Q$ is the capitalized value of the marginal capital investment divided by its replacement cost. Therefore, it is called marginal Tobin's $Q$. However, if there is no market in which firms' capital goods can be traded, the marginal $Q$ cannot be measured actually. Consequently, academics commonly use the average $Q$ as a proxy for the marginal $Q$ in their empirical research since the average $Q$ is observable. According to Erickson and Whited (2000), the average $Q$ is measured by the market value of capital stock divided by its replacement value. Although many empirical studies show that Tobin's $Q$ is a good determinant of corporate investment, some researchers argue that it fails to reflect all information about firms' investment decisions

(Meng, 2013). Ferderer (1993) shows that uncertainty has a stronger effect on corporate investment than the average $Q$.

### 4.1.6.　*Liquidity theory*

When raising external funds, firms have to pay many costs (e.g., agency costs, transaction costs, underwriting costs and administrative and legal costs of bankruptcy) (Myers, 1984). Moreover, due to the information asymmetry between firms and outside investors, external financing is more costly than internal financing (Meyer & Kuh, 1957). When corporate managers have an information advantage to value their firm, they are more likely to finance their investment opportunities by external funds (mainly by issuing new stocks). Outside investors fail to have enough information about the firm; therefore, they think that the firm is overvalued and give lower prices for the firm's stocks. This adverse selection makes external funds become more expensive. Firms have to pay signaling costs if they want to receive the actual price. Consistently, Stiglitz and Weiss (1981) find that asymmetric information also determines how credit is rationed in the credit market. When facing higher costs of external financing, firms mainly use internal funds to finance their capital investment (Fazzari *et al.*, 1988). Moreover, McDonald and Soderstrom (1986) and Myers and Majluf (1984) posit that firms also prefer using residual funds to buy capital goods. The residual funds are available after a firm pays for prior claims on its cash flow.

Firms only use external funds if their internal funds are unstable and the cost of external financing is negligible. Otherwise, they use retained earnings as the major source of their capital investment and thus their investment is determined by their cash flow. When firms are financially constrained due to their low sales and cash flow, they tend to pay lower levels of dividends and save more funds for their capital investment.

### 4.1.7.　*Agency theory*

According to the agency theory, corporate investment depends on the agency problem between corporate managers and shareholders.

Corporate managers are agents who are entrusted with operating their firms on behalf of their shareholders. However, this relationship results in a moral hazard in which corporate managers make decisions to serve their own utility and sacrifice their shareholders' interests (Jensen & Meckling, 1976). In order to maintain their positions, managers tend to build their empire by increasing firm size beyond the optimal level, developing acquisitions and establishing new manufacturing plants. This empire-building mechanism can be conducted through excessive growth and overinvestment (Hope & Thomas, 2008). Overinvestment is not determined by profitable investment opportunities and thus it destroys shareholders' value. When the agency problem is more severe, firms have higher levels of overinvestment.

## 4.2. Determinants of Corporate Investment

### 4.2.1. *Financial characteristics*

#### 4.2.1.1. *Investment opportunities*

One of the most basic principles of corporate finance is that firms make financial decisions to maximize their present value. In a perfect capital market, investment opportunities are the only determinant of corporate investment decisions (Modigliani & Miller, 1958). In the real world, corporate investment decisions are also determined by other factors, but investment opportunities are still an important determinant. Profitable investment opportunities drive controlling shareholders to allocate corporate resources in order to increase firm value and reduce their incentives to use these resources in order to serve their own benefits. When the profitability of investment opportunities is higher, the return of capital investment is higher than the interest from expropriating minority shareholders (Durnev & Kim, 2007). When valuable investment opportunities are less available, controlling shareholders have high incentives to divert corporate resources to increase their private interest and positive-net present value (NPV) investment is lower.

Tobin's $Q$ is the most popular measure of investment opportunities (Hayashi, 1982). In line with Tobin's $Q$ theory, Aggarwal and Zong (2006); Aivazian *et al.* (2005), Ali *et al.* (2022), Ascioglu *et al.* (2008), Chen *et al.* (2017), Erickson and Whited (2000), Liu and Zhang (2019) and Tran (2020c) find that Tobin's $Q$ has a positive effect on corporate capital investment. Moreover, some prior studies also use sales growth as a proxy for investment opportunities (Hu & Liu, 2015; Mulier *et al.*, 2016; Yoon & Ratti, 2011). The positive relationship between sales growth and corporate investment is supported by the accelerator theories.

### 4.2.1.2.  *Cash flow*

Internally generated cash flow is an important fund for finance investment projects. According to Chiu *et al.* (2022), the relationship between cash flow and corporate investment may be explained by two theories, namely, the agency theory and the liquidity theory of corporate investment behavior. First, the agency theory argues that when firms have high levels of free cash flow, their managers overinvest in order to build their empire or serve their own benefits. Corporate managers are controlled and monitored more strictly when using external financing. Therefore, they have high incentives to overinvest when internal funds are available. He *et al.* (2019) find that sufficient internal funds not only reduce corporate underinvestment but also increase overinvestment. Similarly, Chiu *et al.* (2022) document a positive impact of internal cash flow on overinvestment.

Second, according to the liquidity theory, asymmetric information makes external financing more costly than internal financing (Myers and Majluf, 1984). Therefore, firms are more likely to increase their capital investment in profitable opportunities when their cash flows are higher. Fazzari *et al.* (1987) show that cash flow still determines corporate investment after investment opportunities are controlled. Ascioglu *et al.* (2008) show that corporate investment is lower and more sensitive to cash flow when the probability of information asymmetry is high. Mulier *et al.* (2016) show that firms have the highest investment–cash flow sensitivity when they face high financial constraints and costs of debt. Furthermore, many prior studies show that cash flow positively affects corporate investment (Chen *et al.*, 2017; Malmendier *et al.*, 2011; Mills *et al.*, 1995; Pawlina & Renneboog, 2005; Julio Pindado *et al.*, 2011).

### 4.2.1.3.  *Cash holdings*

According to Opler *et al.* (1999), firms hold cash to avoid missing profitable investment opportunities although cash holdings are costly. With a sample of firms listed in the US over the period 1971–1994, they find that corporate cash holdings are positively related to growth opportunities and cash flow volatility, and negatively related to access to capital. Besides, firms save cash to maintain their financial slack and thus avoid high costs of external financing (Myers & Majluf, 1984). High levels of cash holdings enable firms to undertake future investment opportunities despite their low levels of cash flow (Arslan *et al.*, 2006). Acharya *et al.* (2007) show that cash holdings hedge against cash flow shortfalls and thus secure corporate investment. Morcover, Harford *et al.* (2014), Kashyap *et al.* (1994), Lamont (1997) and Tran (2019e) find that corporate cash balances are positively related to corporate investment.

### 4.2.1.4.  *Firm size*

Firm size significantly affects costs of external financing (Driffield & Pal, 2001). Large firms have better reputations, experiences and management capabilities. These signals are important to reduce the information asymmetry between insiders and outside investors. Therefore, larger firms have easier access to external funds, higher credit ratings for their bonds and lower expenses for their bank loans (Gertler & Gilchrist, 1994). In addition, large firms have more stable future profit flows that help them have easier access to external funds and reduce costs of external financing. Ghosal and Loungani (1996) show that industries with the majority of small firms witness a stronger negative impact of uncertainty on corporate investment while other industries have positive or insignificant effects. Ali *et al.* (2022), Dang *et al.* (2018), Ding *et al.* (2018), Elgebeily *et al.* (2021), Fishman and Rob (1999), Kadapakkam *et al.* (1998), Khémiri and Noubbigh (2020) and Muhammad *et al.* (2022) find empirical evidence of the positive relationship between firm size and corporate investment.

### 4.2.1.5.  *Financial leverage*

Financial leverage negatively affects corporate investment through increasing underinvestment and decreasing overinvestment. First, according to Myers (1977), debt may create a negative externality for firms' optimal investment strategy. The agency problem between highly leveraged firms (the agent) and their creditors (the principal) reduces firms' incentives to invest in valuable investment projects as the benefits from their investment mainly or partially belong to their creditors. This implies a positive relationship between financial leverage and underinvestment. Second, due to the agency problem between corporate managers and shareholders, managers tend to overinvest to build their own empire (Jensen, 1986). However, this appropriation is more difficult with external funds. Managers of highly levered firms are controlled strictly by both legal regulations and creditors such as bondholders and banks. Therefore, their overinvestment is lower. Many prior studies show that firms with high debt ratios have low levels of capital investment (Ahn *et al.*, 2006; Aivazian *et al.*, 2005; Ascioglu *et al.*, 2008; Denis & Denis, 1993; Hoshi *et al.*, 1991; Lang *et al.*, 1996; Liu & Zhang, 2019; Umutlu, 2010; Vo, 2019).

### 4.2.1.6.  *Asset tangibility*

According to Almeida and Campello (2007), asset tangibility is an important determinant of firms' financial constraints. Firms with high asset tangibility can offer more collateral to their creditors such as banks and other financial institutions; therefore, they have better access to external funds. This implies that asset tangibility positively affects corporate investment. Several previous studies show supporting evidence for this positive relationship (Boasiako *et al.*, 2022; González, 2016, 2018; Guermazi, 2014; Gupta & Mahakud, 2018).

## 4.2.2. *Corporate governance*

### 4.2.2.1. *Ownership structure*

Ownership structure plays an important role in corporate governance since it reflects the interest of different shareholder groups. Common structure variables used in prior research include ownership concentration, insider ownership, institutional ownership, state ownership and foreign ownership.

According to Stiglitz (1985), high ownership concentration may lead to stronger corporate governance since large blockholders have high incentives to protect their firms' wealth. Gomes (2000), Kaplan and Minton (1994), Lins (2003), Xiaonian Xu and Wang (1997) and Zingales (1995) show that concentrated ownership reduces the conflict of interest between controlling and minority shareholders. However, high ownership concentration may also make this conflict of interest become more severe. In a firm of concentrated ownership, controlling shareholders have more power and thus they are more likely to expropriate minority shareholders (Claessens & Djankov, 1999; Ducassy & Guyot, 2017; Fan & Wong, 2002; Morck *et al.*, 2000). When the alignment effect dominates, firms with high ownership concentration have lower corporate investment since their controlling shareholders have low incentives to overinvest. When the entrenchment effect dominates, ownership concentration has a positive impact on corporate investment through controlling shareholders' overinvestment.

Similarly, Klaus Gugler *et al.* (2008) posit that insider ownership also has both the alignment effect and the entrenchment effect. Corporate managers with high percentages of shares receive more benefits and losses from their right and wrong decisions, respectively. Therefore, they try harder to increase their own benefits through increasing shareholders' wealth (Ross, 1977). Nevertheless, when managers have more shares, they have more discretion to make decisions that benefit themselves rather than other shareholders (Morck *et al.*, 1988). Anas (2015), Julio Pindado and De la Torre (2006) and Pindado *et al.* (2012) find supporting evidence for the entrenchment effect with a positive impact of insider ownership on corporate investment.

In addition, institutional ownership is effective in monitoring corporate managers (Cella, 2020). Unlike small investors, institutional investors are large shareholders and long-term investors. Consequently, they have high incentives to monitor and control corporate managers (Shleifer & Vishny, 1986). Many institutional investors such as financial institutions and large firms have experience and active plans to monitor the management (Jensen, 1993). McCahery *et al.* (2016) conduct a survey to investigate how institutional investors contribute to corporate governance. They find that institutional shareholders can pressure the management to pursue their interests directly by their voice or indirectly by their exit when they are not satisfied with the management's performance. This implies that institutional investors help firms reduce their managers' overinvestment and thus firms have lower levels of investment. Richardson (2003) shows that institutional investors prevent corporate managers from using excess cash for overinvestment by their monitoring activities.

Moreover, the extant literature shows that state ownership may affect corporate investment through two opposite mechanisms. On the one hand, state ownership is a threat to corporate governance. Politicians may sacrifice economic benefits to pursue political or social objectives (Laffont & Tirole, 1993). This provides corporate managers more opportunities to expropriate shareholders' interests. Borisova *et al.* (2012) and Shen and Lin (2009) show that state ownership leads to weak corporate governance. Chen *et al.* (2017) find that firms with state ownership have higher levels of overinvestment. Besides, the government tends to support firms with state ownership to have better access to credit (Kornai, 1979). Several prior studies document that firms with state ownership have lower costs of external financing (Borisova *et al.*, 2015; Borisova & Megginson, 2011; Shailer & Wang, 2015). Therefore, state ownership has a positive effect on corporate investment (Shen *et al.*, 2016). On the other hand, firms with state ownership are more risk-averse and thus they miss profitable investment opportunities. According to John *et al.* (2008), the government prefers low-risk projects since they provide the government a steady base for rent extraction. Boubakri *et al.* (2013) also find that firms with state ownership are less likely to take risk. Boubakri and Cosset (1998), D'souza and Megginson (1999), Jaslowitzer *et al.* (2018) and Megginson *et al.* (1994) show that state ownership has a negative impact on corporate investment.

According to Aggarwal *et al.* (2011) and Gillan and Starks (2003), firms with foreign ownership have stronger corporate governance since foreign investors have better experience, expertise and technology to monitor corporate managers and value firms. Baba (2009), Desender *et al.* (2016), Garner and Kim (2013) and Jeon *et al.* (2011) find supporting evidence for the positive relationship between foreign ownership and corporate governance. However, foreign investors are less effective than local investors in accessing information (Portes & Rey, 2005). Choe *et al.* (2005), Dvořák (2005) and Hau (2001) find that foreign shareholders face informational disadvantage in many countries. This informational disadvantage may restrict their capability to monitor managers.

### 4.2.2.2. *Board structure*

In modern firms, corporate boards are both monitors and advisors. They hire, monitor and fire corporate managers in the interest of shareholders. In addition, they also give advice to managers in making strategic decisions (Ali *et al.*, 2022). Therefore, board structure plays an important role in corporate governance and performance. Common attributes of board structure are board size, board independence and board diversity.

First, prior research shows that board size has two channels to affect corporate investment. On the one hand, firms with larger boards have stronger corporate governance. Corporate boards with more directors have more monitoring activities and committees; therefore, they can improve information transparency (Anderson *et al.*, 2004; Firstenberg & Malkiel, 1994; Klein, 2002). Moreover, when a board has more members, its diversity is higher since new members may have different backgrounds, education, professional expertise and skills. Consequently, the board can monitor the management more effectively and give better advice toward the firm's strategic decisions (Firstenberg & Malkiel, 1994; Kaplan & Reishus, 1990; Kiel & Nicholson, 2003). Besides, a larger board has more seats for independent directors (Ji, 2016). Med bechir and Jouirou (2021) find a positive impact of board size on corporate investment efficiency. On the other hand, a larger board faces obstacles in coordination and communication due to its diversity and this may be an opportunity for corporate managers to expropriate shareholders' interests (Eisenberg *et al.*, 1998; Lipton & Lorsch, 1992).

Second, board independence is a vital guarantee for corporate governance. According to Lu and Wang (2015), board independence has three characteristics: (1) CEO duality is not present, (2) independent directors fail to have employment relationship or affiliation with the firm, (3) independent directors fail to have social ties with the CEO. A board with more independent directors is able to control managers and reduce their conservatism in investment decisions effectively (Knyazeva *et al.*, 2013; Setia-Atmaja, 2009). Tran (2019e) finds that independent directors help firms decrease overinvestment in capital goods and improve investment efficiency. Baysinger *et al.* (1991) and Osma (2008) also document a negative effect of board independence on R&D investment. Lu and Wang (2015) argue that board independence is more effective in controlling managers' overinvestment in physical assets, not R&D. Overinvestment in physical capital goods directly serves managers' private interests while investment in R&D is risky. Therefore, managers are more conservative in R&D investment. Board independence may help firms reduce managerial conservatism to reduce their underinvestment in R&D. As expected, Lu and Wang (2015) find that board independence is negatively related to capital expenditure but positively associated with R&D investment.

Third, board diversity has two opposite impacts on corporate investment. On the one hand, a diverse board helps firms improve their corporate performance. When board members have various backgrounds, knowledge, expertise and skills, they are able to monitor corporate managers from different perspectives (Ali *et al.*, 2022; Williams & O'Reilly, 1998). To have more insights into the role of board diversity, scholars divide diversity characteristics into categories such as surface-level (gender, race, age) and deep-level (education, tenure, experience and expertise) (Harrison *et al.*, 1998; Milliken and Martins, 1996), information-based (education and tenure) and person-related (age and gender) (Midavaine *et al.*, 2016), relation-oriented (gender and age) and task-oriented (education and tenure) (Ullah *et al.*, 2020). Ali *et al.* (2022) find that the surface-level diversity reduces the efficiency of investment decisions while the deep-level diversity increases corporate investment efficiency. Ullah *et al.* (2020) document that tenure diversity reduces investment expenditure in R&D while education diversity and gender diversity result in higher R&D investment. On the other hand, board diversity may lead to many conflicts and disagreements. To solve these problems, firms need more time and costs to collect and process information (Marcel *et al.*, 2011; Ullah *et al.*, 2020). Therefore, they may miss profitable investment opportunities.

### 4.2.2.3. *Managerial characteristics*

Managers are decision-makers in a firm; therefore, their characteristics also determine corporate financial decisions. The literature shows that the characteristics of CEOs (e.g., gender, overconfidence, education and experience) are important determinants of corporate investment.

According to the social feminist theory, males and females have different roles in society and thus their socialization activities shape their different traits (Eagly, 1987). These various traits govern their behaviors, which lead to different outcomes (Fischer *et al.*, 1993). Many prior studies show that females are more honest and ethical than males (Beltramini *et al.*, 1984; Chonko & Hunt, 1985; Glover *et al.*, 1997; Jones & Gautschi, 1988; Ones & Viswesvaran, 1998; Reiss & Mitra, 1998; Ruegger & King, 1992); therefore, female managers are less willing to engage in risk-taking behaviors and take opportunistic actions (Faccio *et al.*, 2016; Khan & Vieito, 2013; Palvia *et al.*, 2015; Zeng & Wang, 2015). Jun Chen *et al.* (2018), Jie Chen *et al.* (2018), Frye and Pham (2018) and Nielsen and Huse (2010) document that female CEOs tend to support strong corporate governance — a guarantee for investment performance. Ullah *et al.* (2021) and Ullah *et al.* (2020) find that female CEOs improve corporate investment efficiency through decreasing overinvestment rather than underinvestment. Consistently, Liu *et al.* (2022) report that female CFOs have a negative impact on overinvestment. Gul *et al.* (2011) also show that female CEOs make better investment decisions, which increase shareholders' wealth, improve public disclosure and enhance stock price informativeness. Furthermore, Faccio *et al.* (2016) find that female CEOs prefer low-risk financing and investment decisions.

In addition, while traditional theories explain CEOs' behaviors mainly based on agency relation and information asymmetry, Malmendier and Tate (2005) posit that CEOs' beliefs are also an important determinant of corporate investment decisions. They argue that when CEOs are overconfident, they tend to estimate higher levels of returns for their investment. If they face no constraints, they tend to overinvest. If they fail to have enough internal funds, they tend to issue stocks since they think that their firms are undervalued. However, they cannot achieve this goal to finance their investment. The overconfidence theory is based on a psychological effect — "better-than-average". An individual tends to perceive that their ability, knowledge and skills are better than the average level (Larwood & Whittaker, 1977). According to Langer (1975) and March and Shapira (1987), CEOs select a project when they believe that they can manage its performance and underestimate the probability of loss. Schrand and Zechman (2012) also find that overconfident CEOs pay less attention to risk. Heaton (2002), Wei Huang *et al.* (2011) and Malmendier and Tate (2005) document that executive overconfidence distorts investment performance.

Moreover, when CEOs have educational backgrounds in business, finance, law and other social sciences, they are more likely to choose investment projects with clear and quantifiable benefits (Gupta, 2022; Zacharias *et al.*, 2015). Barker and Mueller (2002) find that CEOs are less willing to take risks when they have an MBA degree. Gupta *et al.* (2020) show that CEOs with financial education reduce the investment–cash flow sensitivity. Besides, Ullah *et al.* (2022) argue that CEOs with military experience have low incentives to be self-interested or conduct opportunistic behaviors. They find that firms have more efficient investments when their CEOs have military experience. Benmelech and Frydman (2015) posit that CEOs with military experience are more conservative and ethical. They document that the military experience of CEOs results in lower corporate investment. In addition, Jia *et al.* (2021) show that firms have more investment in environmental protection projects when their CEOs' names have moral meanings.

### 4.2.3. *Business environment*

#### 4.2.3.1. *Environmental uncertainty*

According to Bernanke (1983), Bloom (2009) and Dixit *et al.* (1994), a firm's future investment opportunities are considered as "real options". Therefore, waiting and staging flexibility are significantly important in corporate investment decisions. Firms invest in a project when it has a high probability of success. If firms face more uncertainty, they should wait and see how the problem is resolved. Following this irreversible investment framework, Bloom *et al.* (2007) document that higher uncertainty decreases the responsiveness of corporate investment to demand shocks. According to Gilchrist *et al.* (2014), uncertainty influences corporate investment mainly through changes in credit spreads, and they also find a negative association between uncertainty and investment. Gulen and Ion (2015) also find a strong negative effect of the aggregate level of uncertainty related to future policy and regulatory consequences on firms' capital investment. Analyzing how environmental uncertainty affects corporate investment in China, Li *et al.* (2021) show that environmental uncertainty decreases corporate investment directly and indirectly through financing constraints.

Julio and Yook (2012) investigate the effect of political uncertainty on corporate investment and find that political uncertainty makes firms reduce their investment until the electoral uncertainty is eliminated. Examining whether political turnover affects firm investment, An *et al.* (2016) document that political turnover makes firms significantly reduce corporate investment. Jens (2017) finds that the US firms reduce their investment expenditure by 5% before all gubernatorial elections. Especially, firms which are sensitive to political uncertainty have decreases of up to 15% in their investment. Amore and Minichilli (2018) also show that local political uncertainty reduces corporate investment. In addition, Cao *et al.* (2019) investigate how political uncertainty influences cross-border acquisitions. They report that foreign firms are less likely to have inbound acquisitions before a national election in the host country. Akbar *et al.* (2021) find that corporate investments in election years are lower than in years without elections.

Recently, academics have been paying much attention to the role of economic policy uncertainty in corporate investment decisions. Liu and Zhang (2019) and Wang *et al.* (2014) find that economic policy uncertainty leads to lower capital expenditure in China. Kang *et al.* (2014) show that economic policy uncertainty in interaction with firm-level uncertainty has a negative influence on corporate investment in the US. Drobetz *et al.* (2018) find a negative relationship between economic policy uncertainty and capital expenditure across 20 countries. Consistently, Tran (2019d) and Tran (2021a) document that economic policy uncertainty has positive and negative effects on corporate risk-taking and cost of debt financing, respectively. These findings imply that the negative impact of economic policy uncertainty on corporate investment may be transmitted through risk-taking behavior and external financing cost. Akron *et al.* (2020), Altaf (2022) and Chen *et al.* (2020) also find empirical evidence for this relationship. Moreover, Wang *et al.* (2017) show that both policy and market uncertainty deter corporate investment in R&D projects. Phan *et al.* (2019) find that crude oil price uncertainty leads to lower investment.

### 4.2.3.2. *National culture*

According to Hofstede *et al.* (1991), culture is a system of shared values, beliefs and behavioral patterns that govern people in a community. In a firm, most corporate decisions are made by managers; therefore, national culture is more likely to affect corporate financial decisions through managers' views rather than shareholders' views (Bae *et al.*, 2012). Scholars commonly use Hofstede's cultural dimensions to investigate how national culture determines corporate investments in prior studies. Shao *et al.* (2013) show that firms in individualistic cultures have higher investments in long-term assets and R&D projects since their managers are more willing to take risks. Managers in individualistic countries are overconfident and overoptimistic; therefore, they have high incentives to invest in risky projects (Breuer *et al.*, 2014; Hofstede, 2001; Markus & Kitayama, 1991).

Moreover, Zhang *et al.* (2016) find that individualism positively influences investment bias, which decreases investment efficiency, while uncertainty avoidance and masculinity have opposite effects. Managers in individualistic countries tend to have risky and self-interested behaviors; therefore, their firms have high levels of overinvestment. Managers in high uncertainty avoidance countries are less willing to take risks and this leads to lower overinvestment (Li *et al.*, 2013). Managers in high masculinity countries are performance-driven and thus they tend to limit overinvestment (Hofstede, 2001). Kashefi-Pour *et al.* (2020) also argue that national culture determines how managers perceive information asymmetry and agency problems. Their study shows that firms in countries with high uncertainty avoidance, power distance and masculinity have higher levels of investment-cash flow sensitivity than firms in countries with high collectivism. Consistently, Li *et al.* (2021) find that individualism, uncertainty avoidance and masculinity help firms improve their social responsibility and thus increase their investment efficiency. Choi (2020) shows individualism and indulgence positively affect R&D investment while masculinity reduces corporate investment in R&D. Yan *et al.* (2021) document that Confucian values restrict corporate R&D.

### 4.2.3.3. *Legislation*

From the pioneer study of La Porta *et al.* (1998), many empirical studies show that legal protection of shareholders and creditors plays an important role in corporate financial decisions. When shareholder rights are strong, corporate managers' expropriation of shareholders benefits is restricted. Consequently, firms in strong shareholder protection countries have lower overinvestment. McLean *et al.* (2012) show that legal protection of shareholders increases corporate investment efficiency. Xiao (2013) also finds that strong shareholder protection leads to decreases in both underinvestment and overinvestment in R&D. Moreover, legal protection of creditors is effective in controlling firms' risky investment projects. Acharya *et al.* (2011) document a negative relationship between creditor rights and corporate risk-taking. González (2018) finds that healthy firms in countries of strong creditor protection have higher investment efficiency due to lower overinvestment. However, Tran (2020b) argues that firms balance the interest of equity and debt claimants. Investigating the effects of both shareholder and creditor rights on corporate investment efficiency, he finds that creditor rights and shareholder rights are negatively and positively related to investment efficiency, respectively. Furthermore, the effect of creditor (shareholder) protection is more pronounced when shareholder (creditor) protection is stronger.

In addition, prior studies show that employment protection laws are an obstacle to corporate investment decisions. Strong employment legislation increases labor adjustment costs and thus firms are less likely to invest in risky projects to avoid big losses. Calcagnini *et al.* (2014) show that employment protection laws in European countries make firms reduce their investment expenditure. Marciukaityte (2019) finds that the state-level right-to-work laws decrease unionized firms' investment in the US. Similarly, John Bai *et al.* (2020) document that the adoption of laws to protect employees leads to lower levels of corporate investment in the US.

### 4.2.3.4. *Macro-economic issues*

The macro-economic environment is important to firms' investment decisions since it determines the expected return of their investment projects. A high growth economy provides firms with more investment opportunities that mainly drive corporate investment (Modigliani & Miller, 1958). Tran (2020b) finds that firms in countries with higher GDP growth rate have higher levels of capital expenditure. Besides, prior research shows that a financial crisis is a macro-economic shock toward corporate investment since it decreases the availability of investment opportunities, increases external financial constraints and raises environmental uncertainty (Flannery *et al.*, 2013; Roubini, 2007; Shin *et al.*, 2018; Tran *et al.*, 2017). A survey of 1,050 CFOs around the world conducted by Campello *et al.* (2010) shows that their firms intend to have sharp declines in investment during the global financial crisis. Bo *et al.* (2014) and Tran (2019a) also find that the 2008 financial crisis led to lower corporate investment.

# 4.3.　Political Corruption and Risk-Taking

## 4.3.1.　*Corporate managers' risk-taking behavior*

Corporate managers make investment decisions based on both, a project's expected returns and risks (Bluhm & Krahnen, 2014). Therefore, managers' behaviors of choosing and taking risks considerably determines their firms' survival, performance and development (Shapira, 1995). From a theoretical perspective, managers are more likely to take risks when they obtain benefits or they are confident in their decisions.

According to the agency theory, corporate managers tend to use corporate resources to overinvest in high-risk projects in order to build their empire (Hope & Thomas, 2008, Jensen, 1986). Consequently, firms have high levels of risky overinvestment when their managers are not monitored and controlled effectively. Moreover, corporate managers may have high incentives to engage in risk-taking since their compensation depends on firm performance. When a high-risk project is successful, it provides managers with many benefits. However, when it is unsuccessful, shareholders suffer losses instead of managers (Jiraporn *et al.*, 2015). Liu *et al.* (2020) document that firms engage in less risk-taking after compensation claw-back provisions are adopted. Jiraporn *et al.* (2015) and Simon and Houghton (2003) show that firms with strong corporate governance engage in less risk-taking. Acharya *et al.* (2011) also find that legal protection of creditors negatively affects corporate risk-taking since creditor rights are effective in monitoring managers.

However, corporate managers also have another pattern of risk-taking behavior to pursue their own benefits. Amihud and Lev (1981), Hirshleifer and Thakor (1992) and Holmstrom and Costa (1986) posit that managers receive benefits from their positions and thus they tend to avoid risk-taking. While shareholders are able to diversify their portfolios to avoid non-systematic risk, corporate managers' interests are tied to their firms. Facing this under-diversification, corporate managers have low incentives to take risks when making decisions (Fama, 1980). On the contrary, they ignore value-enhancing but risky investment opportunities (Jiraporn *et al.*, 2015). They may be less risk-averse when their tenure is shorter (Farag & Mallin, 2018). Weak corporate governance is an opportunity for managers to design their risk-averse decision-making policies and thus their firms engage in less risk-taking. John *et al.* (2008) and Koirala *et al.* (2020) find supporting evidence for this mechanism.

Besides, managers are willing to take risks due to their confidence. They are more confident when they perceive that their experience, knowledge, skills and relations may increase the probability of success of their decisions. Farag and Mallin (2018) find that CEOs with postgraduate education and board experience are more likely to adopt risk-taking behaviors. Ferris *et al.* (2019) document a positive impact of CEO social capital on corporate risk-taking. CEOs with more social capital are more likely to choose risky investment projects and take risky financial decisions. Moreover, many prior studies show that corporate managers' overconfidence leads to corporate risk-taking (Goldberg *et al.*, 2020; Li & Tang, 2010; Simon & Houghton, 2003). This overconfidence can be explained by the "better-than-average" psychological phenomenon (Larwood & Whittaker, 1977).

## 4.3.2. *The effect of political corruption on corporate risk-taking*

As a business environment factor, political corruption affects corporate managers' risk-taking behavior. There are two opposite mechanisms to explain the relationship between corruption and corporate risk-taking. On the one hand, political corruption increases corporate risk-taking. In a corrupt environment, both shareholders and managers perceive that their firms should pay bribes to speed up administrative procedures or avoid state predation. Since bribes are unofficial payments, corporate managers are more flexible to use corporate resources. This becomes an opportunity for managers to choose risky projects in order to serve their own interests at shareholders' costs (Tran, 2019b). In addition, according to Rose-Ackerman (1999), corrupt behaviors are not only created by public officials (the demand side) but also individuals and organizations that pay bribes (the supply side). When paying bribes to corrupt officials, corporate managers and corrupt officials establish and develop their relationship. This may increase managers' confidence in their financial decisions. Charumilind *et al.* (2006) and Khwaja and Mian (2005) show that firms with political connections have better access to bank credit and need less collateral. Consequently, political corruption positively influences corporate risk-taking.

On the other hand, political corruption reduces managers' incentives to take risks due to concern for their careers (Tran, 2022). Political corruption leads to high operating costs since firms have to pay corrupt officials "grease money" and/or "protection money" (Wei & Kaufmann, 1999). "Grease money" reduces red tape and provides more opportunities to obtain scarce resources while "protection money" mitigates state predation (Xu *et al.*, 2017). Moreover, political corruption increases costs of external financing. Chen *et al.* (2015) find that political corruption has a positive effect on bank risk-taking; therefore, firms in high-corruption environments face high interest rates for their loans. Baxamusa and Jalal (2014) also find that political corruption positively affects cost of debt across 72 countries. When firms have high operating costs and financing costs due to political corruption, unsuccessful projects create bigger losses that are threats to their managers' positions. When corporate managers prefer maintaining their positions, they tend to ignore risky projects (Amihud & Lev, 1981; Hirshleifer & Thakor, 1992; Jensen & Meckling, 1976). Therefore, firms in high-corruption environments engage in less risk-taking. Tran (2022) examines how political corruption influences corporate risk-taking across 20 emerging stock markets from 2006 to 2016. His findings show that firms in highly corrupt countries engage in less risk-taking.

## 4.4.   Political Corruption and Investment Expenditure

Political corruption may sand or grease the wheels of corporate investment. On the one hand, firms in corrupt environments face high levels of operational costs and risks; therefore, they have lower levels of investment (Shleifer & Vishny, 1993). In a corrupt environment, firms have to pay bribes in most stages of their value chains such as business registration, transportation, production and distribution (Hills *et al.*, 2009). Murphy *et al.* (1993) posit that government rent-seeking behavior for public goods, namely, permits, licenses, inspections and patents, is a big obstacle for firms. According to Errath (2006), political corruption increases the cost of doing business by over 10% in several countries. Moreover, firms may take legal risks including being charged large fines or being disqualified from future government procurement when they engage in corrupt business conduct. Besides, firms that fail to pay bribes to corrupt officials have limited access to resources and receive worse public services. Hence, they become less competitive than competitors who pay bribes (Hills *et al.*, 2009). In a pioneering empirical study, Mauro (1995) investigates how political corruption affects investment and growth across countries and finds that corruption hinders corporate investment, thereby reducing economic growth. Using data from the World Business Environment Survey, Asiedu and Freeman (2009) document that political corruption has a negative effect on corporate investment growth and corruption is the most important determinant of corporate investment in transition countries. However, this effect is not significant in two regions including Latin America and Sub-Saharan Africa. Riedel *et al.* (2010) find that corruption fails to have a significant impact on investment decisions of domestic firms but negatively influences multi-national firms' asset investment in Asian countries. Examining the effect of political corruption on fixed capital investment in Russia, Zakharov (2018) shows that political corruption also dampens domestic firms' capital investment and foreign firms' direct investment. Similarly, Javorcik and Wei (2009) find that political corruption reduces inward foreign direct investment and shifts the ownership structure toward joint ventures. Ellis *et al.* (2020) and Huang and Yuan (2021) show that the US firms are less innovative when they face high corruption.

On the other hand, political corruption may grease the wheels of corporate investment. According to Leff (1964), there are economic activities that firms cannot conduct without political impacts. Political corruption is considered an extralegal institution through which firms take advantage of political impacts to follow these economic activities. Lui (1985) proposes a theoretical model of bribery and shows that bribery payment is effective in speeding up a sluggish government. Besides, corrupt officials receive bribes, they can create barriers to prevent new firms from entering an industry and thus existing firms to have economies of scale. This protection may also be an opportunity for weak firms to survive, recover and develop (Heo *et al.*, 2021). Svensson (2003) and Wang and You (2012) find that bribery payment improves firm growth. Ayyagari *et al.* (2014)

show that firms with innovations pay more bribes than those without innovations. Sharma and Mitra (2015) show that bribery has a positive effect on product innovation. Shumetie and Watabaji (2019) also find that political corruption restricts corporate R&D activities. In addition, Heo *et al.* (2021) document that political corruption is positively related to corporate capital expenditure and innovation in emerging economies and advanced economies, respectively. Consistently, Du and Heo (2022) find that firms in countries with high corruption have higher levels of investment expenditure than firms in low corruption states.

## 4.5. Political Corruption and Investment Efficiency

According to Modigliani and Miller (1958), under a perfect market setting, corporate investment is only determined by investment opportunities, and firms achieve their optimal level of investment. However, the real world is imperfect and the existence of many market frictions leads to corporate investment deviating from its optimum. Tran (2019b) posits that corporate managers in corrupt countries have high flexibility in using corporate resources since they have to pay bribes to corrupt officials. Consistently, Thakur and Kannadhasan (2019) and Tran (2020a) document that political corruption increases corporate cash levels across countries. This implies that corporate managers have more opportunities to expropriate shareholders' interests through their overinvestment. Using data from 90 to 140 countries over the period 1995–2004, Swaleheen (2007) finds that political corruption negatively affects investment efficiency. O'Toole and Tarp (2014) argue that informal bribes distort capital allocation efficiency by lowering the marginal return of corporate investment. They document that bribery negatively affects corporate investment efficiency in developing countries and this negative relationship is strongest in domestic small and medium-sized firms. With a sample of 30,074 firms listed in 42 countries, Nguyen and Tran (2022) find that firms in high corruption countries have lower investment efficiency and this relationship is more pronounced when shareholders are strongly protected. On the other hand, political corruption makes firms face higher operation costs, debt financing costs and uncertainty (Baxamusa & Jalal, 2014; Shleifer & Vishny, 1993). If corporate managers are concerned about their careers, they tend to reduce their overinvestment in negative-NPV projects. This leads to higher investment efficiency.

# 4.6.  Anti-Corruption and Investment Decisions

The effect of anti-corruption policies on firms' financial decisions depends on their relationship with corrupt officials. Related firms include politically connected firms, state-owned enterprises (SOEs), firms in regulated industries, targeted firms and firms in targeted industries. Related firms are affected directly by anti-corruption measures since their connected officials or illegal affairs are investigated or excluded. Unrelated firms are influenced indirectly by anti-corruption through an improved business environment.

## 4.6.1.  *The effect of anti-corruption on investment decisions in related firms*

Related firms face direct impacts from anti-corruption efforts. Therefore, their investment decisions are strictly controlled and their investment performance is improved under the anti-corruption campaign. Greusard (2018) employs prosecution in accordance with the Foreign Corrupt Practices Act to examine how anti-corruption influences targeted firms' and their peers' investment expenditure. He finds that prosecution makes targeted firms and the peer group reduce corporate investment. Consistently, Zhang *et al.* (2019) document that anti-corruption measures restrict government-subsidized firms' overinvestment and this effect is more pronounced in state-owned enterprises.

Moreover, Pan and Tian (2020) investigate how the ousting of politicians affects their connected firms. Connected firms are those which pay bribes and have personal relationships with the ousted politicians. Their empirical study shows that compared with unconnected firms, connected firms reduce their investment considerably after the politicians are ousted. The ousting events are more effective for bribing firms and firms located in regions of high corruption. Besides, the ousting of politicians increases connected SOEs' investment efficiency. Consistently, Huang and Peng (2021) find that global financial disclosure laws reduce corporate overinvestment caused by government subsidies in regions with high corruption. Zheng and Xiao (2020) show that government investment in infrastructure is lower when anti-corruption measures such as monitoring, compensation and accountability are improved. Anderson *et al.* (2022) document that China's anti-corruption campaign has negative effects on capital investment and R&D investment of SOEs with financial expert CEOs.

## 4.6.2. *The effect of anti-corruption on investment decisions in unrelated firms*

Anti-corruption measures improve transparency and reduce uncertainty in business environments. Under the impact of anti-corruption campaigns, firms have lower operational costs and risks. Xu and Yano (2017) examine how anti-corruption efforts affect corporate decisions to invest and finance R&D projects in China during the period 2009–2015. They find that anti-corruption drives firms to use newly acquired funds for financing innovation projects and thus create more patents. The positive impact of anti-corruption on R&D investment is mainly from the massive anti-corruption campaign conducted since 2013. Especially, their findings show that the positive impact of anti-corruption is only effective for non-state-owned enterprises, young firms, politically unconnected firms and firms in non-regulated sectors.

Similarly, Gan and Xu (2019) document that anti-corruption intensity positively influences corporate R&D investment. They also show that this relationship is stronger in non-state-owned enterprises. In addition, Liu *et al.* (2021) investigate how anti-corruption influences cross-province M&As. They find that firms in provinces with high corruption have increased opportunities to engage in M&As after an anti-corruption campaign. Besides, Du *et al.* (2018) document that government integrity positively influences corporate investment efficiency by reducing underinvestment in non-SOEs. Kong *et al.* (2020) show that China's anti-corruption campaign has a positive effect on Chinese firms' total factor productivity. Especially, this effect is stronger in non-state-owned firms, politically unconnected firms and firms located in a poor legal environment. Moreover, the anti-corruption campaign also improves corporate investment efficiency and encourages firms' innovativeness.

# Chapter 5

# Political Corruption and Financing Decisions

*This chapter aims to analyze how political corruption affects financing decisions. First, it summarizes the main theories of capital structure such as trade-off theory, pecking order theory, agency theory and market timing theory. Then, it synthesizes prior studies to find key determinants of capital structure. Financial characteristics include corporate income taxes, firm profitability, growth opportunities, liquidity, firm size, asset tangibility, share price performance and business risk. Corporate governance factors are ownership structure, board structure and managerial characteristics. Country-level determinants consist of ownership structure, board structure and managerial characteristics. Finally, the chapter analyzes the effects of corruption on financial leverage and the choice of debt.*

## 5.1. Theories of Capital Structure

Corporate financing behavior is one of the most attractive topics in corporate finance. According to Modigliani and Miller (1958), firm value is not determined by financing decisions in a frictionless capital market (no taxes, no transaction costs and no bankruptcy costs). In other words, equity and debt are perfect substitutes for corporate investment, and firm value is not relevant to the source of finance. Their proposition establishes basic principles for modern corporate financing theories that analyze corporate financing decisions under imperfect market conditions. In the presence of market frictions, firms are not indifferent to internal and external funds since their value is affected by their financing decisions.

## 5.1.1.  *Trade-off theory*

Trade-off theory is developed by eliminating two assumptions including no taxes and no bankruptcy costs in Modigliani–Miller's irrelevance proposition. The theory states that when a firm finances its investment projects by external funds, it obtains benefits from the tax shield and incurs bankruptcy costs. Interest expenses are deductible and thus taxable income of a leveraged firm is lower than that of an unleveraged firm. This tax shield increases firm profitability and leads to higher firm value. Nevertheless, when the firm uses debt financing, it faces both direct and indirect costs of bankruptcy (DeAngelo & Masulis, 1980). The former includes legal fees, trustee fees and other expenses that it has to pay to parties other than equity claimants and debt claimants. The latter includes costs arising from disruption, financial constraint, loss of customers and suppliers. Even if the firm fails to go bankrupt, it still incurs financial distress costs. According to Altman (1984), indirect costs of bankruptcy are equivalent to 17.5% of firm value in the year before the year of bankruptcy. Therefore, the firm tends to seek an optimal capital structure to maximize its value through weighing the marginal costs and benefits of additional debt (Bradley *et al.*, 1984). When the firm has a moderate debt ratio, it has a low probability of bankruptcy and thus tax advantage dominates. However, when its debt ratio increases, the marginal costs of additional debt increase and exceed the marginal benefits. In other words, excessive debt destroys firm value (Kraus & Litzenberger, 1973).

## 5.1.2.  *Pecking order theory*

Myers and Majluf (1984) develop the pecking order theory based on information asymmetry, which does not exist in the Modigliani–Miller proposition. The theory states that information asymmetry between corporate managers and outside investors makes firms have different preferences for sources of funds. Since corporate managers have an information advantage about their firms (e.g., future prospects, risks and firm value) over outside investors, outside investors have high incentives to issue risk securities in order to raise external funds. However, outside investors perceive this issuance as a signal of firm overvaluation. Hence, they rationally give these securities higher discount rates and this results in negative market reactions. Facing outside investors' adverse selection, corporate managers prefer internal funds to external funds in their financing decisions. When internal funds are not available, they have to raise external funds by issuing debt or equity securities. Since debt financing is less influenced by outside investors' adverse selection than equity financing, corporate managers have high incentives to use debt financing instead of equity financing. Equity issuance is the last resort.

Myers (1984) modifies the original pecking order theory by taking the costs of financial distress into consideration. Accordingly, firms may issue equity securities to raise funds before they actually need them. This issuance helps firms have some financial slack and they are able to seize future investment opportunities. The pecking order theory does not support an optimal capital structure.

### 5.1.3.　*Agency theory*

Agency theory was initially developed by Berle and Means (1932) to show how the gap between ownership and control affects modern firms. Agency relationship is defined as an agreement under which a principal entrusts an agent to perform some services. Although agents are not owners of resources, they can manage and control resources. Therefore, agents tend to make decisions in order to benefit themselves instead of maximizing the principals' wealth. According to Jensen and Meckling (1976), there are two types of agency problems. The first is between managers and shareholders and the second is between shareholders and creditors.

In a firm, shareholders hire managers to run their firms on their behalf. This separation of ownership and control leads to agency problems. Corporate managers tend to use the firm's resources to serve their personal wealth instead of maximizing shareholders' interest (Jensen & Meckling, 1976). This expropriation behavior leads to agency costs of equity. The firm tends to choose an optimal level of capital structure that balances the benefits of tax shield, bankruptcy costs and agency costs of equity (Alipour *et al.*, 2015). According to Jensen (1986), when firms have much free cash flow, their managers have higher incentives to expropriate shareholders' interests (Jensen, 1986). Levered firms have to pay interest expenses periodically; therefore, they have less free cash flow at their managers' discretion. This implies that corporate managers prefer internal to external funds and firms can reduce agency costs by external financing.

Moreover, shareholders and creditors also have a conflict of interest. Corporate managers serving their shareholders are more likely to invest in risky projects that provide benefits to shareholders and losses to creditors. This moral hazard leads to agency costs of debt (Jensen & Meckling, 1976). When firms raise external funds, they are monitored and controlled strictly by creditors.

## 5.1.4.  *Market timing theory*

The market timing theory is based on corporate managers' cumulative efforts to time the equity market. Stock prices fluctuate continuously and their fluctuations affect corporate capital structure. According to Baker and Wurgler (2002), firms issue equity or debt securities to raise external funds when their market value is high and they repurchase their stocks when they receive low market value. Consequently, the optimal capital structure does not exist. Baker and Wurgler (2002) propose two versions of equity market timing behavior. First, this behavior is explained by a dynamic form of outside investors' adverse selection developed by Myers and Majluf (1984). When both managers and investors are rational, information asymmetry varies across firms and time periods. This makes investors' adverse selection fluctuate across firms and time. The fluctuation of adverse selection costs changes the market-to-book ratio and this creates market timing opportunities.

Second, the equity market timing behavior is explained by managers' perception of time-varying mispricing. When corporate managers believe that their stock prices are irrationally high, they tend to issue new stocks. However, when they recognize that their stock prices are irrationally low, they tend to repurchase their equity securities. In other words, market timing opportunities are present when corporate managers believe that their firms are mispriced.

Alti (2006) argues that the market-to-book ratio fails to reflect timing attempts comprehensively. They isolate timing attempts in the initial public offering in order to investigate how market timing behavior affects corporate capital structure. They find a negative relationship between market timing and debt ratio in the short term, but this relationship disappears within two years after an IPO. Kayhan and Titman (2007) and Leary and Roberts (2005) also find supporting evidence for the short-term effect of the market timing mechanism.

# 5.2. Determinants of Capital Structure

## 5.2.1. *Financial characteristics*

### 5.2.1.1. *Corporate income taxes*

When a firm uses debt to finance its business activities, interest expenses are considered as deductible costs. Therefore, interest payment is not included in the firm's taxable income. According to the trade-off theory, when corporate income tax rates are higher, firm profitability increases. Consequently, high corporate income tax rates drive firms to use more debt financing. Surveying 392 Chief Financial Officers in the US, Graham and Harvey (2001) find that tax advantages of debt are moderately important in capital structure decisions in the full sample. These advantages are more important for large, regulated and dividend-paying firms. Cheng and Shiu (2007), Gungoraydinoglu and Öztekin (2011), Haugen and Senbet (1986) and Zimmerman (1983) document a positive relationship between income tax rate and debt ratio. Besides, Saif-Alyousfi *et al.* (2020)

investigate how tax shields affect corporate capital structure. They measure the tax shield by total tax expenses divided by earnings before interest and taxes. Consistently, their findings show that tax shields are negatively associated with financial leverage. Köksal and Orman (2015) also find a positive effect of potential debt tax shields on debt ratio. However, Antoniou *et al.* (2008) document that the effective tax rate is negatively related to corporate financial leverage. They explain that this opposite relationship is driven by the country's rules and regulations. Alipour *et al.* (2015) and Moradi and Paulet (2019) also find a negative effect of corporate tax on debt ratio.

Moreover, DeAngelo and Masulis (1980) posit that when non-debt tax shields (e.g., depreciation deductions, depletion allowances and investment tax credits) are present, firms have lower incentives to take advantage of debt tax shields. MacKie-Mason (1990) also emphasizes that different types of tax shields have different roles in corporate financing decisions. In line with the trade-off theory, Brailsford *et al.* (2002), De Miguel and Pindado (2001), Huang and Song (2006), Hussain *et al.* (2020), Leary and Roberts (2005), Matemilola *et al.* (2018), Ramli *et al.* (2019), Sheel (1994) and Wiwattanakantang (1999) find a negative relationship between non-debt tax shields and financial leverage. However, Bradley *et al.* (1984) and Titman and Wessels (1988) find an opposite result.

### 5.2.1.2.  *Firm profitability*

Capital structure theories predict two opposite effects of firm profitability on debt ratio. According to the trade-off theory, highly profitable firms face lower bankruptcy costs and thus they are more likely to use debt in order to take advantage of tax saving. In other words, firm profitability has a positive impact on financial leverage. Al-Ajmi *et al.* (2009), Hewa Wellalage and Locke (2015), Jordan *et al.* (1998), Liang *et al.* (2020), Margaritis and Psillaki (2007), Matemilola *et al.* (2018) and Reinhard and Li (2010) find empirical evidence for this impact. However, the pecking order theory implies that highly profitable firms have lower debt ratios. Firms with high profitability have more internal funds and thus they use retained earnings to finance their investment opportunities before raising external funds. Consequently, they have lower leverage levels. Many empirical studies show that firm profitability negatively influences corporate financial leverage (Abadi *et al.*, 2016; Abdulla, 2017; Abor & Biekpe, 2009; Ahmed Sheikh & Wang, 2012; Al-Fayoumi & Abuzayed, 2009; Al-Najjar & Taylor, 2008; Alipour *et al.*, 2015; Antoniou *et al.*, 2008; Bajaj *et al.*, 2020; Booth *et al.*, 2001; Brailsford *et al.*, 2002; Chen, 2004; Cho *et al.*, 2014; D'Acunto *et al.*, 2018; Drobetz & Wanzenried, 2006; Du & Dai, 2005; Ebeh Ezeoha, 2011; Eldomiaty, 2007; Fama & French, 2002; Feidakis & Rovolis, 2007; Feng *et al.*, 2020; Frank & Goyal, 2009; Gaud *et al.*, 2005; Graham, 2000; Granado-Peiró & López-Gracia, 2017; Haque *et al.*, 2011; Haron, 2016; Huang & Song, 2006; Kim *et al.*, 2006; Köksal & Orman, 2015; Lemmon & Zender, 2010; Li & Islam, 2019; Liang *et al.*, 2020; Morais *et al.*, 2022; Nidar & Sugianti, 2020; Nivorozhkin, 2005; Rajan & Zingales, 1995; Saif-Alyousfi *et al.*, 2020; Sogorb-Mira, 2005; Strebulaev, 2007; Yakubu *et al.*, 2021; Yu & Aquino, 2009).

### 5.2.1.3. *Growth opportunities*

According to the pecking order theory, growth opportunities lead to an increase in the demand on internal funds and pressure firms to use external financing (Hall *et al.*, 2004). This implies a positive relationship between firm growth and financial leverage. In addition, the agency theory states that debt financing is a vehicle to reduce agency costs (Jensen, 1986). High growth firms face more severe agency problems since their managers are more flexible in corporate financial decisions. Therefore, growing firms have high incentives to use external funds. Abor and Biekpe (2009), Al-Fayoumi and Abuzayed (2009), Al-Najjar and Taylor (2008), Alipour *et al.* (2015), Chen (2004), Cho *et al.* (2014), Du and Dai (2005), Fama and French (2002), Ghose and Kabra (2019), Guizani and Abdalkrim (2022), Hall *et al.* (2004), Khémiri and Noubbigh (2018), Li and Islam (2019), Moradi and Paulet (2019), Myers (1977), Smith (2010), Rajan and Zingales (1995), Ramli *et al.* (2019), Yartey (2009) and Yu and Aquino (2009) find supporting evidence for this effect.

However, the trade-off theory suggests a negative effect of growth opportunities on debt ratio. High growth firms face higher costs of financial distress and thus they are less likely to raise external funds (Kraus & Litzenberger, 1973). Abadi *et al.* (2016), Antoniou *et al.* (2008), Balios *et al.* (2016), Brailsford *et al.* (2002), Chen (2004), Dewaelheyns *et al.* (2019), Eriotis *et al.* (2007), Feidakis and Rovolis (2007), Frank and Goyal (2009), Gaud *et al.* (2005), Granado-Peiró and López-Gracia (2017), Hovakimian *et al.* (2004), Huang and Song (2006), Kumar *et al.* (2017), Ramjee and Gwatidzo (2012), Saif-Alyousfi *et al.* (2020), Spitsin *et al.* (2021), Wiwattanakantang (1999) and Wu and Yue (2009) find that firm growth negatively influences debt ratio.

### 5.2.1.4.  *Liquidity*

Liquidity reflects a firm's ability to pay off its debt obligations. The effect of liquidity on capital structure decisions can be explained by two theories. On the one hand, the trade-off theory suggests a positive association between liquidity and financial leverage. Firms with high liquidity ratios incur lower bankruptcy costs and thus they increase their borrowings. Abdulla (2017) finds that liquidity positively affects debt ratio. On the other hand, the pecking order theory implies a negative impact of liquidity on financial leverage. When a firm's liquidity is higher, it has enough resources to finance its investment projects. Therefore, it is less likely to rely on external funds and have low incentives to use external financing. Ahmed Sheikh and Wang (2012), Al-Najjar and Taylor (2008), Alipour *et al.* (2015), Bevan and Danbolt (2002), Deesomsak *et al.* (2004), Eldomiaty and Azim (2008), Eriotis *et al.* (2007), Haron (2016), Khémiri and Noubbigh (2018), Le and Tannous (2016), Ozkan (2001), Rajan and Zingales (1995), Ramli *et al.* (2019) and Saif-Alyousfi *et al.* (2020) find that liquidity negatively affects debt ratio.

### 5.2.1.5.  *Firm size*

Large firms face lower bankruptcy costs since they are more diversified and have less earnings volatility (Titman & Wessels, 1988).

According to the trade-off theory, they should have high levels of financial leverage. In addition, large firms also have better reputation, information disclosure and corporate governance (Black *et al.*, 2006; Fama & Jensen, 1983). According to the pecking order theory and the agency theory, these characteristics help them face lower costs of external financing. Consequently, they are more likely to use external funds. Many empirical studies show a positive impact of firm size on financial leverage (Abadi *et al.*, 2016; Abdulla, 2017; Abor & Biekpe, 2009; Ahmed Sheikh & Wang, 2012; Al-Fayoumi & Abuzayed, 2009; Al-Najjar & Taylor, 2008; Antoniou *et al.*, 2008; Cho *et al.*, 2014; Du & Dai, 2005; Eriotis *et al.*, 2007; Feidakis & Rovolis, 2007; Feng *et al.*, 2020; Frank & Goyal, 2009; Gaud *et al.*, 2005; Granado-Peiró & López-Gracia, 2017; Haque *et al.*, 2011; Hewa Wellalage & Locke, 2015; Huang & Song, 2006; Köksal & Orman, 2015; Le & Tannous, 2016; Li & Islam, 2019; Low & Chen, 2004; Matemilola *et al.*, 2018; Wiwattanakantang, 1999; Yu & Aquino, 2009). On the other hand, the pecking order theory also implies a negative relationship between firm size and debt ratio. Large firms have enough internal funds to finance their investment opportunities (Marsh, 1995). Therefore, they are less likely to use debt financing. Alipour *et al.* (2015), Deloof *et al.* (2010) and Haron (2016) document supporting evidence for this negative relationship.

### 5.2.1.6. *Asset tangibility*

Capital structure theories support a positive effect of asset tangibility on financial leverage. On the one hand, a firm with more tangible assets has more collateral assets to pay off its debt when it goes bankrupt. In line with the trade-off theory, this firm incurs lower bankruptcy costs and thus it tends to raise external funds in order to exploit tax deductibility. Besides, tangible assets also reduce agency costs of debt and thus the firm can face lower costs of debt. Ahmed Sheikh and Wang (2012), Al-Najjar and Taylor (2008), Alipour *et al.* (2015), Booth *et al.* (2001), Cho *et al.* (2014), De Jong *et al.* (2008), Du and Dai (2005), Ebeh Ezeoha (2011), Frank and Goyal (2009), Gaud *et al.* (2005), Hewa Wellalage and Locke (2015),

Huang and Song (2006), Khémiri and Noubbigh (2018), Köksal and Orman (2015), Li and Islam (2019), Matemilola *et al.* (2018), Moradi and Paulet (2019), Ramli *et al.* (2019) and Saif-Alyousfi *et al.* (2020) find that asset tangibility is positively associated with debt ratio.

### 5.2.1.7.  *Share price performance*

The relationship between share price performance and capital structure decisions is explained by the marketing time theory. When the share price of a firm increases, corporate managers perceive that their firms are overvalued. As a result, they are more likely to finance investment opportunities by issuing equity securities instead of using debt. Consistently, Hovakimian *et al.* (2004) find that stock returns have a positive effect on equity issuance but have no significant impact on target leverage. Graham and Harvey (2001) show that firms are reluctant to raise funds by equity issuance when their managers perceive that they are undervalued. Alipour *et al.* (2015), Antoniou *et al.* (2008), Deesomsak *et al.* (2004), Feidakis and Rovolis (2007), Haron (2016) and Hussain *et al.* (2020) find supporting evidence for the negative effect of share price performance on financial leverage.

### 5.2.1.8.  *Business risk*

According to the trade-off theory, business risk negatively affects financial leverage since it increases the expected costs of bankruptcy (Wiwattanakantang, 1999). The pecking order theory also implies that business risk restricts firms' access to credit and increases costs of external financing since it exacerbates outside investors' adverse selection. Abor and Biekpe (2009), Ahmed Sheikh and Wang (2011), Al-Najjar and Taylor (2008), Brailsford *et al.* (2002), Eldomiaty (2007), Feidakis and Rovolis (2007), Haron (2016), Köksal and Orman (2015), Le and Tannous (2016), Low and Chen (2004) and Matemilola *et al.* (2018) find empirical evidence to support the negative effect of business risk on debt ratio. Nevertheless, Fama and French (2002), Hewa Wellalage and Locke (2015), Moradi and Paulet (2019) and Saif-Alyousfi *et al.* (2020) document that business risk is positively associated with financial leverage. This can be explained by the agency costs of debt. Risky firms tend to raise external funds to expropriate their creditors' interests.

### 5.2.1.9. *Firm age*

Older firms face less severe information asymmetry between shareholders and creditors since the market has enough time to understand their business activities and ability to fulfill their obligations. From the pecking order perspective, older firms have better reputations and thus they are more likely to use debt financing. Abor and Biekpe (2009), Hall *et al.* (2004), Khémiri and Noubbigh (2018) and Petersen and Rajan (1994) find a positive relationship between firm age and debt ratio. However, according to the life cycle theory, older firms have fewer investment opportunities and thus they have lower incentives to get into debt. Deloof *et al.* (2010) and Paulo Esperança *et al.* (2003) find a negative impact of firm age on financial leverage. Moreover, Huynh and Petrunia (2010), La Rocca *et al.* (2011), Pfaffermayr *et al.* (2013) and Saif-Alyousfi *et al.* (2020) document an inverse U-shaped relationship between firm age and debt ratio. This can be explained as at the beginning of firms' lives, older firms have more investment opportunities and thus they have higher levels of debt. Then, their age reaches a certain level and investment opportunities are less available and they are less likely to use debt.

## 5.2.2. *Corporate governance*

### 5.2.2.1. *Ownership structure*

When a firm's ownership is concentrated, controlling shareholders' wealth depends on this single investment and thus they are more likely to reduce risk (Farooq, 2015). According to the trade-off theory, debt financing leads to bankruptcy risk. Consequently, firms with high ownership concentration have lower levels of leverage. Besides, the agency theory also implies a negative relationship between ownership concentration and debt ratio. When a firm's ownership is dispersed, shareholders have small stakes and thus have low incentives to monitor managers. Ownership concentration improves corporate governance since controlling shareholders have more power to monitor and even dismiss managers with poor performance (Shleifer & Vishny, 1997). Therefore, firms are less likely to use debt financing as a means to monitor their management. Furthermore, ownership concentration may increase information asymmetry between firms and their creditors. Controlling shareholders tend to follow their own interests and sacrifice creditors' benefits. This increases agency costs of debt and thus firms reduce their financial leverage (Farooq, 2015). Farooq (2015), Santos *et al.* (2014) and Short *et al.* (2002) find supporting evidence for the negative effect of ownership concentration on financial leverage. On the other hand, the agency theory suggests a positive relationship. To maximize their wealth, controlling shareholders force managers to use more debt in order to increase firm profitability (Fosberg, 2004; Qi *et al.*, 2000). Debt financing is also a way to expropriate minority shareholders' interests (Mande *et al.*, 2012). Ahmed Sheikh and Wang (2012), Brailsford *et al.* (2002), Driffield *et al.* (2007), Feng *et al.* (2020), Ganguli (2013), Haque *et al.* (2011) and Margaritis and Psillaki (2010) document that firms with high ownership concentration have higher levels of debt. In addition, Sun *et al.* (2016) show that firms with high institutional ownership use more debt. Consistently, Bhojraj and Sengupta (2003) find a positive effect of concentrated institutional ownership on cost of debt capital.

Prior studies show that the relationship between managerial ownership and corporate capital structure is complicated. High managerial ownership mitigates the agency problem between shareholders and managers. Debt financing is a means to monitor corporate managers. Therefore, firms with high managerial ownership are less likely to finance their investment by debt (Wiwattanakantang, 1999). Ahmed Sheikh and Wang (2012), Al-Fayoumi and Abuzayed (2009), Bokpin and Arko (2009) and Huang and Song (2006) find a negative association between managerial ownership and debt ratio. However, high managerial ownership may also increase managers' incentives to use debt. When corporate managers hold more shares, their behavior focuses more on maximizing shareholders' wealth. Therefore, they tend to use more debt to finance investment opportunities whose success and failure mainly belong to shareholders and creditors, respectively. This mechanism is empirically supported by Bokpin and Arko (2009), Le and Tannous (2016), Leland and Pyle (1977) and Short *et al.* (2002). Moreover, Brailsford *et al.* (2002) argue that the relationship between managerial ownership and debt ratio may be nonlinear. When managerial ownership is low, managers have high incentives to expropriate shareholders' interests and thus firms have to use more debt to restrict this behavior. However, when managerial ownership is high enough, managers and shareholders' benefits are more aligned. This makes firms use less debt to reduce bankruptcy risk and the pressure of interest payment. Brailsford *et al.* (2002), Hewa Wellalage and Locke (2015), Granado-Peiró and López-Gracia (2017) and Sun *et al.* (2016) find an inverse U-shaped relationship between managerial ownership and capital structure.

In addition, state ownership is also an important determinant of corporate capital structure. On the one hand, firms with state ownership face weak corporate governance; therefore, they are more likely to use debt financing in order to monitor their managers effectively (Zou & Xiao, 2006). Feng *et al.* (2020), Huang and Song (2006) and Su (2010) find a negative impact of state ownership on debt ratio. On the other hand, firms with state ownership may receive support from the government to have better access to credit and lower financing costs (Khaw *et al.*, 2019; Kornai, 1979). Consequently, they have higher levels of leverage. DeWenter and Malatesta (2001), Le and Tannous (2016), Li *et al.* (2009) and Liu *et al.* (2011) document a positive relationship between state ownership and corporate capital structure.

Furthermore, foreign ownership also affects corporate financing decisions in different ways. Foreign investors help firms improve their corporate governance (Aggarwal *et al.*, 2011; Gillan & Starks, 2003). Consequently, they are less likely to use debt as a means to monitor their managers. Besides, firms with foreign ownership may have different sources of funds; therefore, they are less likely to rely on debt financing (Allen *et al.*, 2005). Many empirical studies show supporting evidence for the negative relationship between foreign ownership and debt ratio (Anwar & Sun, 2015; Do *et al.*, 2020; Gurunlu & Gursoy, 2010; Huang *et al.*, 2011; Le & Tannous, 2016; Li *et al.*, 2009). However, foreign investors may also affect corporate financing decisions through an opposite mechanism. Since foreign investors focus on firm profitability, they tend to pressure firms to use more debt in order to take advantage of debt tax shields. Moreover, foreign investors may prefer debt to equity since they have less information than local investors (Choe *et al.*, 2005; Dvořák, 2005). Debt financing is a compensation for their weakness in monitoring corporate managers due to their information disadvantage. Brennan and Cao (1997), Phung and Le (2013) and Zou and Xiao (2006) find a positive effect of foreign investors on financial leverage. Remarkably, Zeitun and Goaied (2021) argue that foreign investors' power to control and monitor corporate managers depends on their shareholdings. When foreign ownership is low, their power is weak. Nevertheless, when foreign ownership reaches a threshold, foreign investors' voice is effective in controlling and monitoring managers. Zeitun and Goaied (2021) find supporting evidence for their hypothesis in Japan.

Besides, prior research also shows the role of family ownership in firms' capital choices. Wiwattanakantang (1999) finds that firms with single family ownership have higher debt ratios. These firms mainly focus on profitability and thus increase their leverage to save taxes. Mishra and McConaughy (1999) document that funding family-controlled firms have lower levels of debt than non-funding family controlled ones. Thomsen and Pedersen (2000) find that large shareholders including family, banks and institutional investors are risk-averse; consequently, their firms use less debt and more equity.

### 5.2.2.2. *Board structure*

The extant literature shows two opposite effects of board size on corporate capital structure. On the one hand, large boards improve communication and decision-making processes between board members and thus strengthen corporate governance. Strong corporate governance reduces bankruptcy risk; therefore, firms face lower costs of debt financing (Bokpin & Arko, 2009). Besides, large boards are more effective in monitoring managers' behavior and they tend to pressure managers to use more debt in order to increase their firms' profitability. Abor (2007), Ahmed Sheikh and Wang (2012), Bokpin and Arko (2009) and Feng *et al.* (2020) find a positive effect of board size on financial leverage. On the other hand, large boards may have more conflicts between board members; hence, they could be ineffective in controlling the management. When managers' discretion is higher, they are less likely to use debt (Berger *et al.*, 1997; Granado-Peiró & López-Gracia, 2017; and Vakilifard *et al.*, 2011).

In addition, outside directors help firms improve corporate governance and gain more trust from outside investors and creditors (Pfeffer & Salancik, 2003). Therefore, board independence positively affects debt ratio. Ahmed Sheikh and Wang (2012), Feng *et al.* (2020), Granado-Peiró and López-Gracia (2017) and Tarus and Ayabei (2016) find supporting evidence for this relationship. However, Wen *et al.* (2002) show that firms with more independent boards have lower levels of debt. They explain that corporate managers tend to consume internal funds and use less debt since outside directors pressure them to reduce free cash flow.

### 5.2.2.3. *Managerial characteristics*

Managerial overconfidence significantly determines corporate financial decisions. When managers are overconfident, they are more willing to take risks. Therefore, overconfident managers tend to increase their firms' leverage. Hackbarth (2008) and Mundi and Kaur (2022) document a positive impact of CEO overconfidence on debt ratio. Consistently, Ben-David *et al.* (2007) find that firms with overconfident CFOs have higher levels of leverage.

Moreover, managerial tenure is also important in managers' capital structure choices. When a corporate manager's tenure is longer, they have more opportunities and power to control the internal monitoring mechanism. Therefore, firms with longer managerial tenures have weaker corporate governance. Berger *et al.* (1997), Tarus and Ayabei (2016) and Wen *et al.* (2002) show empirical evidence for the negative relationship between CEO tenure and financial leverage. Besides, Matemilola *et al.* (2018) document that managerial experience positively affects debt ratio. The explanation for this is that managers with more experience are more confident and willing to take risks; therefore, they tend to use more debt financing in order to increase their firms' profitability.

## 5.2.3.   *Business environment*

Corporate financing decisions are not only determined by firm-specific factors but also business environment factors such as uncertainty, culture, legislation and macro-economic issues (De Jong *et al.*, 2008).

### 5.2.3.1.   *Environmental uncertainty*

Uncertainty in the business environment may affect corporate capital structure through supply side and demand side. Uncertainty increases information asymmetry between firms and their creditors and thus they face higher costs of external financing (Ben-Nasr *et al.*, 2020; Francis *et al.*, 2014; Tran, 2021a; Waisman *et al.*, 2015). Besides, uncertainty also increases firms' cash flow volatility (Zhang *et al.*, 2015). Consequently, they are less likely to use debt. From the demand perspective, uncertainty makes firms more conservative in their investment decisions (Bernanke, 1983; Bloom, 2009; Dixit *et al.*, 1994). This reduces their investment expenditure (Akron *et al.*, 2020; Altaf, 2022; Amore & Minichilli, 2018; An *et al.*, 2016; Cao *et al.*, 2019; Chen *et al.*, 2020; Gulen & Ion, 2015; Jens, 2017; Julio & Yook, 2012; Li *et al.*, 2021; Phan *et al.*, 2019). Lower investment reduces the demand for debt. Li and Qiu (2021) and Zhang *et al.* (2015) find that economic policy uncertainty negatively affects financial leverage. Chow *et al.* (2018) also document that when firms face high macro-economic uncertainty, they are less likely to use debt financing. Consistently, Lv and Bai (2019) show that political uncertainty decreases corporate debt financing. Ben-Nasr *et al.* (2020) find that political uncertainty drives firms to use more bank loans over total liabilities since they are cheaper than public debts. Khoo and Cheung (2021) document a negative impact of geopolitical uncertainty on debt ratio.

### 5.2.3.2. *National culture*

As an informal institution, culture governs people's behaviors through shared values and beliefs in society (Williamson, 2000). Therefore, corporate capital decisions reflect cultural values. Sekely and Collins (1988) find that capital structure is different across various groups of countries. Particularly, firms headquartered in the Southeast Asian, the Latin American and the Anglo-American countries have low levels of leverage while those in the Scandinavian, the Mediterranean and the Indian Peninsula countries have high debt ratios. Gleason *et al.* (2000) also show that corporate capital structure varies across four groups of countries classified by their cultural values.

Arosa *et al.* (2014) examine how Hofstede's cultural dimensions, including uncertainty avoidance and power distance, influence corporate capital structure across countries. They find that firms in countries with high uncertainty avoidance and power distance are risk-averse; therefore, they are less likely to use debt financing in order to avoid bankruptcy risk. Besides, uncertainty avoidance and power distance reduce the effect of market timing behavior. Mac an Bhaird and Lucey (2014) also document negative effects of uncertainty avoidance and power distance on debt ratio in SMEs. Moreover, managers in individualistic cultures tend to be overconfident and willing to take risks (Anderson & Galinsky, 2006; Breuer *et al.*, 2014; Hofstede, 2001; Markus & Kitayama, 1991; Zinn, 2009). Therefore, Fauver and McDonald (2015) show that individualism positively affects corporate debt financing.

Chui *et al.* (2002) investigate how two key cultural dimensions of Schwartz (1994) (conservatism and mastery) affect corporate capital structure across 22 countries. They argue that conservatism mainly focuses on three groups of values, including (1) harmonious working relationships, (2) public image and (3) security, conformity and tradition. These values make firms reduce the conflicts of interest between shareholders and managers, perceive higher costs of bankruptcy and prefer financial stability. Consequently, firms in conservative societies tend to use less debt financing. Besides, mastery emphasizes internal control and individual success. Therefore, firms in countries with mastery are less willing to use debt to avoid creditors' control and reduce the risk of bankruptcy. Consistently, Chui *et al.* (2002) find that both conservatism and mastery negatively influence financial leverage. Li *et al.* (2011) also document a negative relationship between mastery and foreign joint ventures' debt ratio in China.

### 5.2.3.3. *Legislation*

Legal regulations on shareholder protection, creditor protection and employment protection are important determinants of corporate capital structure. When shareholders are strongly protected by laws, corporate managers have fewer opportunities to expropriate shareholders' benefits and face high pressure to disgorge cash. Consequently, their firms have lower levels of internal funds and they have to use more debt (Cheng & Shiu, 2007). Investigating the relationship between legal protection of shareholders and financial leverage across countries, Alves and Ferreira (2011) and Cheng and Shiu (2007) find that firms in countries with shareholder rights have higher debt ratios. Consistently, Nguyen *et al.* (2020) show that the US firms tend to have higher financial leverage when shareholder litigation rights are stronger.

Furthermore, creditors are more willing to lend their money when legal protection of creditors is strong. Therefore, firms in countries with strong creditor rights have higher levels of debt. This mechanism is empirically supported by Alves and Ferreira (2011) and Cheng and Shiu (2007). However, Cho *et al.* (2014) and De Jong *et al.* (2008) find an opposite relationship between creditor protection and debt ratio. The explanation for this is that strong creditor rights make debt financing riskier than equity financing. In countries with strong creditor protection, firms face higher probability to be forced to go bankrupt when they have financial distress. Consequently, they have lower incentives to use debt (De Jong *et al.*, 2008).

According to Serfling (2016), employment protection laws may have two opposite effects on capital structure choices. On the one hand, strong employment protection results in high debt ratios. When employees face high risk of dismissal, they tend to require a wage premium as compensation. Using debt financing increases the probability of bankruptcy and thus raises employees' risk of unemployment (Agrawal & Matsa, 2013). Strong employment protection provides employees with more benefits when they are dismissed and thus they are less likely to demand a premium wage. Therefore, firms tend to use more debt when they face strong employment protection. On the other hand, strong employment protection increases firing costs and thus distressed firms face high costs of distress when they dismiss their employees. Besides, strong employment protection improves employees' job safety and their firms face more fixed labor costs. These make firms less likely to use debt. Serfling (2016) finds a negative effect of labor protection laws on financial leverage while Simintzi *et al.* (2015) show a positive effect. Dewaelheyns *et al.* (2019) document that firms have higher debt ratios and have higher incentives to adjust their leverage levels under weak employment protection.

### 5.2.3.4. *Macro-economic issues*

Capital structure theories predict opposite effects of economic growth on debt ratio. High economic growth leads to more investment opportunities. According to the trade-off theory, economic growth increases bankruptcy costs. Firms are valued lower when their investment opportunities exceed the capacity of their tangible assets. Therefore, they are less likely to use debt financing. However, the pecking order theory supports the positive effect of economic growth on financial leverage. When firms have more investment opportunities, their internal funds are not enough and thus they have to raise external funds. Cho *et al.* (2014) and Köksal and Orman (2015) find supporting evidence for the trade-off mechanism while Abadi *et al.* (2016), De Jong *et al.* (2008) and Ramli *et al.* (2019) find supporting evidence for the pecking order mechanism.

Similarly, inflation may also affect financial leverage through two opposite channels. On the one hand, high inflation encourages firms to increase their assets and finance these investments by debt since they obtain benefits from the inflated assets and the fixed debt (Cheng & Shiu, 2007). On the other hand, inflation increases costs of debt financing and firms have lower incentives to use debt. Cho *et al.* (2014), Deesomsak *et al.* (2004), Frank and Goyal (2009) and Köksal and Orman (2015) find a positive relationship between inflation and financial leverage while Cheng and Shiu (2007) document a negative relationship. Moreover, Ramli *et al.* (2019) show that interest rate is negatively related to debt ratio.

In addition, financial market development is also an important determinant of corporate capital structure decisions (Demirgüç-Kunt & Maksimovic, 1996). When the stock market is developed, firms prefer equity to debt. However, when credit and markets are developed, firms are more likely to use debt financing. Cheng and Shiu (2007), De Jong *et al.* (2008), Demirgüç-Kunt and Maksimovic (1999) and Köksal and Orman (2015) find supporting evidence for these mechanisms.

# 5.3. Political Corruption and Capital Structure

Political corruption plays an important role in constructing legal regulations, resource distribution and corporate behaviors (Fan *et al.*, 2012). The extant literature shows that political corruption may have a negative or positive effect on financial leverage through various underlying mechanisms.

## 5.3.1. *The negative effect of political corruption on financial leverage*

### 5.3.1.1. *Bankruptcy risk mechanism*

When political corruption is widespread, firms face higher costs of doing business (Baxamusa & Jalal, 2014). According to Mauro (1995), Shleifer and Vishny (1993), political corruption makes firms face high operating costs, generates uncertainty and destroys their market value. Corrupt officials' rent-seeking is an obstacle for firms' operations when they use public services. Therefore, firms pay "grease money" to government officials in order to reduce red tape, speed up administrative procedures and obtain resources (Wei & Kaufmann, 1999). Besides, they may also pay "protection money" to avoid state predation (Xu *et al.* 2017). Operational disruptions and high operational costs lead to high volatility of cash flow and bankruptcy risk. Although debt financing helps firms save taxes, they are less willing to use debt, which leads to additional bankruptcy risk.

### 5.3.1.2.  *Costs of debt mechanism*

Political corruption increases costs of debt financing through greater information asymmetry and segmentation of equity markets. First, political corruption intensifies the information asymmetry between insiders and outside investors. Chen *et al.* (2010) show that stock analysts are less able to predict firms' earnings in corrupt environments. Similarly, Liu (2016) finds that political corruption makes firms have more opportunistic behaviors such as earnings management, financial fraud and insider trading. Second, Bekaert *et al.* (2011) document that corruption leads to higher segmentation of equity markets. Jain *et al.* (2017) show that corruption reduces foreign portfolio investment. Consistently, Chiou *et al.* (2010) find that political corruption positively and negatively affects risk and equity performance, respectively. Liu *et al.* (2015) show that corruption leads to inefficient allocation of financial resources.

Prior empirical studies show supporting evidence for the positive effect of political corruption on costs of debt financing. Ciocchini *et al.* (2003) investigate how corruption affects borrowing costs across countries. They find that both governments and firms in countries with high corruption incur higher risk premium when they issue bonds. Baxamusa and Jalal (2014) also document that political corruption increases both costs of debt and equity across 72 countries. Moreover, Du *et al.* (2020) examine the relationship between local corruption and corporate financing costs in the US. Their findings show that firms in highly corrupt states face higher credit spreads and tighter debt covenants.

### 5.3.1.3.  *Demand mechanism*

According to Amihud and Lev (1981) and Jensen and Meckling (1976), corporate managers are risk-averse since they want to maintain their positions. Political corruption increases both operational costs and financing costs. In corrupt environments, unsuccessful investment projects lead to higher losses. Therefore, corporate managers are less willing to take risk and more conservative in their investment decisions. Tran (2022) finds that political corruption negatively affects corporate risk-taking. Consistently, Asiedu and Freeman (2009), Mauro (1995) and Zakharov (2018) show that firms have lower levels of investment expenditure in countries with high corruption. Ellis *et al.* (2020) and Huang and Yuan (2021) also find that corruption deteriorates innovation. When corporate investment is low, the demand for debt decreases. In other words, political corruption reduces corporate debt financing.

### 5.3.1.4.  *Liquidity mechanism*

According to Smith (2016), political corruption is an opportunity for firms to obtain benefits when they purchase preferences and favors from corrupt officials. Fisman (2001), Goldman *et al.* (2009) and Wu *et al.* (2018) show that political connectedness increases firm performance. Faccio *et al.* (2006) find that firms with political connection have higher probability to receive government bailouts. Besides, Claessens *et al.* (2008) investigate how firm's contributions to elected politicians affect their performance in Brazil. They document that contributing firms have higher stock returns during election outcomes. Their findings also show that contributions help firms have better access to bank finance. Consequently, firms tend to hold more cash to exchange for political favors. Thakur and Kannadhasan (2019) and Tran (2020a) find that firms in corrupt countries have high cash levels and save more cash from their cash flows. When firms have more internal cash and receive political preferences, they are less likely to use debt financing.

De Carvalho (2009) investigates the impact of political corruption on corporate external financing decisions across 13 federal states in Brazil. They find that firms in highly corrupt states face limited access to bank credit, formal sources and trade credit. This negative effect is more pronounced for the smallest firms. Weill (2011) examines how corruption affects bank lending in Russian firms and shows that corruption reduces bank loans. Furthermore, Jõeveer (2013) examines the effects of firm characteristics, institutional factors and macro-economic factors on corporate capital structure in nine Eastern European countries. Their findings show that firms in countries with high corruption have lower levels of leverage.

## 5.3.2.  *The positive effect of political corruption on financial leverage*

### 5.3.2.1.  *Shielding mechanism*

According to McChesney (1987), corrupt officials may take advantage of complicated tax rules and regulations to solicit bribes and extort firms. Facing the threat of expropriation by government officials, firms tend to use more opaque disclosure policies in order to shield their assets (Stulz, 2005). Smith (2016) defines this reaction as the shielding mechanism. Firms also apply this reaction mechanism when facing pressure from the unions. Klasa *et al.* (2009) find that firms reduce their cash levels to gain advantage when negotiating with unions. Consistently, Smith (2016) and Xu and Li (2018) find that political corruption has a negative impact on corporate cash holdings. Moreover, Matsa (2010) shows that firms restrict their cash flow by increasing debt so that they can use debt as a strategic advantage in the negotiation with unions. Therefore, firms in a corrupt environment tend to reduce their cash holdings and increase debt financing in order to minimize the surplus that can be expropriated by corrupt officials.

### 5.3.2.2.  *Managerial entrenchment mechanism*

In a corrupt environment, paying bribes is necessary to ensure firms' survival and development. Corporate managers are the best bribers since they have full information about how their firms operate and what their firms need. Their connections with corrupt officials provide their firms political favors and they can take advantage of these favors effectively (Du, 2008). However, bribery also creates opportunities for corporate managers to expropriate their shareholders' interests. Since bribes are unofficial payments, managers have more flexibility in corporate liquidity decisions. Moreover, shareholders in a corrupt environment may have lower expected returns on their investment when they are aware of political corruption. When corruption is widespread, corporate managers are more likely to divert their firms' resources into negative-net present value (NPV) projects in order to serve their own interests (Du, 2008; Tran, 2019b). When firms use debt financing, corporate managers are controlled not only by shareholders but also by creditors. Therefore, firms in corrupt environments tend to use more debt in order to reduce corporate managers' opportunistic behaviors. Consistently, Tran (2019b) shows that firms in high corruption countries pay more dividends to disgorge cash.

Demirgüç-Kunt and Maksimovic (1999) investigate the effects of institutions on firm debt maturity across 30 countries. They find that firms in countries with low integrity (high corruption) tend to use more debt financing. Fan *et al.* (2012) also document that firms in countries with higher corruption and weaker laws have higher debt ratios. Smith (2016) investigates how local political corruption determines corporate cash holdings and financial leverage in the US. With data of local corruption from the Department of Justice, he finds that firms in high corruption regions have lower cash holdings and higher financial leverage.

### 5.3.3.  *The effect of political corruption on the choice of debt*

Prior research shows that political corruption affects corporate decisions to choose debt maturity. Fan *et al.* (2008) posit that firms in a corrupt environment prefer short-term debt to long-term debt since the former reduces corporate managers' expropriation of shareholders more effectively than the latter. Short-term debt requires corporate managers to arrange their business activities effectively since it reaches maturity in a short time. Long-term debt provides managers enough time to conduct their opportunistic behaviors. Fan *et al.* (2012) find that firms in highly corrupt countries use short-term debt more than long-term debt when they increase their financial leverage. Besides, Lemma (2015) also finds that political corruption increases short-term leverage and decreases long-term leverage.

In addition, political corruption also creates an opportunity for firms to use bank debt. Government officials are more capable of controlling commercial banks than equity markets (Fan *et al.*, 2008). Levine (1999) finds that political corruption supports a bank-based financial system. Therefore, bribing firms may receive political favors to have better access to bank loans. Du (2008) and Wei and Kong (2017) document that political corruption makes firms rely more on bank loans when they raise external funds.

Moreover, Phan and Archer (2020) investigate how political corruption influences SMEs' decisions to choose sources of finance in Vietnam — a developing economy. They find that political corruption makes firms use more informal debt than formal debt and internal funds. This can be explained as follows. Firms tend to use formal debt to finance their long-term investment while informal debt is used to finance daily business activities. Political corruption increases the costs of formal debt but fails to affect costs of informal debt. Besides, SMEs are less able to pay bribes due to their financial constraints. Consequently, they are more likely to use informal debt when facing widespread corruption.

## 5.4.  Anti-Corruption and Financing Decisions

### 5.4.1.  *The effect of anti-corruption on financing decisions in related firms*

Under the impact of an anti-corruption campaign, related firms lose some advantages created by their relationship with corrupt officials. Common benefits that these firms receive from corrupt officials include better access to credit and lower costs of debt financing (Bliss & Gul, 2012; Bussolo *et al.*, 2022). Therefore, anti-corruption measures tend to reduce related firms' financial leverage.

Fan *et al.* (2008) collect information on 23 corruption cases involving high-profile government officials and the connected firms in order to examine how anti-corruption affects corporate financing choices in China. They find that after corrupt officials are arrested, the related firms have lower levels of debt and debt maturity than unrelated ones. In addition, Hu and Xu (2019) consider the anti-corruption campaign originating from the 18th National Congress of the Communist Party of China as an exogenous shock to compare the effects of anti-corruption on corporate financing decisions between politically connected and unconnected firms. Their findings show that connected firms' yearly new debt ratios are lower than that of firms without connections since the campaign makes the former lose their political connections.

## 5.4.2.  *The effect of anti-corruption on financing decisions in unrelated firms*

In a low corruption environment, firms face low operational costs and fewer operational disruptions (Baxamusa & Jalal, 2014). Consequently, they face low volatility of cash flow and bankruptcy risk. Besides, anti-corruption reduces information asymmetry (between firms and their creditors) and increases capital market efficiency (Chen *et al.*, 2010). Therefore, anti-corruption helps firms have lower costs of debt financing. Moreover, anti-corruption decreases uncertainty in business environments and thus firms are more likely to increase their investment. These mechanisms imply that anti-corruption increases corporate financial leverage.

Wu and Liu (2022) investigate the effect of the anti-corruption campaign on corporate capital structure over the period 2007–2019 in China. They find that firms tend to increase their leverage adjustment speed when senior officials are investigated. The positive relationship between anti-corruption and the adjustment speed is stronger in regions where investigated officials have ruled.

# Chapter 6

# Political Corruption and Dividend Decisions

*This chapter aims to analyze the effect of political corruption on dividend decisions. First, it presents the theoretical background of corporate dividend policy. Dividend theories include signaling theory, agency theory, bird-in-hand theory, transaction cost theory, residual theory, pecking order theory, life cycle theory, catering theory and tax clientele theory. Second, it summarizes determinants of dividend policy based on prior empirical evidence. Finally, it presents the relationship between political corruption and corporate dividend policy. As an important factor of institutional environment, political corruption may positively or negatively affect the propensity to pay dividends and the magnitude of dividends through many mechanisms.*

## 6.1.  Theories of Dividend Policy

According to Miller and Modigliani (1961), firm value is irrelevant to dividend policy in a perfect capital market. They propose a model in which market value is only determined by optimal investment. Net payouts (dividends and equity issues) or share repurchases are a residual after firms use their earnings to finance their investment projects. Dividends can take any value since share issues can offset them. However, in practice, capital markets are not perfect due to many frictions such as information asymmetry, agency problems, transaction costs, firm maturity, catering incentives and taxes. Therefore, dividend policy is a complicated decision-making process. These frictions are reflected in dividend policy theories.

### 6.1.1.  *Signaling theory*

The signaling theory was developed in the late 1970s. It is based on asymmetric information between corporate managers and outside investors. Managers can have more information about expected profitability, which investors cannot observe. Therefore, firms pay dividends to signal their value to outside investors. Heinkel (1978) initially proposed a model to describe the relationship between firm value and cash dividends. The model has two assumptions: (1) the number of firms with high expected profitability is limited and (2) the volatility of firm value is negatively related to the expected profitability. Firms with higher dividend levels are perceived to have better performance than those with lower dividend levels. Investors rely on corporate dividend policy to make investment decisions and value stocks.

In addition, Bhattacharya (1979) assumes there is no agency problem and develops a two-period model. At the beginning of the first period, corporate managers decide to invest in a business opportunity and they have full information on its expected profitability, which is unknown to outside investors. At this moment, managers promise to pay investors a certain amount of dividend. At the end of the first period, if the payoff created by the investment is less than the committed dividend amount, firms need to raise external funds for the second period and incur transaction costs. Therefore, in order to avoid transaction costs arising from external financing, managers tend to distribute high dividends in the first period to signal the quality of their project to outside investors. Bhattacharya (1979) posits that firms pay cash dividends regardless of the tax disadvantage. Moreover, Miller and Rock (1985) provide an additional explanation for this two-period model. They argue that dividend policy does not need to reflect managers' intention to convey information about future performance. At the end of the first period, the investment project generates earnings that are used to pay dividends and finance the second period of investment. Investors fail to have information on both earnings and future investment. At the end of the second period, the project generates earnings again. Therefore, dividend declarations only supply investors with the missing information about corporations' current profits. Then, these profits are used to forecast future earnings.

In addition, John and Williams (1985) argue that information revealed by corporate audits about expected performance is unreliable since it fails to illustrate future investment opportunities comprehensively. Given imperfect information, firms can communicate perfectly with outside investors only by paying cash dividends or issuing new shares. When private information about their future profits is favorable, a dilution of proportional ownership is not beneficial to current stockholders. As a result, insiders acting for existing shareholders' benefits may choose to distribute dividends instead of selling new shares. When outside investors are convinced by these signals, they offer higher prices for their stocks. Tax disadvantages for dividends are compensated by increases in stock prices while insiders maintain their fractional ownership. However, Ambarish *et al.* (1987) criticize that the previous models identify an efficient signaling equilibrium by maximizing shareholders' wealth among all possible respective equilibria. They propose a new model in which corporate managers can communicate with outsiders through two types of combinations: (1) dividend payment and investment disclosure and (2) dividend payment and new stock issuance. Analyzing this model, Ambarish *et al.* (1987) propose two main properties. First, cash dividend declaration increases stock price if investment is fixed. Second, when firms pay fixed dividends, declaration of investment or net new shares on stock prices is negative for those with superior information arising from assets in place and positive for those with superior information chiefly from investment opportunities.

Furthermore, Bar-Yosef and Huffman (1986) developed an incentive-signaling model in which corporate owners have managerial reward–penalty schemes to ensure accurate signals from managers' announcements. They claim that under the optimal equilibrium, the dividend payout is an increasing function of future cash flow. Stulz (1990) examines financing policies of firms with atomistic stockholders and claims that the predictability of dividends about expected cash flows is higher for underinvesting and overinvesting firms. Besides, Eades (1982) and Rozeff (1982) consider cash dividends as a signal of cash flow variability. Bar-Yosef and Huffman (1986) argue that considerable dividend variations across industries are explained by industry risk exposure. Their model describes payout ratio as a function of cash flow volatility. They find that dividend payout ratio negatively affects cash flow volatility. Kale and Noe (1990) posit that dividends are considered as a signal of both systematic and unsystematic uncertainty of cash flows.

## 6.1.2.  *Agency theory*

Jensen and Meckling (1976) posit that there are two types of agency problems. First, the conflict of interest between managers and shareholders leads to agency costs of equity. These agency costs include monitoring costs, bonding costs and residual loss. Monitoring costs are incurred by shareholders to reduce expropriation by managers. Bonding costs are incurred by managers to guarantee that they will not conduct opportunistic behaviors. Residual loss is caused by the divergence between corporate managers' actual decisions and the decisions that they should make to maximize shareholders' wealth. According to Easterbrook (1984), in addition to monitoring costs, shareholders also incur costs from managers' risk-averse behaviors. Shareholders can eliminate non-systematic risk with diversified portfolios and expect managers to make decisions as risk preferers to expropriate creditors. However, managers' personal interest is significantly connected to their firms. When firms have lower profitability or go bankrupt, managers will lose their jobs and relevant benefits. Therefore, they tend to be risk-averse and undertake low-risk projects that have low returns. Furthermore, Jensen (1986) and Rozeff (1982) argue that excessive funds that are available to managers are another source of agency costs. If cash flow exceeds the desired level to finance profitable investment projects, corporate managers have high incentives to invest excessive cash in negative-NPV projects in order to build their empires. Dividend payment is a means to reduce agency costs of equity. Monitoring costs, managerial risk-aversion costs and free cash flow costs are lower when corporate managers have less cash to invest in unprofitable projects (Easterbrook, 1984).

Second, the conflict of interest between shareholders and creditors results in agency costs of debt (Jensen & Meckling, 1976; Myers, 1977). Corporate managers tend to sacrifice creditors' interest in order to benefit shareholders when they make financial decisions. One of these decisions is a dividend policy. When firms pay excessive dividends, internal funds are less available. Therefore, they may have to raise external funds to finance their investment opportunities. In other words, excessive dividend payment increases bankruptcy risk. It transfers wealth from creditors to shareholders. In order to reduce agency costs of debt, debt covenants are structured to constrain both investment-financed and debt-financed dividends.

## 6.1.3.  *Bird-in-hand theory*

According to Gordon and Lintner (1956), investors prefer dividends to retained earnings since they are risk-averse. Dividends — a bird in the hand — are certain, while gains on future earnings — a bird in the bush — may be uncertain. "A bird in hand is worth more than two in the bush" goes the old adage, since the birds in the bush may fly away (Gordon, 1959). Easterbrook (1984) argues that dividends are really a bird in the hand when investors use them to pay their living costs or to buy Treasury bills. Dividends are not a bird in the hand when investors use them to reinvest in a firm. Consistently, Brennan and Thakor (1990) find that minority shareholders prefer dividend payment if the effective income tax rates imposed on their dividends are not too high. Moreover, La Porta *et al.* (2000) show that weakly protected shareholders want to obtain dividends although their firms have many investment opportunities.

## 6.1.4.   *Transaction cost theory, residual theory and pecking order theory*

Three theories of dividends, including transaction cost theory, residual theory and pecking order theory, describe the roles of investing and financing decisions in corporate dividend policy. First, firms and investors have to incur transaction costs when firms resort to raising external funds or selling their non-cash assets to finance their investment (Manos, 2001). If transaction costs are significant, firms tend to retain more earnings and thus their dividend levels are low. According to Higgins (1972) and Rozeff (1982), firms paying more dividends face higher transaction costs for external financing.

Second, the residual theory asserts that firms only pay dividends after financing all available investment opportunities (Weston & Brigham, 1979). According to Higgins (1972), dividends should be considered as a residual because investments maximize owners' wealth in an environment of differential taxes and significant transaction costs. This indicates that firms with more positive-NPV projects have high intention rates (Ghosh & Woolridge, 1989).

Third, the pecking order theory also postulates that firms prefer internal equity to external funds when they finance dividend payment and investments. Even if external financing is necessary, firms prefer debt to new share issues. Donaldson (1961) explains these preferences by significant flotation costs. However, Myers and Majluf (1984) argue that the net benefits of raising funds from debt in terms of tax shield and financial distress may exceed flotation costs. Firms prefer internal equity since they want to maximize the wealth of shareholders. Myers and Majluf (1984) propose a model describing managerial decisions on investment and capital structure when corporate managers have an information advantage about their firms' current investment and future opportunities. The model suggests that firms should not distribute dividends if they have to recover cash through issuing new shares or other risky securities. On the other hand, limiting dividends is one way to create financial slack and cash can be saved as tradable securities or reserve power.

## 6.1.5.  *Life cycle theory*

Examining why dividends have disappeared in the US market, Fama and French (2001) find that firms with high profitability and low growth are more likely to pay dividends while those with low profitability and high growth tend to retain more earnings. Grullon *et al.* (2002) investigate dividend change announcements in the US stock market and find two remarkable results. First, there is a decrease instead of an increase in firm profitability after a dividend increase. This is inconsistent with the signaling theory. Second, dividend-increasing firms experience decreases in systematic risk which reduces the cost of capital. They assert that the dividend smoothing theory proposed by Lintner (1956) and the free cash flow hypothesis suggested by Jensen (1986) cannot explain the two findings completely. Hence, they developed a new model to explain these phenomena based on firm maturity.

According to the life cycle theory, firms have more profitable projects in the growth phase; therefore, they have high levels of economic profits, capital expenditure, growth in retained earnings and low levels of free cash flow. If their growth is maintained, more competitors enter the industry. Hence, existing firms have fewer positive-NPV projects, lower levels of capital expenditure and higher levels of free cash flow. When growth opportunities are less available, assets become more important to determine firm value and systematic risk is reduced.

The life cycle theory suggests that mature and established firms tend to pay more dividends due to fewer investment opportunities and abundant resources while young firms with limited resources tend to retain more earnings to finance abundant investment projects. These arguments are implicitly or explicitly based on the trade-off between the costs (e.g., flotation costs) and the benefits of dividend payment (e.g., reducing agency costs of free cash flow). When firms are more mature, more profits are accumulated and investment opportunities decline. Accordingly, the benefits of dividend distribution tend to exceed the costs of dividend payment. This drives firms to pay more dividends (DeAngelo & DeAngelo, 2006; Grullon *et al.*, 2002).

## 6.1.6.   *Catering theory*

The catering theory was initially developed by Baker and Wurgler (2004b). The essence of this theory is that managers follow investors' demand. They loosen the assumption of market efficiency in the dividend irrelevance proposition. They argue that investors' demand for dividend payers varies over time; therefore, the relative prices of dividend payers and non-payers fluctuate. Consequently, corporate managers tend to satisfy this demand by initiating dividends when investors offer relatively high prices for dividend-paying stocks and omitting dividends when investors prefer non-paying stocks.

Li and Lie (2006) criticize Baker and Wurgler's model on account of the fact that it only explains dividend initiations or omissions, and cannot explain dividend changes. In practice, managers make decisions related to changes in dividend payouts, which are more informative than dividend initiations or omissions. They argue that firms should be classified not only by their paying decisions but also their dividend levels. Therefore, they extend the catering theory with continuous dividend levels. In other words, corporate managers undertake dividend policies to satisfy investors' demand.

## 6.1.7.   *Tax clientele theory*

The tax clientele theory was developed by Brennan (1970) with an initial after-tax capital assets pricing model. Then, Litzenberger and Ramaswamy (1979) extended this model by eliminating some assumptions. This theory states that dividend yield and systematic risk are two determinants of after-tax expected returns, and that dividends fail to provide investors with optimal benefits due to tax-related reasons. Income tax rates for dividends are commonly higher than those for long-term capital gains. This tax policy makes investors prefer a low dividend payout to a high dividend payout. Therefore, if firms want to maximize their shareholders' wealth, they should minimize their dividends.

Black and Scholes (1974) argue that the effect of taxes is not uniform for all investors since different groups of investors face different tax rates for dividends and capital gains. Investors for whom dividends are taxed at lower effective brackets than capital gains prefer dividends. However, investors whose dividends are tax disadvantaged tend to prefer retained earnings. Investors for whom taxes on dividends and capital gains are effectively equal are indifferent to them.

# 6.2.  Determinants of Dividend Policy

## 6.2.1.  *Financial characteristics*

### 6.2.1.1.  *Firm profitability*

Firms distribute dividends from their earnings. Kent Baker and Jabbouri (2016) conduct a survey to investigate corporate managers' views about determinants of dividend policy. They find that current earnings and their stability are the most important determinants. High profitability increases free cash flow. This is an opportunity for managers to expropriate shareholders' benefits. Therefore, shareholders of high-profitability firms pressure managers to increase dividends in order to reduce agency costs of equity (Jensen, 1986; Rozeff, 1982). Many prior studies show a positive relationship between firm profitability and corporate dividend policy (Abreu & Gulamhussen, 2013; Aivazian *et al.*, 2003; Baker *et al.*, 2020; Benjamin & Biswas, 2019; Boshnak, 2021; Byrne & O'Connor, 2012; Denis & Osobov, 2008; Fama & French, 2001; Gyapong *et al.*, 2021; Ho, 2003; Howatt *et al.*, 2009; Jabbouri, 2016; Kilincarslan, 2021; Kilincarslan & Demiralay, 2021; Koo *et al.*, 2017; Labhane, 2018; Labhane & Mahakud, 2016; Lam *et al.*, 2012; Nissim & Ziv, 2001; Tran, 2021b).

### 6.2.1.2.  *Cash holdings*

According to DeAngelo *et al.* (2006), the relationship between cash holdings and dividend decisions is ambiguous. On the one hand, the agency theory implies that firms with high cash levels pay more dividends to restrict corporate managers' opportunistic behaviors. On the other hand, cash holdings are also considered a signal of potential growth opportunities. Firms hold more cash since they have many future investment opportunities to finance. Consequently, they are less likely to pay dividends although their cash holdings are high. Agrawal and Jayaraman (1994), Chen *et al.* (2014), Lam *et al.* (2012), Lang and Litzenberger (1989), Subramaniam *et al.* (2011) and Tran (2021b) find that corporate cash holdings are positively related to dividend policy. However, Koo *et al.* (2017), Tran *et al.* (2017) and Ucar (2019) show a negative relationship.

### 6.2.1.3.  *Free cash flow*

According to Jensen (1986), free cash flows make the agency problem between shareholders and corporate managers more severe. When firms have more free cash flows, their managers are more flexible in their investment decisions. Therefore, they tend to divert free cash flows into value-destroying projects in order to serve their own benefits. Recognizing this opportunistic behavior, shareholders insist on dividend distribution to reduce free cash flows. Holder *et al.* (1998) initially use free cash flows to investigate the agency problem in dividend decisions. They find that firms pay more dividends when they have high levels of free cash flows. Adjaoud and Ben-Amar (2010), Ain *et al.* (2021), Amidu and Abor (2006), Fairchild (2010), Koo *et al.* (2017), Labhane (2018), Lang and Litzenberger (1989) and Sawicki (2009) also show supporting evidence for the positive effect of free cash flow on dividend policy. However, Al-Najjar and Hussainey (2009) and Jabbouri (2016) find that firms with more free cash flows have lower payout ratios. This can be explained as free cash flows reflect managers' power and control in their firms. When managers are respected by shareholders, they can have more free cash flows and face lower pressure to disgorge cash.

### 6.2.1.4.  *Investment opportunities*

Both corporate investment and dividend payment consume corporate cash resources. Due to transaction costs and information asymmetry, external financing is more expensive than internal financing. When firms have more investment opportunities, their cash resources are mainly used for investment projects rather than dividend payment. Ain *et al.* (2021), Alli *et al.* (1993), Amidu and Abor (2006), Baker *et al.* (2007, 2020), Byrne and O'Connor (2012), Chang and Rhee (1990), Denis and Osobov (2008), Fama and French (2001), Gyapong *et al.* (2021), Higgins (1972), Holder *et al.* (1998), Jabbouri (2016), Jiraporn *et al.* (2011), Kilincarslan (2021), Kim *et al.* (2020), Koo *et al.* (2017), Labhane (2018), Labhane and Mahakud (2016), Lam *et al.* (2012) and Rozeff (1982) find a negative effect of investment opportunities on corporate dividend policy. Nevertheless, Gonzalez *et al.* (2017) document a positive relationship between investment opportunities and dividend decisions. This can be explained as when more investment opportunities are available, firms are more likely to send positive signals to outside investors by increasing dividends.

### 6.2.1.5. *Financial leverage*

Highly levered firms face higher risk of bankruptcy. Consequently, they are financially constrained and face high costs of external financing. They have high incentives to hold cash and low incentives to pay dividends. Ain *et al.* (2021), Aivazian *et al.* (2003), Al-Malkawi (2007), Boshnak (2021), Fan and Sundaresan (2000), Gonzalez *et al.* (2017), Gyapong *et al.* (2021), Harada and Nguyen (2011), Jabbouri (2016), Jensen *et al.* (1992), John and Muthusamy (2010), Kilincarslan (2021), Kim *et al.* (2020), Koo *et al.* (2017), Kowalewski *et al.* (2007), Labhane (2018), Labhane and Mahakud (2016), Lam *et al.* (2012), Mehdi *et al.* (2017), Setia-Atmaja (2010) and Thanatawee (2011) document that debt ratio negatively influences dividend payment decisions. However, some studies show a positive relationship between financial leverage (Aggarwal *et al.*, 2011; Chang & Rhee, 1990; Jiraporn *et al.*, 2011; Utami & Inanga, 2011; Zhang, 2008). This can be explained as levered firms are monitored and controlled strictly by their creditors. Therefore, their managers have fewer opportunities to divert cash into value-destroying projects. When firms have excessive cash, they are more likely to pay dividends.

### 6.2.1.6.  *Firm size*

Large firms have better reputations and better relationships with financial institutions. They are also well-organized and thus their corporate governance is stronger. These characteristics enable large firms to have better access to credit and incur lower costs of external financing. Consequently, they are more likely to pay dividends. Abreu and Gulamhussen (2013), Adjaoud and Ben-Amar (2010), Ain *et al.* (2021), Aivazian *et al.* (2003), Al Shabibi and Ramesh (2011), Al-Malkawi (2007), Al-Najjar and Hussainey (2009), Baker *et al.* (2020), Benjamin and Biswas (2019), Byrne and O'Connor (2012), Chang and Rhee (1990), Denis and Osobov (2008), Gonzalez *et al.* (2017), Harada and Nguyen (2011), Ho (2003), Jabbouri (2016), Kilincarslan (2021), Kim *et al.* (2020), Koo *et al.* (2017), Kowalewski *et al.* (2007), Labhane (2018), Labhane and Mahakud (2016), Mollah (2001), Setia-Atmaja (2010) and Thanatawee (2011) find that firm size has a positive impact on corporate dividend policy. However, Arora and Srivastava (2019) and Boshnak (2021) show that firm size is negatively related to dividend decisions. This can be explained as large firms have more investment opportunities and thus they tend to retain more earnings to finance their investment projects instead of paying dividends.

### 6.2.1.7.  *Asset tangibility*

Tangible assets are used as collaterals when firms borrow from banks. Firms with more tangible assets have lower agency costs of debt (Titman & Wessels, 1988). They are more likely to pay dividends since debt financing is cheaper. Arko *et al.* (2014), Labhane (2018) and Rajesh Kumar and Sujit (2018) show a positive relationship between asset tangibility and dividend payment.

### 6.2.1.8.  *Firm maturity*

According to the life cycle theory, mature firms have fewer investment opportunities and thus pay more dividends to disgorge cash (DeAngelo & DeAngelo, 2006; Grullon *et al.*, 2002). Prior research measures firm maturity by the earned/contributed capital mix. DeAngelo *et al.* (2006) and Denis and Osobov (2008) find that mature firms have higher likelihood of dividend payment. Consistently, Brockman and Unlu (2009), Denis and Osobov (2008), Koo *et al.* (2017), Labhane (2018) and Labhane and Mahakud (2016) show a positive relationship between firm maturity and corporate dividend decisions.

### 6.2.1.9. *Business risk*

Firms with higher risk face higher costs of external financing. Moreover, firms with unstable earnings fail to have good prediction of future earnings. Therefore, they are more likely to retain earnings and reduce their dividend payments. Baker and Jabbouri (2016), Balachandran *et al.* (2019), Bartram *et al.* (2015), Harada and Nguyen (2011), Ho (2003), Koo *et al.* (2017), Labhane (2018), Labhane and Mahakud (2016), Mehdi *et al.* (2017), Rozeff (1982), Sawicki (2009) and Setia-Atmaja (2010) find empirical evidence for the negative effect of business risk on corporate dividend policy.

### 6.2.1.10. *Firm age*

Firm age may positively affect corporate dividend decisions through two mechanisms. First, young firms have less reputation and experience than mature firms. Therefore, young firms face higher information asymmetry between insiders and outside investors. This makes them incur higher costs of external financing and thus they have lower incentives to pay dividends. Second, the life cycle theory predicts that young firms are less willing to pay dividends since they have more investment opportunities. Al-Najjar and Kilincarslan (2017), Benjamin and Biswas (2019), Boshnak (2021), Koo *et al.* (2017) and Mehdi *et al.* (2017) find a positive impact of firm age on dividend policy.

### 6.2.1.11. *Catering incentives*

Baker and Wurgler (2004b) initially test the catering theory of dividends by investigating how dividend premium affects firms' decisions to initiate and omit dividends. Dividend premium is defined as the difference between payers' and non-payers' stock prices. They find that dividend premium has positive and negative effects on dividend initiation and omission, respectively. Furthermore, Baker and Wurgler (2004a) and Li and Lie (2006) analyze how catering incentives influence the likelihood to pay dividends and find consistent results in the US market. Byrne and O'Connor (2017) and Ferris *et al.* (2006) also show supporting evidence for the catering theory. However, some prior studies fail to find significant catering incentives in corporate dividend policy (Denis & Osobov, 2008; Ferris *et al.*, 2009; von Eije & Megginson, 2008).

### 6.2.1.12.  *Taxes*

Pettit (1977) examines how tax clientele effects dividend policy and finds that there are two groups of investors who prefer high dividend yield stocks: (1) investors who have low tax rates and (2) investors who face a big gap between their ordinary income and capital gains. Bolster and Janjigian (1991), Casey and Dickens (2000), Litzenberger and Ramaswamy (1979), Means *et al.* (1992), Papaioannou and Savarese (1994), Poterba and Summers (1984) and Saadi and Chkir (2008) also show that tax rates determine investors' preferences toward dividends. However, Black and Scholes (1974), Lewellen *et al.* (1978) and Miller and Scholes (1982) fail to find empirical support for the tax clientele theory.

## 6.2.2.  *Corporate governance*

According to the agency theory, corporate governance helps firms reduce conflicts of interest between shareholders and managers. Therefore, corporate governance is important in corporate dividend decisions (Rozeff, 1982). Adjaoud and Ben-Amar (2010), Baker *et al.* (2020), Bebczuk (2005), Jiraporn (2006) and Kowalewski *et al.* (2007) find that strong corporate governance leads to high corporate payout ratios. Prior studies show that ownership structure, board structure and managerial characteristics are three common proxies of corporate governance.

### 6.2.2.1. *Ownership structure*

Ownership structure determines firms' ability to monitor and control their managers' opportunistic behaviors. According to Harada and Nguyen (2011), ownership concentration influences dividend policy through two opposite mechanisms. On the one hand, concentrated ownership is an opportunity for large shareholders to control corporate managers effectively (Shleifer & Vishny, 1986). Consequently, managers cannot accumulate much cash for their overinvestment. Even when corporate managers invest firm resources in unprofitable projects, ownership concentration still helps large shareholders reduce the wasted resources. In other words, firms with high ownership concentration have stronger corporate governance and thus pay more dividends. Arora and Srivastava (2019), Brunzell *et al.* (2014), Kilincarslan (2021) and Rozeff (1982) find a positive relationship between ownership concentration and corporate dividend policy. On the other hand, concentrated ownership also creates an opportunity for large shareholders to expropriate minority shareholders (Johnson *et al.*, 2000; Shleifer & Vishny, 1997). Large shareholders pressure managers to hold and divert corporate resources to serve their own benefits and sacrifice minority shareholders' interests. As a result, firms with high ownership concentration have low levels of dividends. Gonzalez *et al.* (2017), Gyapong *et al.* (2021), Harada and Nguyen (2011) and Mehdi *et al.* (2017) document a negative impact of ownership concentration on dividend policy.

In addition, the effect of insider ownership on corporate dividend decisions is also a debatable topic. Firms with high insider ownership may face less severe agency problems since insiders' benefits are more aligned with those of shareholders (Jensen *et al.*, 1992). When corporate managers have high incentives to serve shareholders, they are less likely to retain earnings for low-quality investment projects. This leads to an increase in dividend payment. Balachandran *et al.* (2019) and Benjamin and Biswas (2019) show that insider ownership is positively associated with dividend decisions. However, firms with high insider ownership may decrease their dividends since their managers face lower pressure from shareholders to disgorge cash. Besides, their managers may also take advantage of their ownership to expropriate shareholders' benefits. Al-Malkawi (2007), Alli *et al.* (1993), Chen *et al.* (2005), Espen Eckbo and Verma (1994) and Rozeff (1982) find supporting evidence for the negative effect of insider ownership on dividend policy. Moreover, the relationship between insider ownership and dividend policy may be nonlinear. When insider ownership is low, insiders have high incentives to serve shareholders. Therefore, they are more likely to pay dividends and disgorge cash. When insider ownership reaches a high level, insiders have high incentives to adopt opportunistic behaviors. As a result, high insider ownership implies higher payout ratios. Farinha (2003), Farinha and Lopez-De-Foronda (2009), Kim *et al.* (2020), McConnell and Servaes (1990) and Morck *et al.* (1988) find that insider ownership has an inverse U-shaped relationship with dividend policy.

Furthermore, institutional investors are also important in corporate governance. Institutional investors have more knowledge, skills, technology and information than individual investors; therefore, they are more effective in monitoring and controlling corporate managers. When corporate managers have fewer opportunities to overinvest in unprofitable projects, their firms have higher payout ratios. Bataineh (2021), Chang *et al.* (2016), Crane *et al.* (2016), Jacob and Jijo Lukose (2018), Mehdi *et al.* (2017) and Short *et al.* (2002) find a positive relationship between institutional ownership and dividend decisions.

According to Gugler (2003), firms with state ownership face a "double principal–agent problem". Besides the agency problem between corporate managers and shareholders, they also face the problem between politicians and citizens. Politicians may pursue social objectives to maintain their positions and ignore economic objectives; therefore, they fail to have active monitoring activities. Weak corporate governance provides corporate managers with many opportunities to expropriate shareholders' interests. Consequently, firms with state ownership have lower payout ratios. Al-Najjar and Kilincarslan (2016) and Musallam and Lin (2019) show a negative relationship between state ownership and dividend payment. On the other hand, state ownership may affect corporate dividend decisions in an opposite channel. According to Kornai (1979), firms with state ownership may be supported by the government in raising external funds. Many prior studies show that they have better access to bank loans (Cong *et al.*, 2018; Megginson *et al.*, 2014) and lower costs of debt (Borisova *et al.*, 2015; Shailer & Wang, 2015). Besides, firms with state ownership face high pressure from investors to disgorge cash since investors are concerned about weak corporate governance. Therefore, state ownership has a positive impact on corporate dividend policy. This mechanism is empirically supported by Al-Malkawi (2007), Gonzalez *et al.* (2017), Gugler (2003), Lam *et al.* (2012), Tran (2021b), Wang *et al.* (2011) and Wei *et al.* (2004).

Moreover, foreign investors also affect corporate governance through shareholder activism and board representation (Lam *et al.*, 2012). They have advantages and disadvantages in monitoring corporate managers. They may have better experience, expertise and technology, but they may not have much information about local firms. When their advantages dominate, foreign investors help firms improve their corporate governance. Hence, their firms have higher payout ratios. However, when their disadvantages dominate, firms with foreign ownership face weaker corporate governance and thus their dividends are lower. Baba (2009), Balachandran *et al.* (2019), Gonzalez *et al.* (2017) and Jeon *et al.* (2011) find that foreign ownership is positively related to dividend policy while Bataineh (2021) and Lam *et al.* (2012) show the opposite relationship.

Furthermore, family ownership is a determinant of dividend policy. Family investors tend to have consistent behaviors. Therefore, the mechanisms through which family ownership may affect corporate dividend decisions are similar to those of concentrated ownership. Gonzalez *et al.* (2017), Kilincarslan (2021) and Setia-Atmaja (2010) find that firms with high family ownership have high levels of dividends. However, Attig *et al.* (2016) and Setiawan *et al.* (2016) show a negative impact of family ownership on dividend levels. Besides, Benjamin *et al.* (2016) and Sikalidis *et al.* (2022) document a U-shaped relationship between family ownership and dividend payments.

### 6.2.2.2.  *Board structure*

Board members hire corporate managers and monitor their behaviors. Board size may affect corporate dividend policy positively or negatively. A large board may improve corporate governance when its members cooperate to control managers. However, it may weaken corporate governance when its members have many conflicts in communication and decision-making. Ain *et al.* (2021), Benjamin and Biswas (2019), Kilincarslan (2021), Roy (2015) and Thompson and Adasi Manu (2021) find a positive relationship between board size and dividend decisions.

In addition, board independence may also have two opposite effects on dividend policy. On the one hand, independent directors monitor corporate managers and thus reduce their expropriation of shareholders' benefits. Firms with high board independence have strong corporate governance. Therefore, they pay more dividends. Borokhovich *et al.* (2005), Boshnak (2021), Kaplan and Reishus (1990), Mehdi *et al.* (2017), Schellenger *et al.* (1989) and Thompson and Adasi Manu (2021) find a positive impact of board independence on corporate dividend decisions. On the other hand, independent directors weaken corporate governance if their monitoring role is not effective. Independent members without appropriate expertise and experience are "rubber stamps" and thus managers have more opportunities to expropriate shareholders' benefits. Kilincarslan (2021), Roy (2015) and Setia-Atmaja (2010) find that firms with high board independence have lower payout ratios.

Moreover, board diversity is important to improve corporate governance. The social feminist theory states that men and women have different cognitive and socio-psychological characteristics. Prior research shows that women are more honest and ethical than men (Chonko & Hunt, 1985; Glover *et al.*, 1997; Reiss & Mitra, 1998). Besides, they are more conservative, risk-averse, hardworking and competent than men (Faccio *et al.*, 2016; Ittonen *et al.*, 2010; Palvia *et al.*, 2015; Pucheta-Martínez & Bel-Oms, 2016; Zeng & Wang, 2015). Consequently, female directors are more effective in monitoring corporate managers and improving corporate governance. Ain *et al.* (2021), Benjamin and Biswas (2019), Gyapong *et al.* (2021)

and Thompson and Adasi Manu (2021) find that firms with more female directors are more likely to pay dividends.

### 6.2.2.3. *Managerial characteristics*

Corporate managers make most financial decisions. Consequently, their characteristics are also determinants of corporate financial decisions. According to Schrand and Zechman (2012), overconfident managers tend to increase their investment expenditure. Consistently, Hackbarth (2008) and Mundi and Kaur (2022) find that managerial overconfidence positively influences financial leverage. Therefore, firms with overconfident managers have low incentives to pay dividends. Deshmukh *et al.* (2013) find that CEO overconfidence has a negative effect on corporate dividend policy. On the other hand, overconfident managers may believe that they can raise external funds easily and thus increase their dividends to signal their stellar performance to outside investors. Nguyen *et al.* (2021) document a positive relationship between CEO overconfidence and dividend payment.

In addition, Onali *et al.* (2016) argue that CEOs with power are more likely to expropriate shareholders' benefits through dividend policy. They find that CEO power negatively affects dividend payout. Barros, Guedes, Santos and Sarmento (2022) posit that CEO turnover is mainly caused by CEOs' retirement and poor performance; therefore, CEO turnover is a signal of better performance. They document that firms tend to pay dividends after a CEO turnover.

## 6.2.3. *Business environment characteristics*

### 6.2.3.1. *Environmental uncertainty*

Uncertainty in the business environment may have two opposite effects on corporate dividend policy. On the one hand, environmental uncertainty makes firms face higher costs of external financing and thus they have low incentives to pay dividends. Lei *et al.* (2015)

find that political uncertainty reduces non-paying firms' propensity to initiate dividends and paying firms' payout ratios. Huang *et al.* (2015) document that global political crises increase payers' probability of dividend payment and decrease non-payers' probability of dividend initiation. Sarwar and Hassan (2021) also find that firms are more likely to stop paying dividends over the period of high economic policy uncertainty.

On the other hand, environmental uncertainty increases investors' preference to obtain dividends; therefore, they are more likely to force corporate managers to distribute dividends. Buchanan *et al.* (2017) find that non-payers tend to initiate dividend payment and payers have higher levels of dividends before they face a tax increase. Attig *et al.* (2018) also show that firms in countries with high economic policy uncertainty pay more dividends. Similarly, Farooq and Ahmed (2019) document that firms extract more earnings to distribute dividends when they face high political uncertainty. Tran (2020) finds that economic policy uncertainty is positively associated with bank dividend policy.

### 6.2.3.2. *National culture*

Culture may affect both managers' and shareholders' views and thus influence corporate financial decisions. Many prior studies use Hofstede's dimensions to analyze the relationship between national culture and corporate dividend policy. Uncertainty avoidance culture drives corporate managers to hold more cash as a buffer for difficult situations while it increases shareholders' bird-in-hand motive. Aggarwal and Goodell (2014) and Bae *et al.* (2012) find that firms in countries with uncertainty avoidance culture have low incentives to pay dividends while Chang *et al.* (2020) show a positive relationship.

In addition, individualism drives people to follow their own interests (Hofstede, 2001). Corporate managers in individualistic countries are more likely to expropriate shareholders' benefits and thus they tend to hold cash for their overinvestment. However, investors in these countries also focus on their benefits and pressure managers to pay dividends. If managers' views are more effective in corporate dividend policy, their firms have low payout ratios. If investors' views dominate corporate dividend policy, their firms have high levels of dividends. Bae *et al.* (2012), Byrne and O'Connor (2017) and Chang *et al.* (2020) document a positive effect of individualism on dividend decisions. Nevertheless, Naeem and Khurram (2020) find that firms with individualistic CEOs have higher probability of dividend payment. Consistently, Tahir *et al.* (2020) show that multinational corporations tend to repatriate dividends from countries with high individualism.

Moreover, according to Hofstede (2001), people in high power distance cultures are more likely to recognize a hierarchical order and people in high masculinity cultures concentrate more on outcomes and performance. This implies that power distance cultures and masculinity cultures provide corporate managers more discretion in dividend decisions. Consequently, they tend to retain earnings instead of paying dividends. Aggarwal and Goodell (2014), Bae *et al.* (2012) and Chang *et al.* (2020) find that both power distance and masculinity have negative effects on dividend policy. Besides, Bae *et al.* (2012) and Chang *et al.* (2020) document that firms in countries with long-term orientation have high payout ratios.

Furthermore, Shao *et al.* (2010) examine the effects of Schwartz's cultural dimensions (conservatism and mastery) on corporate dividend decisions. They argue that in a conservative community, both managers and shareholders respect group relationships. Dividend payment is a means to reduce the conflict of interest between the two sides and strengthen these relationships. Besides, a conservative culture appreciates in value in the public image; hence, corporate managers are more likely to use dividends in order to build their firms' reputation. Shareholders in countries with conservatism focus more on security and thus prefer dividends to retained earnings. In addition, Shao *et al.* (2010) posit that a mastery culture respects independence and success. The former creates opportunities for corporate managers to hold more cash for their overinvestment in low-quality projects. The latter drives managers to use more earnings for financing profitable investment opportunities in order to improve their firms' performance. Using data from 21 countries, Shao *et al.*

(2010) find that conservatism and mastery have positive and negative impacts on corporate dividend policy, respectively.

Cao *et al.* (2016) find that firms in Buddhist and Taoist communities have high levels of dividends since these religions focus on sharing wealth, sacrifice and the next life. Nishikawa *et al.* (2021) postulate that languages with strong future-time reference decrease their speakers' concern about the future. Corporate dividend policy is determined by both current and expected future earnings. Consequently, firms tend to pay more dividends when their headquarters are located in countries with strong future-time languages. Nishikawa *et al.* (2021) also find empirical evidence for their hypothesis.

### 6.2.3.3. *Legislation*

In a pioneering study to investigate how legal protection of shareholders affects corporate dividend policy around the world, La Porta *et al.* (2000) propose two opposite mechanisms. First, the outcome mechanism shows a positive relationship between shareholder rights and dividend payment. Strong legal protection of shareholders is effective in controlling corporate managers; therefore, their firms are more likely to distribute dividends. Second, the substitute mechanism implies a negative relationship between shareholder rights and dividend policy. Corporate managers may use dividends as compensation for weak shareholder rights. Consequently, firms in countries with strong shareholder rights have low incentives to pay dividends. Many prior studies show supporting evidence for the outcome mechanism (Bae *et al.*, 2012; Brockman & Unlu, 2009; Byrne & O'Connor, 2017; Chang *et al.*, 2020; La Porta *et al.*, 2000; Shao *et al.*, 2010; Shao *et al.*, 2013; Tran *et al.*, 2017).

In addition, Brockman and Unlu (2009) examine how creditor rights influence dividend policies. In line with the substitute mechanism, they find a positive relationship between legal protection of creditors and dividend decisions. Byrne and O'Connor (2017) and Tran *et al.* (2017) document consistent empirical findings. Tran (2019c) shows that the positive impact of creditor rights on corporate dividend policy is explained by debt covenants rather than firms' reputation-building motive. Furthermore, Shao *et al.* (2013) postulate that corporate managers tend to balance shareholders' and creditors' benefits through their dividend decisions. Shao *et al.* (2013) find that the positive effect of shareholder (creditor) rights on dividend policy is stronger when creditors (shareholders) are strongly protected. Besides, Tran *et al.* (2017) document that the effects of both shareholder and creditor rights on dividend decisions are weaker under the impact of the global financial crisis.

### 6.2.3.4. *Macro-economic issues*

National income is a measure of economic development. Rich countries have more transparent and fair business environments; therefore, their firms face lower costs of external financing. Moreover, firms also have better access to external funds if the stock market is highly developed. Chang *et al.* (2020) and Shao *et al.* (2010) find that both national income and stock market development positively affect corporate dividend policy. Furthermore, many academics posit that a financial crisis is an exogenous shock toward corporate financial policies and thus they investigate its effect on corporate dividend decisions. A financial crisis makes firms face more external financial constraints, higher uncertainty and lower expected returns. Consistently, Ankudinov and Lebedev (2016), Chang *et al.* (2020) and Hauser (2013) find that both the probability of dividend payment and the dividend magnitude are lower under the impact of the global financial crisis.

# 6.3.  Political Corruption and Dividend Policy

## 6.3.1.  *The negative effect of political corruption on dividend policy*

### 6.3.1.1. *External financing mechanism*

Political corruption reduces the transparency and increases the segmentation of financial markets (Bekaert *et al.*, 2011; Chen *et al.*,

2010; Jain *et al.*, 2017; Liu, 2016). Therefore, firms in a corrupt environment face more difficulties in raising external funds and higher costs of external financing. Ciocchini *et al.* (2003) document that political corruption makes firms face high risk premium if they raise external funds by issuing bonds. Consistently, Baxamusa and Jalal (2014) and Du *et al.* (2020) find a positive relationship between political corruption and cost of debt. Furthermore, many prior studies show that firms in high corruption countries or regions have lower financial leverage (De Carvalho, 2009; Jõeveer, 2013; Weill, 2011).

When external funds become less available and more expensive, firms have high incentives to hold cash for two reasons. First, they need cash as a safety buffer. High cash holdings help firms meet unpredictable contingencies and avoid missing potential investment opportunities (Almeida *et al.*, 2004; Opler *et al.*, 1999). Second, firms save cash to avoid high transaction costs. When firms fail to have enough cash for their business activities, they tend to sell their non-cash assets. However, this transaction may lead to some costs. If these transaction costs are significant, firms are more likely to retain earnings. Consequently, firms in highly corrupt countries or regions tend to pay dividends and have large dividend magnitudes.

### 6.3.1.2.  *Cash trading mechanism*

In order to survive and develop in a corrupt environment, firms have to pay "grease money" and/or "protection money". Therefore, corporate managers have high incentives to trade cash for preferences and privileges from corrupt officials (Smith, 2016). Many prior studies also find that firms with political connections have higher likelihood of obtaining government bailouts (Faccio *et al.*, 2006) and more government procurement contracts (Goldman *et al.*, 2008). Therefore, they have better performance (Claessens *et al.*, 2008; Fisman, 2001; Goldman *et al.*, 2009; Wu *et al.*, 2018). Consistently, Thakur and Kannadhasan (2019) and Tran (2020a) find that firms in countries with high corruption have high levels of cash. Chen (2011) shows that firms have higher asset liquidity when political corruption is widespread. As a result, firms in a highly corrupt environment are less likely to pay dividends.

### 6.3.1.3. *Managerial entrenchment mechanism*

In a corrupt environment, corporate managers are entrusted to pay bribes since they need to develop a strong relationship with government officials in order to support business activities (Du, 2008). However, corporate managers may exploit this opportunity to expropriate shareholders' interests. As bribes are unofficial payments, shareholders fail to monitor their firms' liquidity policy strictly. Managers may use the pretext of paying bribes to insist on more flexibility and discretion in their liquidity decisions (Tran, 2019b).

Moreover, a culture of corruption is highly contagious. Corporate managers may perceive and apply bureaucratic procedures in their business activities. This weakens corporate governance and provides them more chances to conduct opportunistic behaviors (Dass *et al.*, 2017; Xu & Li, 2018). Besides, a strong relationship between corporate managers and government officials makes external controlling mechanisms less effective in the long run (Xu & Li, 2018). As a result, corporate managers in countries or regions with high corruption retain more earnings to serve their overinvestment instead of paying dividends.

Yensu and Adusei (2016) investigate the relationship between political corruption and corporate dividend policy across 13 African countries. They find that political corruption negatively affects dividend decisions. Consistently, Dong *et al.* (2022) and Lu and Zhang (2020) document a negative effect of local corruption on dividend policy of Chinese listed firms. Besides, Tahir *et al.* (2020) show that foreign subsidiaries located in countries with high corruption tend to hold more cash and reduce dividend repatriation.

## 6.3.2. *The positive effect of political corruption on dividend policy*

### 6.3.2.1. *Shielding mechanism*

In a corrupt environment, public servants have more opportunities for rent-seeking (Kusnadi *et al.*, 2015). Therefore, firms use their financial policies to prevent corrupt officials' rent-seeking

(McChesney, 1987; Stulz, 2005). Myers and Rajan (1998) posit extracting anonymous liquid assets is more difficult and expensive than extracting hard assets. Durnev and Fauver (2008) also argue that firms use information disclosure to prevent their liquid assets from being extracted by corrupt officials. Caprio *et al.* (2013) find that firms tend to reduce their liquid assets by converting them into harder-to-extract assets and paying dividends when they face high political extraction. Harder-to-extract assets include property, plant, equipment and inventory. According to Smith (2016), firms have many channels to avoid political extraction: lower cash holdings, higher debt ratios and more acquisitions. They empirically find that firms in countries with high political corruption tend to save more cash and use more debt financing. Similarly, Xu and Li (2018) show that local corruption has a negative effect on corporate cash holdings. When the shielding mechanism is effective, firms tend to pay more dividends to reduce their liquid assets.

### 6.3.2.2.  *Bird-in-hand mechanism*

Political corruption is a good opportunity for corporate managers to expropriate shareholders' benefits. However, political corruption also increases shareholders' bird-in-hand motive. In a corrupt environment, investors face high uncertainty and information disadvantage (Kuncoro, 2006). This makes shareholders focus on short-term benefits rather than long-term benefits. Moreover, shareholders recognize that agency costs of equity are higher when corporate managers have higher flexibility in liquidity policy. Consequently, firms in highly corrupt countries or regions face high pressure from shareholders to disgorge cash (Tran, 2019b). In other words, political corruption positively influences corporate dividend policy.

### 6.3.2.3.  *Empirical evidence*

Tran (2019b) investigates how political corruption determines corporate dividend policy across 47 countries. He finds that firms in countries with high corruption have high probability of dividend payment and payout levels. Consistently, Hossain *et al.* (2021) and Tran

(2021b) show that local corruption has a positive impact on dividend decisions in Vietnam and the US, respectively.

# 6.4.   Anti-Corruption and Dividend Decisions

In a corrupt environment, related firms have better access to credit and lower cost of debt due to the support of corrupt officials. Hence, they are more confident to pay dividends. However, when anti-corruption efforts are effective in controlling corrupt behaviors and eliminating corrupt officials, related firms are less likely to pay dividends in order to save cash for future investment. Qing (2018) finds that when the Chinese government's anti-corruption campaign restricts and terminates the connection between related firms and government officials, these firms react to this political incident by reducing their payout ratios.

Moreover, anti-corruption efforts may lead to a more transparent economic environment for unrelated firms. On the one hand, anti-corruption may drive firms to hold more cash and reduce dividends. Firms in a low-corruption environment have low incentives to shield their liquid assets and high incentives to increase their investment. Their investors are also less driven by the bird-in-hand motive and thus they are less likely to pressure corporate managers to pay dividends. Cai *et al.* (2022) show that firms increase their cash levels after their local politicians are investigated for corrupt cases. On the other hand, anti-corruption may make firms pay more dividends. In a less corrupt environment, firms have lower costs of debt and agency costs of equity. They also have fewer opportunities to trade cash for favorable treatment from the government. Consequently, firms are more likely to pay dividends when anti-corruption is effective. Xie and Zhang (2020) investigate how anti-corruption affects corporate liquidity policy. They find that firms in regions with strong anti-corruption intensity tend to hold less cash.

# Conclusions

Political corruption arises from misuse of public power. Government officials tend to use public power to serve their own benefits and individuals/organizations also tend to bribe for better public services and more favorable treatments. Political corruption is a challenging problem for the government around the world since it has strong effects on political, economic and socio-cultural issues in a society. Especially, developing countries face more severe corruption due to their weak public governance mechanisms and, therefore, many efforts and action plans have been made to prevent, limit and respond to corrupt behaviors domestically and internationally.

Corporate financial decisions are determined by both firm-specific characteristics and the external business environment. This book presents theories of corporate finance, determinants of corporate financial decisions and then describes the mechanisms through which political corruption may affect corporate financial decisions. There are also many empirical studies supporting the effects of political corruption on corporate investment, financing and dividend payment decisions across countries.

We hope that our book has provided a relatively comprehensive understanding of political corruption, corporate finance and their relationship. It is a potential reference for academics, researchers and practitioners in corporate finance. In addition, it may provide implications for policymakers when they make anti-corruption action plans and political policies. Although we have spared no efforts to finish this book, we understand that our work is not perfect and may have many mistakes. Therefore, we look forward to receiving comments from readers so that we can improve it in the future.

# References


Abadi, F., Bany-Ariffin, A. N., Kokoszczynski, R., & Azman-Saini, W. N. W. (2016). The impact of banking concentration on firm leverage in emerging markets. *International Journal of Emerging Markets, 11*(4), 550–568. doi:10.1108/IJoEM-02-2015-0035

Abdulla, Y. (2017). Capital structure in a tax-free economy: evidence from UAE. *International Journal of Islamic and Middle Eastern Finance and Management, 10*(1), 102–116. doi:10.1108/IMEFM-11-2015-0144

Abed, G. T., & Davoodi, H. R. (2000). Corruption, structural reforms, and economic performance in the transition economies. IMF Working Paper 132. https://www.imf.org/external/pubs/ft/wp/2000/wp00132.pdf

Abor, J. (2007). Corporate governance and financing decisions of Ghanaian listed firms. *Corporate Governance: The International Journal of Business in Society, 7*(1), 83–92. doi:10.1108/14720700710727131

Abor, J., & Biekpe, N. (2009). How do we explain the capital structure of SMEs in sub-Saharan Africa? *Journal of Economic Studies, 36*(1), 83–97. doi:10.1108/01443580910923812

Abreu, J. F., & Gulamhussen, M. A. (2013). Dividend payouts: evidence from U.S. bank holding companies in the context of the financial crisis. *Journal of Corporate Finance, 22*, 54–65. https://doi.org/10.1016/j.jcorpfin.2013.04.001

Acharya, V. V., Almeida, H., & Campello, M. (2007). Is cash negative debt? A hedging perspective on corporate financial policies. *Journal of Financial Intermediation, 16*(4), 515–554. http://dx.doi.org/10.1016/j.jfi.2007.04.001

Acharya, V. V., Amihud, Y., & Litov, L. (2011). Creditor rights and corporate risk-taking. *Journal of Financial Economics, 102*(1), 150–166. http://dx.doi.org/10.1016/j.jfineco.2011.04.001

Achim, M. V. (2016). Cultural dimension of corruption: a cross-country survey. *International Advances in Economic Research, 22*(3), 333–345. doi:10.1007/s11294-016-9592-x

Adem, G. (2021). Determinants of corruption: the case of sub-Saharan Africa. *Ankara Üniversitesi SBF Dergisi, 76*(2), 523–546.

Ades, A., & Di Tella, R. (1999). Rents, competition, and corruption. *American Economic Review, 89*(4), 982–993.

Adjaoud, F., & Ben-Amar, W. (2010). Corporate governance and dividend policy: shareholders' protection or expropriation? *Journal of Business Finance & Accounting, 37*(5–6), 648–667. doi:10.1111/j.1468-5957.2010.02192.x

Adserà, A., Boix, C., & Payne, M. (2003). Are you being served? Political accountability and quality of government. *The Journal of Law, Economics, and Organization, 19*(2), 445–490. doi:10.1093/jleo/ewg017

Aggarwal, R., Erel, I., Ferreira, M., & Matos, P. (2011). Does governance travel around the world? Evidence from institutional investors. *Journal of Financial Economics, 100*(1), 154–181. http://dx.doi.org/10.1016/j.jfineco.2010.10.018

Aggarwal, R., & Goodell, J. W. (2014). Cross-national differences in access to finance: influence of culture and institutional environments. *Research in International Business and Finance, 31*, 193–211. https://doi.org/10.1016/j.ribaf.2013.09.004

Agrawal, A., & Jayaraman, N. (1994). The dividend policies of all-equity firms: a direct test of the free cash flow theory. *Managerial & Decision Economics, 15*(2), 139–148.

Aggarwal, R., & Zong, S. (2006). The cash flow–investment relationship: international evidence of limited access to external finance. *Journal of Multinational Financial Management, 16*(1), 89–104. http://dx.doi.org/10.1016/j.mulfin.2005.04.009

Agrawal, A. K., & Matsa, D. A. (2013). Labor unemployment risk and corporate financing decisions. *Journal of Financial Economics*, *108*(2), 449–470. https://doi.org/10.1016/j.jfineco.2012.11.006

Ahlin, C. R. (2001). Corruption: political determinants and macroeconomic effects. Vanderbilt University Department of Economics Working Paper 0126. https://ideas.repec.org/p/van/wpaper/0126.html

Ahmed Sheikh, N., & Wang, Z. (2011). Determinants of capital structure: an empirical study of firms in manufacturing industry of Pakistan. *Managerial Finance*, *37*(2), 117–133. doi:10.1108/03074351111103668

Ahmed Sheikh, N., & Wang, Z. (2012). Effects of corporate governance on capital structure: empirical evidence from Pakistan. *Corporate Governance: The International Journal of Business in Society*, *12*(5), 629–641. doi:10.1108/14720701211275569

Ahn, S., Denis, D. J., & Denis, D. K. (2006). Leverage and investment in diversified firms. *Journal of Financial Economics*, *79*(2), 317–337. https://doi.org/10.1016/j.jfineco.2005.03.002

Aidt, T. S. (2009). Corruption, institutions, and economic development. *Oxford Review of Economic Policy*, *25*(2), 271–291. doi:10.1093/oxrep/grp012

Ain, Q. U., Yuan, X., Javaid, H. M., Zhao, J., & Xiang, L. (2021). Board gender diversity and dividend policy in chinese listed firms. *SAGE Open*, *11*(1), 2158244021997807. doi:10.1177/2158244021997807

Aivazian, V., Booth, L., & Cleary, S. (2003). Do emerging market firms follow different dividend policies from U.S. firms? *Journal of Financial Research*, *26*(3), 371–387. doi:10.1111/1475-6803.00064

Aivazian, V. A., Ge, Y., & Qiu, J. (2005). The impact of leverage on firm investment: Canadian evidence. *Journal of Corporate Finance*, *11*(1), 277–291. https://doi.org/10.1016/S0929-1199(03)00062-2

Ajaz, T., & Ahmad, E. (2010). The effect of corruption and governance on tax revenues. *The Pakistan Development Review*, 405–417.

Akbar, Z., Bashir, M. F., & Tariq, Y. B. (2021). An analysis of political uncertainty and corporate investment cycles in Pakistan. *Quality & Quantity, 55*(6), 2271–2293. doi:10.1007/s11135-021-01116-8

Akdede, S. H. (2006). Corruption and tax evasion. *Doğuş Üniversitesi Dergisi, 7*(2), 141–149.

Akhbari, R., & Nejati, M. (2019). The effect of corruption on carbon emissions in developed and developing countries: empirical investigation of a claim. *Heliyon, 5*(9), e02516. https://doi.org/10.1016/j.heliyon.2019.e02516

Akhter, S. H. (2004). Is globalization what it's cracked up to be? Economic freedom, corruption, and human development. *Journal of World Business, 39*(3), 283–295. https://doi.org/10.1016/j.jwb.2004.04.007

Akron, S., Demir, E., Díez-Esteban, J. M., & García-Gómez, C. D. (2020). Economic policy uncertainty and corporate investment: evidence from the U.S. hospitality industry. *Tourism Management, 77*, 104019. https://doi.org/10.1016/j.tourman.2019.104019

Al Shabibi, B. K., & Ramesh, G. (2011). An empirical study on the determinants of dividend policy in the UK. *International Research Journal of Finance & Economics* (80), 105–120.

Al-Fayoumi, N. A., & Abuzayed, B. M. (2009). Ownership structure and corporate financing. *Applied Financial Economics, 19*(24), 1975–1986. doi:10.1080/09603100903266807

Al-Malkawi, H.-A. N. (2007). Determinants of corporate dividend policy in jordan: an application of the tobit model. *journal of Economic and Administrative Sciences, 23*(2), 26. doi:10.1108/10264116200700007

Al-Marhubi, F. A. (2000). Corruption and inflation. *Economics Letters, 66*(2), 199–202. https://doi.org/10.1016/S0165-1765(99)00230-X

Al-Najjar, B., & Hussainey, K. (2009). The association between dividend payout and outside directorships. *Journal of Applied Accounting Research, 10*(1), 15. doi: 10.1108/09675420910963360

Al-Najjar, B., & Kilincarslan, E. (2016). The effect of ownership structure on dividend policy: evidence from Turkey. *Corporate*

*Governance: The International Journal of Business in Society*, *16*(1), 135–161. doi:10.1108/CG-09-2015-0129

Al-Najjar, B., & Kilincarslan, E. (2017). Corporate dividend decisions and dividend smoothing. *International Journal of Managerial Finance*, *13*(3), 304–331. doi:10.1108/IJMF-10-2016-0191

Al-Najjar, B., & Taylor, P. (2008). The relationship between capital structure and ownership structure: new evidence from Jordanian panel data. *Managerial Finance*, *34*(12), 919–933. doi:10.1108/03074350810915851

Al-Ajmi, J., Abo Hussain, H., & Al-Saleh, N. (2009). Decisions on capital structure in a Zakat environment with prohibition of riba: the case of Saudi Arabia. *The Journal of Risk Finance*, *10*(5), 460–476. doi:10.1108/15265940911001376

Albornoz, F., & Cabrales, A. (2013). Decentralization, political competition and corruption. *Journal of Development Economics*, *105*, 103–111. https://doi.org/10.1016/j.jdeveco.2013.07.007

Alesina, A., & Angeletos, G.-M. (2005). Corruption, inequality, and fairness. *Journal of Monetary Economics*, *52*(7), 1227–1244. https://doi.org/10.1016/j.jmoneco.2005.05.003

Alesina, A., & Perotti, R. (1996). Income distribution, political instability, and investment. *European Economic Review*, *40*(6), 1203–1228. https://doi.org/10.1016/0014-2921(95)00030-5

Alhassan-Alolo, N. (2007). Gender and corruption: testing the new consensus. *Public Administration and Development*, *27*(3), 227–237. https://doi.org/10.1002/pad.455

Ali, A. M., & Isse, H. S. (2002). Determinants of economic corruption: a cross-country comparison. *Cato Journal*, *22*, 449.

Ali, F., Ullah, M., Ali, S. T., Yang, Z., & Ali, I. (2022). Board diversity and corporate investment decisions: evidence from China. *SAGE Open*, *12*(2), 21582440221104089. doi:10.1177/21582440221104089

Ali, M. S. B., & Krammer, S. M. (2016). The role of institutions in economic development. *Economic Development in the Middle East and North Africa* (pp. 1–25). Springer.

Alipour, M., Mohammadi, M. F. S., & Derakhshan, H. (2015). Determinants of capital structure: an empirical study of firms in Iran.

*International Journal of Law and Management, 57*(1), 53–83. https://doi.org/10.1108/IJLMA-01-2013-0004

Allen, F., Qian, J., & Qian, M. (2005). Law, finance, and economic growth in China. *Journal of Financial Economics, 77*(1), 57–116. http://dx.doi.org/10.1016/j.jfineco.2004.06.010

Alli, K. L., Khan, A. Q., & Ramirez, G. G. (1993). Determinants of corporate dividend policy: a factorial analysis. *Financial Review, 28*(4), 523–547. doi:10.1111/j.1540-6288.1993.tb01361.x

Alm, J., Martinez-Vazquez, J., & McClellan, C. (2016). Corruption and firm tax evasion. *Journal of Economic Behavior & Organization, 124*, 146–163.

Almeida, H., & Campello, M. (2007). Financial constraints, asset tangibility, and corporate investment. *The Review of Financial Studies, 20*(5), 1429–1460. doi:10.1093/rfs/hhm019

Almeida, H., Campello, M., & Weisbach, M. S. (2004). The cash flow sensitivity of cash. *The Journal of Finance, 59*(4), 1777–1804.

Alt, J. E., & Lassen, D. D. (2003). The political economy of institutions and corruption in American States. *Journal of Theoretical Politics, 15*(3), 341–365. doi:10.1177/0951692803015003006

Alt, J. E., & Lassen, D. D. (2014). Enforcement and public corruption: evidence from the American States. *The Journal of Law, Economics, and Organization, 30*(2), 306–338. doi:10.1093/jleo/ews036

Altaf, N. (2022). Economic policy uncertainty and corporate investment: evidence from Indian hospitality firms. *Journal of Policy Research in Tourism, Leisure and Events*, 1–14. doi:10.1080/19407963.2022.2029462

Alti, A. (2006). How persistent is the impact of market timing on capital structure? *The Journal of Finance, 61*(4), 1681–1710. https://doi.org/10.1111/j.1540-6261.2006.00886.x

Altman, E. I. (1984). A further empirical investigation of the bankruptcy cost question. *The Journal of Finance, 39*(4), 1067–1089.

Alves, P. F. P., & Ferreira, M. A. (2011). Capital structure and law around the world. *Journal of Multinational Financial Management, 21*(3), 119–150. http://dx.doi.org/10.1016/j.mulfin.2011.02.001

Ambarish, R., John, K., & Williams, J. (1987). Efficient signalling with dividends and investments. *Journal of Finance, 42*(2), 321–343.

Amenta, E., & Ramsey, K. M. (2010). Institutional theory. In *Handbook of Politics* (pp. 15–39). Springer.

Amidu, M., & Abor, J. (2006). Determinants of dividend payout ratios in Ghana. *Journal of Risk Finance, 7*(2), 136–145. doi:10.1108/15255940610648580

Amihud, Y., & Lev, B. (1981). Risk reduction as a managerial motive for conglomerate mergers. *The Bell Journal of Economics, 12*(2), 605–617.

Amin, M., & Soh, Y. C. (2019). Corruption and country size: evidence using firm-level survey data. *World Bank Policy Research Working Paper* (8864).

Amoh, J. K., & Ali-Nakyea, A. (2019). Does corruption cause tax evasion? Evidence from an emerging economy. *Journal of Money Laundering Control, 22*(2), 217–232. doi:10.1108/JMLC-01-2018-0001

Amore, M. D., & Minichilli, A. (2018). Local political uncertainty, family control, and investment behavior. *Journal of Financial and Quantitative Analysis, 53*(4), 1781–1804. doi:10.1017/S002210901800025X

An, H., Chen, Y., Luo, D., & Zhang, T. (2016). Political uncertainty and corporate investment: evidence from China. *Journal of Corporate Finance, 36,* 174–189. https://doi.org/10.1016/j.jcorpfin.2015.11.003

Anas, E. (2015). The impact of ownership concentration, structure, and corporate governance to the firm's performance and credit rating: Indonesian case study. *Structure, and Corporate Governance to the Firm's Performance and Credit Rating: Indonesian Case Study* (July 27, 2015).

Andersen, T. B. (2009). E-Government as an anti-corruption strategy. *Information Economics and Policy, 21*(3), 201–210. https://doi.org/10.1016/j.infoecopol.2008.11.003

Andersen, T. B., Bentzen, J., Dalgaard, C.-J., & Selaya, P. (2011). Does the internet reduce corruption? evidence from U.S. States and across countries. *The World Bank Economic Review, 25*(3), 387–417. doi:10.1093/wber/lhr025

Anderson, C., & Galinsky, A. D. (2006). Power, optimism, and risk-taking. *European Journal of Social Psychology, 36*(4), 511–536. https://doi.org/10.1002/ejsp.324

Anderson, C. J., & Tverdova, Y. V. (2003). Corruption, political allegiances, and attitudes toward government in contemporary democracies. *American Journal of Political Science, 47*(1), 91–109.

Anderson, H. D., Liao, J., & Yue, S. (2022). Financial expert CEOs, political intervention, and corporate investment decisions: evidence from the anti-corruption campaign. *International Journal of Managerial Finance, 18*(3), 562–593. doi:10.1108/IJMF-12-2020-0622

Anderson, R. C., Mansi, S. A., & Reeb, D. M. (2004). Board characteristics, accounting report integrity, and the cost of debt. *Journal of Accounting and Economics, 37*(3), 315–342. http://dx.doi.org/10.1016/j.jacceco.2004.01.004

Andres, A. R., & Ramlogan-Dobson, C. (2011). Is corruption really bad for inequality? Evidence from Latin America. *The Journal of Development Studies, 47*(7), 959–976. doi:10.1080/00220388.2010.509784

Andvig, J. C., & Moene, K. O. (1990). How corruption may corrupt. *Journal of Economic Behavior & Organization, 13*(1), 63–76. https://doi.org/10.1016/0167-2681(90)90053-G

Anh, N. N., Minh, N. N., & Tran-Nam, B. (2016). Corruption and economic growth, with a focus on Vietnam. *Crime, Law and Social Change, 65*(4), 307–324. doi:10.1007/s10611-016-9603-0

Ankudinov, A. B., & Lebedev, O. V. (2016). Dividend payouts and company ownership structure amid the global financial crisis: evidence from Russia. *Post-Communist Economies, 28*(3), 384–404. doi:10.1080/14631377.2016.1196882

Antoniou, A., Guney, Y., & Paudyal, K. (2008). The determinants of capital structure: capital market-oriented versus bank-oriented institutions. *Journal of Financial and Quantitative Analysis, 43*(1), 59–92. doi:10.1017/S0022109000002751

Anwar, S., & Sun, S. (2015). Can the presence of foreign investment affect the capital structure of domestic firms? *Journal of Corporate Finance, 30*, 32–43. https://doi.org/10.1016/j.jcorpfin.2014.11.003

Apergis, N., Dincer, O. C., & Payne, J. E. (2012). Live free or bribe: on the causal dynamics between economic freedom and corruption in U.S. states. *European Journal of Political Economy*, *28*(2), 215–226. https://doi.org/10.1016/j.ejpoleco.2011.10.001

Appolloni, A., & Nshombo, J. M. M. (2014). Public procurement and corruption in Africa: a literature review. In F. Decarolis & M. Frey (eds), *Public Procurement's Place in the World: The Charge towards Sustainability and Innovation* (pp. 185–208). London: Palgrave Macmillan UK.

Arif, I., & Rawat, A. S. (2018). Corruption, governance, and tax revenue: evidence from EAGLE countries. *Journal of Transnational Management*, *23*(2–3), 119–133. doi:10.1080/15475778.2018.1469912

Arikan, G. G. (2004). Fiscal decentralization: a remedy for corruption? *International Tax and Public Finance*, *11*(2), 175–195. doi:10.1023/B:ITAX.0000011399.00053.a1

Arko, C. A., Abor, J., Adjasi, K. D. C., & Amidu, M. (2014). What influence dividend decisions of firms in sub-Saharan African? *Journal of Accounting in Emerging Economies*, *4*(1), 57–78. doi:10.1108/JAEE-12-2011-0053

Aristotle. (1932). The politics. *Jowett* (p. 59). The Modern Library: New York, 1943.

Arora, R. K., & Srivastava, A. (2019). Ownership concentration and dividend payout in emerging markets: evidence from India. *Global Business Review*, *22*(5), 1276–1288. doi:10.1177/0972150918824953

Arosa, C. M. V., Richie, N., & Schuhmann, P. W. (2014). The impact of culture on market timing in capital structure choices. *Research in International Business and Finance*, *31*, 178–192. http://dx.doi.org/10.1016/j.ribaf.2013.06.007

Arslan, Ö., Florackis, C., & Ozkan, A. (2006). The role of cash holdings in reducing investment–cash flow sensitivity: evidence from a financial crisis period in an emerging market. *Emerging Markets Review*, *7*(4), 320–338. https://doi.org/10.1016/j.ememar.2006.09.003

Ascioglu, A., Hegde, S. P., & McDermott, J. B. (2008). Information asymmetry and investment–cash flow sensitivity. *Journal of Banking & Finance, 32*(6), 1036–1048. https://doi.org/10.1016/j.jbankfin.2007.09.018

Asiedu, E., & Freeman, J. (2009). The effect of corruption on investment growth: evidence from firms in Latin America, Sub-Saharan Africa, and transition countries. *Review of Development Economics, 13*(2), 200–214.

Asongu, S. (2014). Globalization (fighting), corruption and development. *Journal of Economic Studies, 41*(3), 346–369. doi:10.1108/JES-04-2012-0048

Attig, N., Boubakri, N., El Ghoul, S., & Guedhami, O. (2016). The global financial crisis, family control, and dividend policy. *Financial Management, 45*(2), 291–313. doi:10.1111/fima.12115

Attig, N., El Ghoul, S., Guedhami, O., & Zheng, X. (2018). Dividends and economic policy uncertainty: international evidence. *Available at SSRN 3295228.*

Aurore, G. (2013). Political instability and the interventions of IMF and the World Bank in non-democratic regimes. Paper presented at the *6th Annual Conference of The Political Economy of International Organizations.*

Ayyagari, M., Demirgüç-Kunt, A., & Maksimovic, V. (2014). Bribe payments and innovation in developing countries: are innovating firms disproportionately affected? *Journal of Financial and Quantitative Analysis, 49*(1), 51–75. doi:10.1017/S002210901400026X

Baba, N. (2009). Increased presence of foreign investors and dividend policy of Japanese firms. *Pacific-Basin Finance Journal, 17*(2), 163–174. http://dx.doi.org/10.1016/j.pacfin.2008.04.001

Badinger, H., & Nindl, E. (2012). Globalization, inequality, and corruption. Department of Economics Working Paper Series 138. Wirtschaftsuniversität Vienna.

Bae, S. C., Chang, K., & Kang, E. (2012). Culture, corporate governance, and dividend policy: international evidence. *Journal of Financial Research, 35*(2), 289–316. doi:10.1111/j.1475-6803.2012.01318.x

Bai, J., Fairhurst, D., & Serfling, M. (2020). Employment protection, investment, and firm growth. *The Review of Financial Studies, 33*(2), 644–688. doi:10.1093/rfs/hhz066

Bai, J., Jayachandran, S., Malesky, E. J., & Olken, B. A. (2019). Firm growth and corruption: empirical evidence from Vietnam. *The Economic Journal, 129*(618), 651–677. doi:10.1111/ecoj.12560

Bajada, C., & Shashnov, M. (2019). The effects of economic development and the evolution of social institutions on the level of corruption: comparing the Asia-Pacific with other regional blocs. *Asia Pacific Business Review, 25*(4), 470–500. doi:10.1080/13602381.2019.1589768

Bajaj, Y., Kashiramka, S., & Singh, S. (2020). Capital structure dynamics: China and India (Chindia) perspective. *European Business Review, 32*(5), 845–868.

Baker, H. K., Dewasiri, N. J., Premaratne, S. P., & Yatiwelle Koralalage, W. (2020). Corporate governance and dividend policy in Sri Lankan firms: a data triangulation approach. *Qualitative Research in Financial Markets, 12*(4), 543–560. doi:10.1108/QRFM-11-2019-0134

Baker, H. K., & Jabbouri, I. (2016). How Moroccan managers view dividend policy. *Managerial Finance, 42*(3), 270–288. doi:10.1108/MF-07-2015-0211

Baker, H. K., Saadi, S., Dutta, S., & Gandhi, D. (2007). The perception of dividends by Canadian managers: new survey evidence. *International Journal of Managerial Finance, 3*(1), 70–91. doi:10.1108/17439130710721662

Baker, M., & Wurgler, J. (2002). Market timing and capital structure. *The Journal of Finance, 57*(1), 1–32.

Baker, M., & Wurgler, J. (2004a). Appearing and disappearing dividends: the link to catering incentives. *Journal of Financial Economics, 73*(2), 271–288. http://dx.doi.org/10.1016/j.jfineco.2003.08.001

Baker, M., & Wurgler, J. (2004b). A catering theory of dividends. *Journal of Finance, 59*(3), 1125–1165. doi:10.1111/j.1540-6261.2004.00658.x

Balachandran, B., Khan, A., Mather, P., & Theobald, M. (2019). Insider ownership and dividend policy in an imputation tax environment. *Journal of Corporate Finance, 54*, 153–167. https://doi.org/10.1016/j.jcorpfin.2017.01.014

Balios, D., Daskalakis, N., Eriotis, N., & Vasiliou, D. (2016). SMEs capital structure determinants during severe economic crisis: the case of Greece. *Cogent Economics & Finance*, *4*(1), 1145535. doi:10.1080/23322039.2016.1145535

Bar-Yosef, S., & Huffman, L. (1986). The information content of dividends: a signalling approach. *Journal of Financial & Quantitative Analysis*, *21*(1), 47–58.

Bardhan, P. (1997). Corruption and development: a review of issues. *Journal of economic literature*, *35*(3), 1320–1346.

Barenstein, M., & Fund, I. M. (2001). *Fiscal decentralization and governance: a cross-country analysis*. International Monetary Fund.

Barker, V. L., & Mueller, G. C. (2002). CEO characteristics and firm R&D spending. *Management Science*, *48*(6), 782–801. Retrieved from http://www.jstor.org/stable/822629

Barnes, T. D., Beaulieu, E., & Saxton, G. W. (2018). Restoring trust in the police: why female officers reduce suspicions of corruption. *Governance*, *31*(1), 143–161. https://doi.org/10.1111/gove.12281

Barr, A., Lindelow, M., & Serneels, P. (2009). Corruption in public service delivery: an experimental analysis. *Journal of Economic Behavior & Organization*, *72*(1), 225–239. https://doi.org/10.1016/j.jebo.2009.07.006

Barr, A., & Serra, D. (2010). Corruption and culture: an experimental analysis. *Journal of Public Economics*, *94*(11), 862–869. https://doi.org/10.1016/j.jpubeco.2010.07.006

Barros, V., Guedes, M. J., Santos, P., & Sarmento, J. M. (2022). Does CEO turnover influence dividend policy? *Finance Research Letters*, *44*, 102085. https://doi.org/10.1016/j.frl.2021.102085

Bartram, S. M., Brown, G. W., & Waller, W. (2015). How important is financial risk? *Journal of Financial and Quantitative Analysis*, *50*(4), 801–824. doi:10.1017/S0022109015000216

Basabose, J. d. D. (2019). Conventional Anti-corruption Measures. In J. d. D. Basabose (ed), *Anti-corruption Education and Peacebuilding: The Ubupfura Project in Rwanda* (pp. 47–59). Cham: Springer International Publishing.

Bataineh, H. (2021). The impact of ownership structure on dividend policy of listed firms in Jordan. *Cogent Business & Management*, *8*(1), 1863175. doi:10.1080/23311975.2020.1863175

Bauhr, M., Charron, N., & Wägnerud, L. (2019). Exclusion or interests? Why females in elected office reduce petty and grand corruption. *European Journal of Political Research*, *58*(4), 1043–1065. https://doi.org/10.1111/1475-6765.12300

Baxamusa, M., & Jalal, A. (2014). The effects of corruption on capital structure: when does it matter? *The Journal of Developing Areas*, *48*(1), 315–335.

Baysinger, B. D., Kosnik, R. D., & Turk, T. A. (1991). Effects of board and ownership structure on corporate R&D strategy. *Academy of Management Journal*, *34*(1), 205–214.

Bebczuk, R. N. (2005). Corporate governance and ownership: measurement and impact on corporate performance and dividend policies in Argentina. Retrieved from http://www.depeco. econo.unlp.edu.ar/doctrab/doc59.pdf

Becker, G. S. (2000). Crime and punishment: an economic approach. In N. G. Fielding, A. Clarke, & R. Witt (eds), *The Economic Dimensions of Crime* (pp. 13–68). London: Palgrave Macmillan UK.

Becker, G. S., & Stigler, G. J. (1974). Law enforcement, malfeasance, and compensation of enforcers. *The Journal of Legal Studies*, *3*(1), 1–18.

Bekaert, G., Harvey, C. R., Lundblad, C. T., & Siegel, S. (2011). What segments equity markets? *The Review of Financial Studies*, *24*(12), 3841–3890. doi:10.1093/rfs/hhr082

Belle, N., & Cantarelli, P. (2017). What causes unethical behavior? A meta-analysis to set an agenda for public administration research. *Public Administration Review*, *77*(3), 327–339. https://doi.org/10.1111/puar.12714

Beltramini, R. F., Peterson, R. A., & Kozmetsky, G. (1984). Concerns of college students regarding business ethics. *Journal of Business Ethics*, *3*(3), 195–200. doi:10.1007/BF00382919

Ben Ali, M. S., & Sassi, S. (2016). The corruption-inflation nexus: evidence from developed and developing countries. *The B.E. Journal of Macroeconomics*, *16*(1), 125–144. doi:10.1515/bejm-2014-0080

Ben-David, I., Graham, J. R., & Harvey, C. R. (2007). *Managerial overconfidence and corporate policies*. Retrieved from National Bureau of Economic Research.

Ben-Nasr, H., Bouslimi, L., Ebrahim, M. S., & Zhong, R. (2020). Political uncertainty and the choice of debt sources. *Journal of International Financial Markets, Institutions and Money, 64*, 101142. https://doi.org/10.1016/j.intfin.2019.101142

Benjamin, S. J., & Biswas, P. (2019). Board gender composition, dividend policy and COD: the implications of CEO duality. *Accounting Research Journal, 32*(3), 454–476. doi:10.1108/ARJ-02-2018-0035

Benjamin, S. J., Wasiuzzaman, S., Mokhtarinia, H., & Rezaie Nejad, N. (2016). Family ownership and dividend payout in Malaysia. *International Journal of Managerial Finance, 12*(3), 314–334. doi:10.1108/IJMF-08-2014-0114

Benmelech, E., & Frydman, C. (2015). Military CEOs. *Journal of Financial Economics, 117*(1), 43–59. https://doi.org/10.1016/j.jfineco.2014.04.009

Berger, P. G., Ofek, E. L. I., & Yermack, D. L. (1997). Managerial entrenchment and capital structure decisions. *The Journal of Finance, 52*(4), 1411–1438. https://doi.org/10.1111/j.1540-6261.1997.tb01115.x

Berle, A. A., & Means, G. C. (1932). *The Modern Corporation and Private Property*. New York: The Macmillan Company.

Berman, H. J. (1977). *The Use of Law to Guide People to Virtue: A comparison of Soviet and US Perspectives*. Holt, Rinehart and Winston.

Bernanke, B. S. (1983). Irreversibility, uncertainty, and cyclical investment. *The Quarterly Journal of Economics, 98*(1), 85–106. doi:10.2307/1885568

Bevan, A. A., & Danbolt, J. (2002). Capital structure and its determinants in the UK — a decompositional analysis. *Applied Financial Economics, 12*(3), 159–170. doi:10.1080/09603100110090073

Bhatnagar, S. C. (2003). E-government and access to information. *Global Corruption Report* (pp. 24–32).

Bhattacharya, S. (1979). Imperfect information, dividend policy, and "the bird in the hand" fallacy. *Bell Journal of Economics, 10*(1), 259–270.

Bhattacharyya, S., & Jha, R. (2013). Economic growth, law, and corruption: evidence from India. *Comparative Economic Studies, 55*(2), 287–313. doi:10.1057/ces.2013.4

Bhojraj, S., & Sengupta, P. (2003). Effect of corporate governance on bond ratings and yields: the role of institutional investors and outside directors. *The Journal of Business, 76*(3), 455–475. doi:10.1086/344114

Billger, S. M., & Goel, R. K. (2009). Do existing corruption levels matter in controlling corruption?: cross-country quantile regression estimates. *Journal of Development Economics, 90*(2), 299–305. https://doi.org/10.1016/j.jdeveco.2008.07.006

Bird, R. M., Martinez-Vazquez, J., & Torgler, B. (2008). Tax Effort in developing countries and high income countries: the impact of corruption, voice and accountability. *Economic Analysis and Policy, 38*(1), 55–71. https://doi.org/10.1016/S0313-5926(08)50006-3

Bischoff, C. W. (1972). *The Effect of Alternative Lag Distributions*. Cowles Foundation for Research in Economics at Yale University.

Biswas, A. K., Farzanegan, M. R., & Thum, M. (2012). Pollution, shadow economy and corruption: theory and evidence. *Ecological Economics, 75*, 114–125. https://doi.org/10.1016/j.ecolecon.2012.01.007

Black, B. S., Jang, H., & Kim, W. (2006). Predicting firms' corporate governance choices: evidence from Korea. *Journal of Corporate Finance, 12*(3), 660–691. https://doi.org/10.1016/j.jcorpfin.2005.08.001

Black, F., & Scholes, M. (1974). The effects of dividend yield and dividend policy on common stock prices and returns. *Journal of Financial Economics, 1*(1), 1–22. http://dx.doi.org/10.1016/0304-405X(74)90006-3

Blackburn, K., & Powell, J. (2011). Corruption, inflation and growth. *Economics Letters, 113*(3), 225–227. https://doi.org/10.1016/j.econlet.2011.06.015

Bliss, M. A., & Gul, F. A. (2012). Political connection and leverage: some Malaysian evidence. *Journal of Banking & Finance, 36*(8), 2344–2350. https://doi.org/10.1016/j.jbankfin.2012.04.012

Bloom, N. (2009). The impact of uncertainty shocks. *Econometrica,* *77*(3), 623–685.

Bloom, N., Bond, S., & Van Reenen, J. (2007). Uncertainty and investment dynamics. *The Review of Economic Studies, 74*(2), 391–415. doi:10.1111/j.1467-937X.2007.00426.x

Bluhm, M., & Krahnen, J. P. (2014). Systemic risk in an interconnected banking system with endogenous asset markets. *Journal of Financial Stability, 13*, 75–94. https://doi.org/10.1016/j.jfs.2014.04.002

Bo, H., Driver, C., & Lin, H.-C. M. (2014). Corporate investment during the financial crisis: evidence from China. *International Review of Financial Analysis, 35*, 1–12. https://doi.org/10.1016/j.irfa.2014.07.002

Boasiako, K. A., Manu, S. A., & Antwi-Darko, N. Y. (2022). Does financing influence the sensitivity of cash and investment to asset tangibility? *International Review of Financial Analysis, 80*, 102055.

Bokpin, G. A., & Arko, A. C. (2009). Ownership structure, corporate governance and capital structure decisions of firms. *Studies in Economics and Finance, 26*(4), 246–256. doi:10.1108/10867370910995708

Bolster, P. J., & Janjigian, V. (1991). Dividend policy and valuation effects of the tax reform act of 1986. *National Tax Journal, 44*(4), 511–518. doi:10.2307/41788937

Bolzendahl, C. (2009). Making the implicit explicit: gender influences on social spending in twelve industrialized democracies, 1980–99. *Social Politics: International Studies in Gender, State & Society, 16*(1), 40–81. doi:10.1093/sp/jxp002

Bonaglia, F., De Macedo, J. B., & Bussolo, M. (2009). How globalisation improves governance. *The Law and Economics of Globalisation.* Edward Elgar Publishing.

Booth, L., Aivazian, V., Demirguc-Kunt, A., & Maksimovic, V. (2001). Capital structures in developing countries. *The Journal of Finance, 56*(1), 87–130. https://doi.org/10.1111/0022-1082.00320

Borisova, G., Brockman, P., Salas, J. M., & Zagorchev, A. (2012). Government ownership and corporate governance: evidence from the EU. *Journal of Banking & Finance, 36*(11), 2917–2934. https://doi.org/10.1016/j.jbankfin.2012.01.008

Borisova, G., Fotak, V., Holland, K., & Megginson, W. L. (2015). Government ownership and the cost of debt: evidence from government investments in publicly traded firms. *Journal of Financial Economics, 118*(1), 168–191. https://doi.org/10.1016/j.jfineco.2015.06.011

Borisova, G., & Megginson, W. L. (2011). Does government ownership affect the cost of debt? Evidence from privatization. *The Review of Financial Studies, 24*(8), 2693–2737. doi:10.1093/rfs/hhq154

Borokhovich, K. A., Brunarski, K. R., Harman, Y., & Kehr, J. B. (2005). Dividends, corporate monitors and agency costs. *Financial Review, 40*(1), 37–65. doi:10.1111/j.0732-8516.2005.00092.x

Boshnak, H. A. (2021). The impact of board composition and ownership structure on dividend payout policy: evidence from Saudi Arabia. *International Journal of Emerging Markets*. doi:10.1108/IJOEM-05-2021-0791

Boubakri, N., & Cosset, J.-C. (1998). The financial and operating performance of newly privatized firms: evidence from developing countries. *The Journal of Finance, 53*(3), 1081–1110. doi:10.1111/0022-1082.00044

Boubakri, N., Cosset, J.-C., & Saffar, W. (2013). The role of state and foreign owners in corporate risk-taking: evidence from privatization. *Journal of Financial Economics, 108*(3), 641–658.

Bowler, S., & Karp, J. A. (2004). Politicians, scandals, and trust in government. *Political Behavior, 26*(3), 271–287. doi:10.1023/B:POBE.0000043456.87303.3a

Brada, J. C., Drabek, Z., Mendez, J. A., & Perez, M. F. (2019). National levels of corruption and foreign direct investment. *Journal of Comparative Economics, 47*(1), 31–49. https://doi.org/10.1016/j.jce.2018.10.005

Brademas, J., & Heimann, F. (1998). Tackling international corruption: no longer taboo. *Foreign affairs, 77*(5), 1722.

Bradley, M., Jarrell, G. A., & Kim, E. H. (1984). On the existence of an optimal capital structure: theory and evidence. *Journal of Finance, 39*(3), 857–878.

Brailsford, T. J., Oliver, B. R., & Pua, S. L. H. (2002). On the relation between ownership structure and capital structure. *Accounting & Finance*, *42*(1), 1–26. https://doi.org/10.1111/1467-629X.00001

Brainard, W. C., & Tobin, J. (1968). Pitfalls in financial model building. *The American Economic Review*, *58*(2), 99–122.

Bratton, K. A., & Ray, L. P. (2002). Descriptive representation, policy outcomes, and municipal day-care coverage in Norway. *American Journal of Political Science*, *46*(2), 428–437. doi:10.2307/3088386

Braun, M., & Di tella, R. (2004). Inflation, Inflation Variability, and Corruption. *Economics & Politics*, *16*(1), 77–100. https://doi.org/10.1111/j.1468-0343.2004.00132.x

Breen, M., Gillanders, R., McNulty, G., & Suzuki, A. (2017). Gender and corruption in business. *The Journal of Development Studies*, *53*(9), 1486–1501. doi:10.1080/00220388.2016.1234036

Brennan, M. (1970). Tax reform and the stock market: an asset price approach. *American Economic Review*, *23*(4), 417–427.

Brennan, M. J., & Cao, H. H. (1997). International portfolio investment flows. *The Journal of Finance*, *52*(5), 1851–1880.

Brennan, M. J., & Thakor, A. V. (1990). Shareholder preferences and dividend policy. *The Journal of Finance*, *45*(4), 993–1018. https://doi.org/10.1111/j.1540-6261.1990.tb02424.x

Breuer, W., Riesener, M., & Salzmann, A. J. (2014). Risk aversion vs. individualism: what drives risk taking in household finance? *The European Journal of Finance*, *20*(5), 446–462. doi:10.1080/1351847X.2012.714792

Broadman, H. G., & Recanatini, F. (2001). Seeds of corruption — do market institutions matter? *MOST: Economic Policy in Transitional Economies*, *11*(4), 359–392. doi:10.1023/A:1015264312632

Broadman, H. G., & Recanatini, F. (2002). Corruption and policy: back to the roots. *The Journal of Policy Reform*, *5*(1), 37–49. doi:10.1080/13841280212381

Brockman, P., & Unlu, E. (2009). Dividend policy, creditor rights, and the agency costs of debt. *Journal of Financial Economics*, *92*(2), 276–299. http://dx.doi.org/10.1016/j.jfineco.2008.03.007

Brunetti, A., & Weder, B. (2003). A free press is bad news for corruption. *Journal of Public Economics*, *87*(7), 1801–1824. https://doi.org/10.1016/S0047-2727(01)00186-4

Brunzell, T., Liljeblom, E., Löflund, A., & Vaihekoski, M. (2014). Dividend policy in Nordic listed firms. *Global Finance Journal, 25*(2), 124–135. https://doi.org/10.1016/j.gfj.2014.06.004

Buchanan, B. G., Cao, C. X., Liljeblom, E., & Weihrich, S. (2017). Uncertainty and firm dividend policy — a natural experiment. *Journal of Corporate Finance, 42*, 179–197. https://doi.org/10.1016/j.jcorpfin.2016.11.008

Bussolo, M., de Nicola, F., Panizza, U., & Varghese, R. (2022). Politically connected firms and privileged access to credit: evidence from Central and Eastern Europe. *European Journal of Political Economy, 71*, 102073. https://doi.org/10.1016/j.ejpoleco.2021.102073

Byrne, J., & O'Connor, T. (2012). Creditor rights and the outcome model of dividends. *Quarterly Review of Economics and Finance, 52*(2), 227–242. doi:10.1016/j.qref.2012.04.002

Byrne, J., & O'Connor, T. (2017). Creditor rights, culture and dividend payout policy. *Journal of Multinational Financial Management, 39*, 60–77. https://doi.org/10.1016/j.mulfin.2016.12.002

Cai, W., Hu, F., Xu, F., & Zheng, L. (2022). Anti-corruption campaign and corporate cash holdings: evidence from China. *Emerging Markets Review, 51*, 100843. https://doi.org/10.1016/j.ememar.2021.100843

Calcagnini, G., Ferrando, A., & Giombini, G. (2014). Does employment protection legislation affect firm investment? The European case. *Economic Modelling, 36*, 658–665. https://doi.org/10.1016/j.econmod.2013.06.036

Cameron, L., Chaudhuri, A., Erkal, N., & Gangadharan, L. (2009). Propensities to engage in and punish corrupt behavior: experimental evidence from Australia, India, Indonesia and Singapore. *Journal of Public Economics, 93*(7), 843–851. https://doi.org/10.1016/j.jpubeco.2009.03.004

Campello, M., Graham, J. R., & Harvey, C. R. (2010). The real effects of financial constraints: evidence from a financial crisis. *Journal of Financial Economics, 97*(3), 470–487. http://dx.doi.org/10.1016/j.jfineco.2010.02.009

Cao, C., Jia, F., Zhang, X., & Chan, K. C. (2016). Does religion matter to dividend policy? Evidence from Buddhism and Taoism in

China. *Nankai Business Review International, 7*(4), 510–541. doi:10.1108/NBRI-12-2015-0033

Cao, C., Li, X., & Liu, G. (2019). Political uncertainty and cross-border acquisitions. *Review of Finance, 23*(2), 439–470. doi:10.1093/rof/rfx055

Caprio, L., Faccio, M., & McConnell, J. J. (2013). Sheltering corporate assets from political extraction. *The Journal of Law, Economics, and Organization, 29*(2), 332–354. doi:10.1093/jleo/ewr018

Casey, K. M., & Dickens, R. N. (2000). The effects of tax and regulatory changes on commercial bank dividend policy. *The Quarterly Review of Economics and Finance, 40*(2), 279–293. http://dx.doi.org/10.1016/S1062-9769(99)00051-4

Castro, C., & Nunes, P. (2013). Does corruption inhibit foreign direct investment? *Política. Revista de Ciencia Política, 51*(1), 61–83.

Catão, L. A. V., & Terrones, M. E. (2005). Fiscal deficits and inflation. *Journal of Monetary Economics, 52*(3), 529–554. https://doi.org/10.1016/j.jmoneco.2004.06.003

Catterberg, G., & Moreno, A. (2006). The individual bases of political trust: trends in new and established democracies. *International Journal of Public Opinion Research, 18*(1), 31–48. doi:10.1093/ijpor/edh081

Cella, C. (2020). Institutional investors and corporate investment. *Finance Research Letters, 32*, 101169.

Chafuen, A., & Guzman, E. (2000). Economic freedom and corruption. *2000 Index of Economic Freedom*, 51–63.

Chang, E. C. C., & Chu, Y.-h. (2006). Corruption and trust: exceptionalism in asian democracies? *The Journal of Politics, 68*(2), 259–271. doi:10.1111/j.1468-2508.2006.00404.x

Chang, E. C. C., & Golden, M. A. (2007). Electoral systems, district magnitude and corruption. *British Journal of Political Science, 37*(1), 115–137. doi:10.1017/S0007123407000063

Chang, K., Kang, E., & Li, Y. (2016). Effect of institutional ownership on dividends: an agency-theory-based analysis. *Journal of Business Research, 69*(7), 2551–2559. https://doi.org/10.1016/j.jbusres.2015.10.088

Chang, M., Chang, B., & Dutta, S. (2020). National culture, firm characteristics, and dividend policy. *Emerging Markets Finance and Trade, 56*(1), 149–163. doi:10.1080/1540496X.2019.167518

Chang, R. P., & Rhee, S. G. (1990). The impact of personal taxes on corporate dividend policy and capital structure decisions. *FM: The Journal of the Financial Management Association, 19*(2), 21–31.

Charoensukmongkol, P., & Sexton, S. (2011). The effect of corruption on exports and imports in Latin America and the Caribbean. *Latin American Business Review, 12*(2), 83–98. doi:10.1080/10978526.2011.592800

Charron, N. (2009). The impact of socio-political integration and press freedom on corruption. *The Journal of Development Studies, 45*(9), 1472–1493. doi:10.1080/00220380902890243

Charumilind, C., Kali, R., & Wiwattanakantang, Y. (2006). Connected lending: Thailand before the financial crisis. *The Journal of Business, 79*(1), 181–218.

Cheibub, J. A. & Przeworski, A. (1999). Democracy, elections, and accountability for economic outcomes. *Democracy, Accountability, and Representation, 2*, 222–250.

Chen, R., El Ghoul, S., Guedhami, O., & Wang, H. (2017). Do state and foreign ownership affect investment efficiency? Evidence from privatizations. *Journal of Corporate Finance, 42*, 408–421.

Chen, C. J. P., Ding, Y., & Kim, C. (2010). High-level politically connected firms, corruption, and analyst forecast accuracy around the world. *Journal of International Business Studies, 41*(9), 1505–1524. doi:10.1057/jibs.2010.27

Chen, J., Dong, W., Tong, J. Y., & Zhang, F. F. (2018). Corporate philanthropy and investment efficiency: empirical evidence from China. *Pacific-Basin Finance Journal, 51*, 392–409. https://doi.org/10.1016/j.pacfin.2018.08.008

Chen, J., Leung, W. S., & Evans, K. P. (2018). Female board representation, corporate innovation and firm performance. *Journal of Empirical Finance, 48*, 236–254. https://doi.org/10.1016/j.jempfin.2018.07.003

Chen, J. J. (2004). Determinants of capital structure of Chinese-listed companies. *Journal of Business Research, 57*(12), 1341–1351. https://doi.org/10.1016/S0148-2963(03)00070-5

Chen, M., Jeon, B. N., Wang, R., & Wu, J. (2015). Corruption and bank risk-taking: evidence from emerging economies.

*Emerging Markets Review, 24*, 122–148. https://doi.org/10.1016/j.ememar.2015.05.009

Chen, N. (2011). Securities laws, control of corruption, and corporate liquidity: international evidence. *Corporate Governance: An International Review, 19*(1), 3–24. https://doi.org/10.1111/j.1467-8683.2010.00823.x

Chen, S.-S., Chou, R. K., & Lee, Y.-C. (2014). The long-term performance following dividend initiations and resumptions revisited. *Journal of Economics and Finance, 38*(4), 643–657. doi:10.1007/s12197-012-9243-x

Chen, X., Le, C. H. A., Shan, Y., & Taylor, S. (2020). Australian policy uncertainty and corporate investment. *Pacific-Basin Finance Journal, 61*, 101341. https://doi.org/10.1016/j.pacfin.2020.101341

Chen, Z., Cheung, Y.-L., Stouraitis, A., & Wong, A. W. S. (2005). Ownership concentration, firm performance, and dividend policy in Hong Kong. *Pacific-Basin Finance Journal, 13*(4), 431–449. http://dx.doi.org/10.1016/j.pacfin.2004.12.001

Chenery, H. B. (1952). Overcapacity and the acceleration principle. *Econometrica: Journal of the Econometric Society*, 1–28.

Cheng, S.-R., & Shiu, C.-Y. (2007). Investor protection and capital structure: international evidence. *Journal of Multinational Financial Management, 17*(1), 30–44. https://doi.org/10.1016/j.mulfin.2006.03.002

Chiou, W.-J. P., Lee, A. C., & Lee, C.-F. (2010). Stock return, risk, and legal environment around the world. *International Review of Economics & Finance, 19*(1), 95–105. https://doi.org/10.1016/j.iref.2009.05.001

Chiu, C.-J., Ho, A. Y.-F., & Tsai, L.-F. (2022). Effects of financial constraints and managerial overconfidence on investment-cash flow sensitivity. *International Review of Economics & Finance, 82*, 135–155. https://doi.org/10.1016/j.iref.2022.06.008

Cho, S.-S., El Ghoul, S., Guedhami, O., & Suh, J. (2014). Creditor rights and capital structure: evidence from international data. *Journal of Corporate Finance, 25*, 40–60. http://dx.doi.org/10.1016/j.jcorpfin.2013.10.007

Choe, H., Kho, B.-C., & Stulz, R. M. (2005). Do domestic investors have an edge? The trading experience of foreign investors in Korea. *The Review of Financial Studies, 18*(3), 795–829.

Choi, J. P., & Thum, M. (2005). Corruption and the shadow economy. *International Economic Review, 46*(3), 817–836.

Choi, K.-S. (2020). National culture and R&D investments. *The European Journal of Finance, 26*(6), 500–531. doi:10.1080/1351847X.2019.1697324

Chonko, L. B., & Hunt, S. D. (1985). Ethics and marketing management: an empirical examination. *Journal of Business Research, 13*(4), 339–359.

Chow, Y. P., Muhammad, J., Bany-Ariffin, A. N., & Cheng, F. F. (2018). Macroeconomic uncertainty, corporate governance and corporate capital structure. *International Journal of Managerial Finance, 14*(3), 301–321. doi:10.1108/IJMF-08-2017-0156

Chowdhury, S. K. (2004). The effect of democracy and press freedom on corruption: an empirical test. *Economics Letters, 85*(1), 93–101. https://doi.org/10.1016/j.econlet.2004.03.024

Chui, A. C., Lloyd, A. E., & Kwok, C. C. (2002). The determination of capital structure: is national culture a missing piece to the puzzle? *Journal of International Business Studies, 33*(1), 99–127.

Ciocchini, F., Durbin, E., & Ng, D. T. C. (2003). Does corruption increase emerging market bond spreads? *Journal of Economics and Business, 55*(5), 503–528. https://doi.org/10.1016/S0148-6195(03)00052-3

Claessens, S., & Djankov, S. (1999). Ownership concentration and corporate performance in the Czech Republic. *Journal of Comparative Economics, 27*(3), 498–513.

Claessens, S., Feijen, E., & Laeven, L. (2008). Political connections and preferential access to finance: the role of campaign contributions. *Journal of Financial Economics, 88*(3), 554–580.

Clark, J. M. (1917). Business acceleration and the law of demand: a technical factor in economic cycles. *Journal of Political Economy, 25*(3), 217–235.

Cohen, D. V., & Nelson, K. A. (1992). *Multinational Ethics Programs: Cases in Corporate Practice*. Bentley College.

Cohn, A., Maréchal, M. A., Tannenbaum, D., & Zünd, C. L. (2019). Civic honesty around the globe. *Science, 365*(6448), 70–73.

Cole, M. A. (2007). Corruption, income and the environment: an empirical analysis. *Ecological Economics, 62*(3), 637–647. https://doi.org/10.1016/j.ecolecon.2006.08.003

Cong, L. W., Gao, H., Ponticelli, J., & Yang, X. (2018). Credit allocation under economic stimulus: evidence from China. *Buffett Institute Global Poverty Research Lab Working Paper* (pp. 17–108).

Cooray, A., & Schneider, F. (2016). Does corruption promote emigration? An empirical examination. *Journal of Population Economics, 29*(1), 293–310. doi:10.1007/s00148-015-0563-y

Corrado, G., & Rossetti, F. (2018). Public corruption: a study across regions in Italy. *Journal of Policy Modeling, 40*(6), 1126–1139. https://doi.org/10.1016/j.jpolmod.2018.01.001

Crane, A. D., Michenaud, S., & Weston, J. P. (2016). The effect of institutional ownership on payout policy: evidence from index thresholds. *The Review of Financial Studies, 29*(6), 1377–1408. doi:10.1093/rfs/hhw012

D'Acunto, F., Liu, R., Pflueger, C., & Weber, M. (2018). Flexible prices and leverage. *Journal of Financial Economics, 129*(1), 46–68. https://doi.org/10.1016/j.jfineco.2018.03.009

D'souza, J., & Megginson, W. L. (1999). The financial and operating performance of privatized firms during the 1990s. *The Journal of Finance, 54*(4), 1397–1438.

Damania, R., Fredriksson, P. G., & Mani, M. (2004). The persistence of corruption and regulatory compliance failures: theory and evidence. *Public Choice, 121*(3), 363–390. doi:10.1007/s11127-004-1684-0

Dang, C., Li, Z., & Yang, C. (2018). Measuring firm size in empirical corporate finance. *Journal of Banking & Finance, 86*, 159–176. https://doi.org/10.1016/j.jbankfin.2017.09.006

Das, A., & Parry, M. (2011). Greasing or sanding? GMM estimation of the corruption-investment relationship. *International Journal of Environmental Research, 2*(2), 95–108.

Das, J., & DiRienzo, C. (2009). The nonlinear impact of globalization on corruption. *The International Journal of Business and Finance Research, 3*(2), 33–46.

Dass, N., Nanda, V., & Xiao, S. C. (2017). Is there a local culture of corruption in the US. Georgia Institute of Technology Working Paper.

Davidson, W. H. (1980). The location of foreign direct investment activity: country characteristics and experience effects. *Journal of International Business Studies*, *11*(2), 9–22. doi:10.1057/palgrave.jibs.8490602

Davis, J. (2004). Corruption in public service delivery: experience from South Asia's water and sanitation sector. *World Development*, *32*(1), 53–71. https://doi.org/10.1016/j.worlddev.2003.07.003

Davis, J. H., & Ruhe, J. A. (2003). Perceptions of country corruption: antecedents and outcomes. *Journal of Business Ethics*, *43*(4), 275–288. doi:10.1023/A:1023038901080

De Carvalho, A. G. (2009). The effect of institutions on the external financing of Brazilian firms. *Revista Brasileira de Finanças*, *7*(1), 1–27.

De Jong, A., Kabir, R., & Nguyen, T. T. (2008). Capital structure around the world: the roles of firm- and country-specific determinants. *Journal of Banking & Finance*, *32*(9), 1954–1969. https://doi.org/10.1016/j.jbankfin.2007.12.034

De Jong, E., & Bogmans, C. (2011). Does corruption discourage international trade? *European Journal of Political Economy*, *27*(2), 385–398. https://doi.org/10.1016/j.ejpoleco.2010.11.005

De Miguel, A., & Pindado, J. (2001). Determinants of capital structure: new evidence from Spanish panel data. *Journal of Corporate Finance*, *7*(1), 77–99. http://dx.doi.org/10.1016/S0929-1199(00)00020-1

De Tocqueville, A. (1988). *Democracy in America* (1840). Trans. George Lawrence. New York: Harper Perennial.

DeAngelo, H., & DeAngelo, L. (2006). The irrelevance of the MM dividend irrelevance theorem. *Journal of Financial Economics*, *79*(2), 293–315. http://dx.doi.org/10.1016/j.jfineco.2005.03.003

DeAngelo, H., DeAngelo, L., & Stulz, R. M. (2006). Dividend policy and the earned/contributed capital mix: a test of the life-cycle theory. *Journal of Financial Economics*, *81*(2), 227–254. http://dx.doi.org/10.1016/j.jfineco.2005.07.005

DeAngelo, H., & Masulis, R. W. (1980). Optimal capital structure under corporate and personal taxation. *Journal of Financial Economics*, *8*(1), 3–29. http://dx.doi.org/10.1016/0304-405X(80)90019-7

Debski, J., Jetter, M., Mösle, S., & Stadelmann, D. (2018). Gender and corruption: the neglected role of culture. *European Journal of Political Economy, 55*, 526–537. https://doi.org/10.1016/j.ejpoleco.2018.05.002

Deesomsak, R., Paudyal, K., & Pescetto, G. (2004). The determinants of capital structure: evidence from the Asia Pacific region. *Journal of Multinational Financial Management, 14*(4), 387–405. https://doi.org/10.1016/j.mulfin.2004.03.001

Delavallade, C. (2006). Corruption and distribution of public spending in developing countries. *Journal of Economics and Finance, 30*(2), 222–239. doi:10.1007/BF02761488

Dell'Anno, R., & Teobaldelli, D. (2015). Keeping both corruption and the shadow economy in check: the role of decentralization. *International Tax and Public Finance, 22*(1), 1–40. doi:10.1007/s10797-013-9298-4

Deloof, M., Roggeman, A., & van Overfelt, W. (2010). Bank affiliations and corporate dividend policy in pre-World War I Belgium. *Business History, 52*(4), 590–616. doi:10.1080/000767910 03753178

Demirgüç-Kunt, A., & Maksimovic, V. (1996). Stock market development and financing choices of firms. *The World Bank Economic Review, 10*(2), 341–369. doi:10.1093/wber/10.2.341

Demirgüç-Kunt, A., & Maksimovic, V. (1999). Institutions, financial markets, and firm debt maturity. *Journal of Financial Economics, 54*(3), 295–336. http://dx.doi.org/10.1016/S0304-405X(99)00039-2

Denis, D. J., & Denis, D. K. (1993). Managerial discretion, organizational structure, and corporate performance: a study of leveraged recapitalizations. *Journal of Accounting and Economics, 16*(1), 209–236. https://doi.org/10.1016/0165-4101 (93)90011-4

Denis, D. J., & Osobov, I. (2008). Why do firms pay dividends? International evidence on the determinants of dividend policy. *Journal of Financial Economics, 89*(1), 62–82. http://dx.doi.org/10.1016/j.jfineco.2007.06.006

Desender, K. A., Aguilera, R. V., Lópezpuertas-Lamy, M., & Crespi, R. (2016). A clash of governance logics: foreign ownership and board monitoring. *Strategic Management Journal, 37*(2), 349–369.

Deshmukh, S., Goel, A. M., & Howe, K. M. (2013). CEO overconfidence and dividend policy. *Journal of Financial Intermediation, 22*(3), 440–463. https://doi.org/10.1016/j.jfi.2013.02.003

Dewaelheyns, N., Van Hulle, C., & Van Landuyt, Y. (2019). Employment protection and SME capital structure decisions. *Journal of Small Business Management, 57*(4), 1232–1251. https://doi.org/10.1111/jsbm.12383

DeWenter, K. L., & Malatesta, P. H. (2001). State-owned and privately owned firms: an empirical analysis of profitability, leverage, and labor intensity. *American Economic Review, 91*(1), 320–334. doi:10.1257/aer.91.1.320

Dimant, E., Krieger, T., & Meierrieks, D. (2013). The effect of corruption on migration,1985–2000. *Applied Economics Letters, 20*(13), 1270–1274. doi:10.1080/13504851.2013.806776

Dincer, O. (2019). Does corruption slow down innovation? Evidence from a cointegrated panel of U.S. states. *European Journal of Political Economy, 56*, 1–10. https://doi.org/10.1016/j.ejpoleco.2018.06.001

Dincer, O. C. (2008). Ethnic and religious diversity and corruption. *Economics Letters, 99*(1), 98–102. https://doi.org/10.1016/j.econlet.2007.06.003

Dincer, O. C., & Gunalp, B. (2005). *Corruption, Income Inequality and Growth: Evidence from US States.* Department of Commerce, Massey University at Albany.

Dincer, O. C., & Johnston, M. (2014). Corruption issues in state and local politics: is political culture a deep determinant? *Edmond J. Safra Working Papers* (48).

Ding, S., Kim, M., & Zhang, X. (2018). Do firms care about investment opportunities? Evidence from China. *Journal of Corporate Finance, 52*, 214–237. https://doi.org/10.1016/j.jcorpfin.2018.07.003

Dinh Nguyen, D., To, T. H., Nguyen, D. V., & Phuong Do, H. (2021). Managerial overconfidence and dividend policy in Vietnamese enterprises. *Cogent Economics & Finance, 9*(1), 1885195. doi:10.1080/23322039.2021.1885195

Dixit, A. K., Dixit, R. K., & Pindyck, R. S. (1994). *Investment Under Uncertainty.* New Haven: Princeton University Press.

Dizaji, S. F., Farzanegan, M. R., & Naghavi, A. (2016). Political institutions and government spending behavior: theory and evidence from Iran. *International Tax and Public Finance, 23*(3), 522–549. doi:10.1007/s10797-015-9378-8

Do, T. K., Lai, T. N., & Tran, T. T. (2020). Foreign ownership and capital structure dynamics. *Finance Research Letters, 36,* 101337.

Dollar, D., Fisman, R., & Gatti, R. (2001). Are women really the "fairer" sex? Corruption and women in government. *Journal of Economic Behavior & Organization, 46*(4), 423–429. https://doi.org/10.1016/S0167-2681(01)00169-X

Dominik, H., & Heldman, C. (2017). Causes and consequences of corruption: an overview of empirical results. *IW Report.* Cologne: Institute der Deutschen Wirtschaft Köln.

Donaldson, G. (1961). *Corporate Debt Capacity: A Study of Corporate Debt Policy and the Determination of Corporate Debt Capacity.* Boston: Harvard Graduate School of Business Administration.

Donchev, D., & Ujhelyi, G. (2014). What do corruption indices measure? *Economics & Politics, 26*(2), 309–331. https://doi.org/10.1111/ecpo.12037

Donfouet, H. P. P., Jeanty, P. W., & Malin, E. (2018). Analysing spatial spillovers in corruption: a dynamic spatial panel data approach. *Papers in Regional Science, 97*(S1), S63–S78. https://doi.org/10.1111/pirs.12231

Dong, B., Chen, Y., & Fan, C. (2022). Local corruption and dividend policy: evidence from China. *Finance Research Letters, 47,* 102698. https://doi.org/10.1016/j.frl.2022.102698

Dong, B., & Torgler, B. (2011). Democracy, property rights, income equality, and corruption. Nota Di Lavoro. Global Challenges Series. Fondazione Eni Enrico Mattei.

Dong, B., & Torgler, B. (2013). Causes of corruption: evidence from China. *China Economic Review, 26,* 152–169. https://doi.org/10.1016/j.chieco.2012.09.005

Douglas Beets, S. (2007). Global corruption and religion: an empirical examination. *Journal of Global Ethics, 3*(1), 69–85. doi:10.1080/17449620600991614

Dreher, A., & Gassebner, M. (2013). Greasing the wheels? The impact of regulations and corruption on firm entry. *Public Choice, 155*(3–4), 413–432.

Dreher, A., & Herzfeld, T. (2005). The economic costs of corruption: a survey and new evidence. Available at SSRN 734184.

Dreher, A., Kotsogiannis, C., & McCorriston, S. (2008). How do institutions affect corruption and the shadow economy? *International Tax and Public Finance, 16*(6), 773. doi:10.1007/s10797-008-9089-5

Dreher, A., & Schneider, F. (2010). Corruption and the shadow economy: an empirical analysis. *Public Choice, 144*(1), 215–238. doi:10.1007/s11127-009-9513-0

Driffield, N., Mahambare, V., & Pal, S. (2007). How does ownership structure affect capital structure and firm value Recent evidence from East Asia. *Economics of Transition and Institutional Change, 15*(3), 535–573. https://doi.org/10.1111/j.1468-0351.2007.00291.x

Driffield, N., & Pal, S. (2001). The East Asian crisis and financing corporate investment: is there a cause for concern? *Journal of Asian Economics, 12*(4), 507–527. http://dx.doi.org/10.1016/S1049-0078(01)00099-9

Drobetz, W., El Ghoul, S., Guedhami, O., & Janzen, M. (2018). Policy uncertainty, investment, and the cost of capital. *Journal of Financial Stability, 39*, 28–45. https://doi.org/10.1016/j.jfs.2018.08.005

Drobetz, W., & Wanzenried, G. (2006). What determines the speed of adjustment to the target capital structure? *Applied Financial Economics, 16*(13), 941–958. doi:10.1080/09603100500426358

Du, J. (2008). Corruption and corporate finance patterns: an international perspective. *Pacific Economic Review, 13*(2), 183–208. https://doi.org/10.1111/j.1468-0106.2008.00396.x

Du, J., & Dai, Y. (2005). Ultimate corporate ownership structures and capital structures: evidence from East Asian economies. *Corporate Governance: An International Review, 13*(1), 60–71. https://doi.org/10.1111/j.1467-8683.2005.00403.x

Du, J., Li, W., Lin, B., & Wang, Y. (2018). Government integrity and corporate investment efficiency. *China Journal of Accounting Research, 11*(3), 213–232. https://doi.org/10.1016/j.cjar.2017.03.002

Du, Q., Hasan, I., Wang, Y., & Wei, K. (2020). Local corruption, whistleblowing, and debt financing. *Whistleblowing, and Debt Financing* (May 1, 2020).

Du, Q., & Heo, Y. (2022). Political corruption, Dodd–Frank whistleblowing, and corporate investment. *Journal of Corporate Finance, 73,* 102145. https://doi.org/10.1016/j.jcorpfin.2021.102145

Ducassy, I., & Guyot, A. (2017). Complex ownership structures, corporate governance and firm performance: the French context. *Research in International Business and Finance, 39,* 291–306.

Durnev, A., & Fauver, L. (2008). Stealing from thieves: firm governance and performance when states are predatory. *CEI Working Paper Series 2008–12.* Center for Economic Institutions, Institute of Economic Research, Hitotsubashi University.

Durnev, A., & Kim, E. H. (2007). Explaining differences in the quality of governance among companies: evidence from emerging markets. *Journal of Applied Corporate Finance, 19*(1), 16–24.

Dutt, P., & Traca, D. (2010). Corruption and bilateral trade flows: extortion or evasion? *The Review of Economics and Statistics, 92*(4), 843–860. doi:10.1162/REST_a_00034

Dvořák, T. (2005). Do domestic investors have an information advantage? Evidence from Indonesia. *The Journal of Finance, 60*(2), 817–839.

Dwiputri, I. N., Arsyad, L., & Pradiptyo, R. (2018). *The Corruption-Income Inequality Trap: A Study of Asian Countries.* Retrieved from Economics Discussion Papers.

Eades, K. M. (1982, 1982/11). *Empirical Evidence on Dividends as a Signal of Firm Value.*

Eagly, A. H. (1987). Sex differences in social behavior: a social-role analysis. *Hillsdale, NJ: Lawrence Erlbaum.* doi:10.0146167204271177

Eagly, A. H., & Wood, W. (2016). Social role theory of sex differences. *The Wiley Blackwell Encyclopedia of Gender and Sexuality Studies* (pp. 1–3). Malden, MA: Wiley-Blackwell.

Easterbrook, F. H. (1984). Two agency-cost explanations of dividends. *American Economic Review, 74*(4), 650.

Ebeh Ezeoha, A. (2011). Firm versus industry financing structures in Nigeria. *African Journal of Economic and Management Studies, 2*(1), 42–55. doi:10.1108/20400701111110768

Edgardo Campos, J., Lien, D., & Pradhan, S. (1999). The impact of corruption on investment: predictability matters. *World Development*, *27*(6), 1059–1067. https://doi.org/10.1016/S0305-750X(99)00040-6

Egger, P., & Winner, H. (2005). Evidence on corruption as an incentive for foreign direct investment. *European Journal of Political Economy*, *21*(4), 932–952. https://doi.org/10.1016/j.ejpoleco.2005.01.002

Egger, P., & Winner, H. (2006). How corruption influences foreign direct investment: a panel data study. *Economic Development and Cultural Change*, *54*(2), 459–486. doi:10.1086/497010

Eisenberg, T., Sundgren, S., & Wells, M. T. (1998). Larger board size and decreasing firm value in small firms. *Journal of Financial Economics*, *48*(1), 35–54. http://dx.doi.org/10.1016/S0304-405X(98)00003-8

Elbahnasawy, N. G. (2014). E-government, internet adoption, and corruption: an empirical investigation. *World Development*, *57*, 114–126. https://doi.org/10.1016/j.worlddev.2013.12.005

Elbahnasawy, N. G., & Revier, C. F. (2012). The determinants of corruption: cross-country-panel-data analysis. *The Developing Economies*, *50*(4), 311–333. https://doi.org/10.1111/j.1746-1049.2012.00177.x

Eldomiaty, T. I. (2007). Determinants of corporate capital structure: evidence from an emerging economy. *International Journal of Commerce and Management*, *17*(1/2), 25–43. doi:10.1108/10569210710774730

Eldomiaty, T. I., & Azim, M. H. (2008). The dynamics of capital structure and heterogeneous systematic risk classes in Egypt. *International Journal of Emerging Markets*, *3*(1), 7–37. doi:10.1108/17468800810849204

Elgebeily, E., Guermat, C., & Vendrame, V. (2021). Managerial optimism and investment decision in the UK. *Journal of Behavioral and Experimental Finance*, *31*, 100519. https://doi.org/10.1016/j.jbef.2021.100519

Elliott, K. A. (1997). *Corruption and the Global Economy*. Peterson Institute.

Elliott, K. A. (2017). Corruption as an international policy problem. *Political Corruption* (pp. 925–942). London: Routledge.

Ellis, J., Smith, J., & White, R. (2020). Corruption and corporate innovation. *Journal of Financial and Quantitative Analysis, 55*(7), 2124–2149. doi:10.1017/S0022109019000735

Erickson, T., & Whited, T. M. (2000). Measurement error and the relationship between investment and q. *Journal of Political Economy, 108*(5), 1027–1057.

Eriotis, N., Vasiliou, D., & Ventoura-Neokosmidi, Z. (2007). How firm characteristics affect capital structure: an empirical study. *Managerial Finance, 33*(5), 321–331. doi:10.1108/0307435071 0739605

Errath, B. (2006). Business against corruption: case stories and examples. Implementation of the *10th United Nations Global Compact Principle Against Corruption* Birgit Errath (ed). United Nations Global Compact Office.

Esarey, J., & Schwindt-Bayer, L. A. (2018). Women's representation, accountability and corruption in democracies. *British Journal of Political Science, 48*(3), 659–690. doi:10.1017/S0007123416000478

Espen Eckbo, B., & Verma, S. (1994). Managerial shareownership, voting power, and cash dividend policy. *Journal of Corporate Finance, 1*(1), 33–62. http://dx.doi.org/10.1016/ 0929-1199(94)90009-4

Ettema, J. S. (2007). Journalism as reason-giving: deliberative democracy, institutional accountability, and the news media's mission. *Political Communication, 24*(2), 143–160. doi:10.1080/10584600701312860

Faccio, M., Marchica, M.-T., & Mura, R. (2016). CEO gender, corporate risk-taking, and the efficiency of capital allocation. *Journal of Corporate Finance, 39*, 193–209. http://dx.doi.org/10.1016/ j.jcorpfin.2016.02.008

Faccio, M., Masulis, R. W., & McConnell, J. J. (2006). Political connections and corporate bailouts. *The Journal of Finance, 61*(6), 2597–2635. doi:10.1111/j.1540-6261.2006.01000.x

Fairchild, R. (2010). Dividend policy, signalling and free cash flow: an integrated approach. *Managerial Finance, 36*(5), 394–413. doi:10.1108/03074351011039427

Fama, E. F. (1980). Agency problems and the theory of the firm. *Journal of Political Economy. April,* 288–307.

Fama, E. F., & French, K. R. (2001). Disappearing dividends: changing firm characteristics or lower propensity to pay? *Journal of Financial Economics, 60*(1), 3–43. http://dx.doi.org/10.1016/S0304-405X(01)00038-1

Fama, E. F., & French, K. R. (2002). Testing trade-off and pecking order predictions about dividends and debt. *The Review of Financial Studies, 15*(1), 1–33. doi:10.1093/rfs/15.1.1

Fama, E. F., & Jensen, M. C. (1983). Agency problems and residual claims. *The Journal of Law and Economics, 26*(2), 327–349.

Fan, C. S., Lin, C., & Treisman, D. (2009). Political decentralization and corruption: evidence from around the world. *Journal of Public Economics, 93*(1), 14–34. https://doi.org/10.1016/j.jpubeco.2008.09.001

Fan, H., & Sundaresan, S. M. (2000). Debt valuation, renegotiation, and optimal dividend policy. *Review of Financial Studies, 13*(4), 1057–099. Retrieved from http://www.scopus.com/inward/record.url?eid=2-s2.0-0039004405&partnerID=40&md5=250313f4ca4edc1db498e4b8bab0107c

Fan, J. P., Titman, S., & Twite, G. (2012). An international comparison of capital structure and debt maturity choices. *Journal of Financial Quantitative Analysis, 47*(1), 23–56.

Fan, J. P., & Wong, T. J. (2002). Corporate ownership structure and the informativeness of accounting earnings in East Asia. *Journal of Accounting and Economics, 33*(3), 401–425.

Fan, J. P. H., Rui, O. M., & Zhao, M. (2008). Public governance and corporate finance: evidence from corruption cases. *Journal of Comparative Economics, 36*(3), 343–64. https://doi.org/10.1016/j.jce.2008.05.001

Farag, H., & Mallin, C. (2018). The influence of CEO demographic characteristics on corporate risk-taking: evidence from Chinese IPOs. *The European Journal of Finance, 24*(16), 1528–1551. doi:10.1080/1351847X.2016.1151454

Färdigh, M. A., Andersson, E., & Oscarsson, H. (2011). Re-examining the relationship between press freedom and corruption. *QoG Working Paper Series, 13*, 1–32.

Farinha, J. (2003). Dividend policy, corporate governance and the managerial entrenchment hypothesis: an empirical analysis.

*Journal of Business Finance and Accounting, 30*(9-10), 1173–1209. doi:10.1111/j.0306-686X.2003.05624.x

Farinha, J., & Lopez-De-Foronda, O. (2009). The relation between dividends and insider ownership in different legal systems: international evidence. *European Journal of Finance, 15*(2), 169–189. doi:10.1080/13518470802588718

Farooq, O. (2015). Effect of ownership concentration on capital structure: evidence from the MENA region. *International Journal of Islamic and Middle Eastern Finance and Management, 8*(1), 99–113. doi:10.1108/IMEFM-10-2013-0115

Farooq, O., & Ahmed, N. (2019). Dividend policy and political uncertainty: evidence from the US presidential elections. *Research in International Business and Finance, 48*, 201–209. https://doi.org/10.1016/j.ribaf.2019.01.003

Farzanegan, M. R., & Witthuhn, S. (2017). Corruption and political stability: does the youth bulge matter? *European Journal of Political Economy, 49*, 47–70. https://doi.org/10.1016/j.ejpoleco.2016.12.007

Fauver, L., & McDonald, M. B. (2015). Culture, agency costs, and governance: international evidence on capital structure. *Pacific-Basin Finance Journal, 34*, 1–23. https://doi.org/10.1016/j.pacfin.2015.05.001

Fazzari, S., Hubbard, R. G., & Petersen, B. C. (1987). *Financing Constraints and Corporate Investment.* Cambridge, MA: National Bureau of Economic Research.

Fazzari, S., Hubbard, R. G., & Petersen, B. (1988). Investment, financing decisions, and tax policy. *The American economic review, 78*(2), 200–205.

Feidakis, A., & Rovolis, A. (2007). Capital structure choice in European Union: evidence from the construction industry. *Applied Financial Economics, 17*(12), 989–1002. doi:10.1080/09603100600749311

Feng, Y., Hassan, A., & Elamer, A. A. (2020). Corporate governance, ownership structure and capital structure: evidence from Chinese real estate listed companies. *International Journal of Accounting & Information Management, 28*(4), 759–783. doi:10.1108/IJAIM-04-2020-0042

Ferderer, J. P. (1993). The impact of uncertainty on aggregate investment spending: an empirical analysis. *Journal of Money, Credit and Banking, 25*(1), 30–48.

Ferris, S. P., Javakhadze, D., & Rajkovic, T. (2019). An international analysis of CEO social capital and corporate risk-taking. *European Financial Management, 25*(1), 3–37. https://doi.org/10.1111/eufm.12156

Ferris, S. P., Jayaraman, N., & Sabherwal, S. (2009). Catering effects in corporate dividend policy: the international evidence. *Journal of Banking & Finance, 33*(9), 1730–1738. http://dx.doi.org/10.1016/j.jbankfin.2009.04.005

Firstenberg, P. B., & Malkiel, B. G. (1994). The twenty-first century boardroom: who will be in charge? *MIT Sloan Management Review, 36*(1), 27.

Fischer, E. M., Reuber, A. R., & Dyke, L. S. (1993). A theoretical overview and extension of research on sex, gender, and entrepreneurship. *Journal of Business Venturing, 8*(2), 151–168. https://doi.org/10.1016/0883-9026(93)90017-Y

Fishman, A., & Rob, R. (1999). The size of firms and R&D investment. *International Economic Review, 40*(4), 915–931.

Fisman, R. (2001). Estimating the value of political connections. *American Economic Review, 91*(4), 1095–1102. doi:10.1257/aer.91.4.1095

Fisman, R., & Gatti, R. (2000). Decentralization and corruption. *Policy Research Working Paper* (2290).

Fisman, R., & Gatti, R. (2002a). Decentralization and corruption: evidence across countries. *Journal of Public Economics, 83*(3), 325–345. https://doi.org/10.1016/S0047-2727(00)00158-4

Fisman, R., & Gatti, R. (2002b). Decentralization and corruption: evidence from U.S. federal transfer programs. *Public Choice, 113*(1), 25–35. doi:10.1023/A:1020311511787

Fisman, R., & Miguel, E. (2007). Corruption, norms, and legal enforcement: evidence from diplomatic parking tickets. *Journal of Political Economy, 115*(6), 1020–1048. doi:10.1086/527495

Fjelde, H. (2009). Buying peace? Oil wealth, corruption and civil war, 1985–99. *Journal of Peace Research, 46*(2), 199–218. doi:10.1177/0022343308100715

Fjelde, H., & Hegre, H. (2014). Political corruption and institutional stability. *Studies in Comparative International Development, 49*(3), 267–299. doi:10.1007/s12116-014-9155-1

Flannery, M. J., Kwan, S. H., & Nimalendran, M. (2013). The 2007–2009 financial crisis and bank opaqueness. *Journal of Financial Intermediation, 22*(1), 55–84.

Flyvbjerg, B. (2007). Cost overruns and demand shortfalls in urban rail and other infrastructure. *Transportation Planning and Technology, 30*(1), 9–30. doi:10.1080/03081060701207938

Fosberg, R. H. (2004). Agency problems and debt financing: leadership structure effects. *Corporate Governance: The International Journal of Business in Society, 4*(1), 31–38. doi:10.1108/14720700410521943

Francis, B. B., Hasan, I., & Zhu, Y. (2014). Political uncertainty and bank loan contracting. *Journal of Empirical Finance, 29*, 281–286. https://doi.org/10.1016/j.jempfin.2014.08.004

Frank, M. Z., & Goyal, V. K. (2009). Capital structure decisions: which factors are reliably important? *Financial Management, 38*(1), 1–37.

Fredriksson, P. G., List, J. A., & Millimet, D. L. (2003). Bureaucratic corruption, environmental policy and inbound US FDI: theory and evidence. *Journal of Public Economics, 87*(7), 1407–1430. https://doi.org/10.1016/S0047-2727(02)00016-6

Fredriksson, P. G., Vollebergh, H. R. J., & Dijkgraaf, E. (2004). Corruption and energy efficiency in OECD countries: theory and evidence. *Journal of Environmental Economics and Management, 47*(2), 207–231. https://doi.org/10.1016/j.jeem.2003.08.001

Freille, S., Haque, M. E., & Kneller, R. (2007). A contribution to the empirics of press freedom and corruption. *European Journal of Political Economy, 23*(4), 838–862. https://doi.org/10.1016/j.ejpoleco.2007.03.002

Friedman, E., Johnson, S., Kaufmann, D., & Zoido-Lobaton, P. (2000). Dodging the grabbing hand: the determinants of unofficial activity in 69 countries. *Journal of Public Economics, 76*(3), 459–493. https://doi.org/10.1016/S0047-2727(99)00093-6

Frye, M. B., & Pham, D. T. (2018). CEO gender and corporate board structures. *The Quarterly Review of Economics and Finance, 69*, 110–124. https://doi.org/10.1016/j.qref.2017.12.002

Galtung, F., & Pope, J. (1999). *The Global Coalition Against Corruption: Evaluating Transparency International* (pp. 257–282). Boulder, CO: Lynne Rienner Publishers.

Gan, W., & Xu, X. (2019). Does anti-corruption campaign promote corporate R&D investment? Evidence from China. *Finance Research Letters, 30*, 292–296. https://doi.org/10.1016/j.frl.2018.10.012

Ganguli, S. K. (2013). Capital structure — does ownership structure matter? Theory and Indian evidence. *Studies in Economics and Finance, 30*(1), 56–72. doi:10.1108/10867371311300982

Garner, J. L., & Kim, W. Y. (2013). Are foreign investors really beneficial? Evidence from South Korea. *Pacific-Basin Finance Journal, 25*, 62–84. https://doi.org/10.1016/j.pacfin.2013.08.003

Gaud, P., Jani, E., Hoesli, M., & Bender, A. (2005). The capital structure of swiss companies: an empirical analysis using dynamic panel data. *European Financial Management, 11*(1), 51–69. https://doi.org/10.1111/j.1354-7798.2005.00275.x

Gerring, J., & Thacker, S. C. (2005). Do neoliberal policies deter political corruption? *International Organization, 59*(1), 233–254. doi:10.1017/S0020818305050083

Gertler, M., & Gilchrist, S. (1994). Monetary policy, business cycles, and the behavior of small manufacturing firms. *The Quarterly Journal of Economics, 109*(2), 309–340.

Getz, K. A., & Volkema, R. J. (2001). Culture, perceived corruption, and economics: a model of predictors and outcomes. *Business & society, 40*(1), 7–30.

Ghaniy, N., & Hastiadi, F. F. (2017). Political, social and economic determinants of corruption. *International Journal of Economics and Financial Issues, 7*(4), 144–149.

Ghosal, V., & Loungani, P. (1996). Firm size and the impact of profit-margin uncertainty on investment: do financing constraints play a role? *International Finance Discussion Papers 557*, Board of Governors of the Federal Reserve System (U.S.).

Ghose, B., & Kabra, K. C. (2019). Firm profitability and adjustment of capital structure: Indian evidence. *Vision, 23*(3), 297–308. doi:10.1177/0972262919855804

Ghosh, C., & Woolridge, J. R. (1989). Stock-market reaction to growth-induced dividend cuts: are investors myopic? *Managerial & Decision Economics, 10*(1), 25–35.

Gil-Pareja, S., Llorca-Vivero, R., & Martínez-Serrano, J. A. (2019). Corruption and international trade: a comprehensive analysis with gravity. *Applied Economic Analysis, 27*(79), 3–20. doi:10.1108/AEA-06-2019-0003

Gilchrist, S., Sim, J. W., & Zakrajšek, E. (2014). *Uncertainty, Financial Frictions, and Investment Dynamics*. National Bureau of Economic Research.

Gillan, S., & Starks, L. T. (2003). Corporate governance, corporate ownership, and the role of institutional investors: a global perspective. *Journal of Applied Finance, 13*(2).

Glaeser, E. L., & Saks, R. E. (2006). Corruption in America. *Journal of Public Economics, 90*(6), 1053–1072. https://doi.org/10.1016/j.jpubeco.2005.08.007

Gleason, K. C., Mathur, L. K., & Mathur, I. (2000). The interrelationship between culture, capital structure, and performance: evidence from european retailers. *Journal of Business Research, 50*(2), 185–191. https://doi.org/10.1016/S0148-2963(99)00031-4

Glover, S. H., Bumpus, M. A., Logan, J. E., & Ciesla, J. R. (1997). Re-examining the influence of individual values on ethical decision making. In M. Fleckenstein, M. Maury, L. Pincus, & P. Primeaux (eds), *From the Universities to the Marketplace: The Business Ethics Journey: The Second Annual International Vincentian Conference Promoting Business Ethics* (pp. 109–119). Dordrecht: Springer Netherlands.

Goel, R. K., & Budak, J. (2006). Corruption in transition economies: effects of government size, country size and economic reforms. *Journal of Economics and Finance, 30*(2), 240–250. doi:10.1007/BF02761489

Goel, R. K., Herrala, R., & Mazhar, U. (2013). Institutional quality and environmental pollution: MENA countries versus the rest of the world. *Economic Systems, 37*(4), 508–521. https://doi.org/10.1016/j.ecosys.2013.04.002

Goel, R. K., & Nelson, M. A. (1998). Corruption and government size: a disaggregated analysis. *Public Choice, 97*(1), 107–120. doi:10.1023/A:1004900603583

Goel, R. K., & Nelson, M. A. (2010). Causes of corruption: history, geography and government. *Journal of Policy Modeling, 32*(4), 433–447. https://doi.org/10.1016/j.jpolmod.2010.05.004

Goel, R. K., & Nelson, M. A. (2011). Measures of corruption and determinants of US corruption. *Economics of Governance, 12*(2), 155–176. doi:10.1007/s10101-010-0091-x

Goel, R. K., Nelson, M. A., & Naretta, M. A. (2012). The internet as an indicator of corruption awareness. *European Journal of Political Economy, 28*(1), 64–75. https://doi.org/10.1016/j.ejpoleco.2011.08.003

Goel, R. K., & Saunoris, J. W. (2014). Global corruption and the shadow economy: spatial aspects. *Public Choice, 161*(1), 119–139. doi:10.1007/s11127-013-0135-1

Gokcekus, O. (2008). Is it protestant tradition or current protestant population that affects corruption? *Economics Letters, 99*(1), 59–62. https://doi.org/10.1016/j.econlet.2007.05.029

Gokcekus, O., & Ekici, T. (2020). Religion, religiosity, and corruption. *Review of Religious Research, 62*(4), 563–581. doi:10.1007/s13644-020-00421-2

Goldberg, C. S., Graham, C. M., & Ha, J. (2020). CEO overconfidence and corporate risk taking: evidence from pension policy. *Journal of Corporate Accounting & Finance, 31*(4), 135–153. https://doi.org/10.1002/jcaf.22470

Goldman, E., Rocholl, J., & So, J. (2008). *Political connections and the allocation of procurement contracts.* Indiana University Working Paper (pp. 1–37).

Goldman, E., Rocholl, J., & So, J. (2009). Do politically connected boards affect firm value? *The Review of Financial Studies, 22*(6), 2331–2360. doi:10.1093/rfs/hhn088

Goldsmith, A. A. (1999). Slapping the grasping hand. *American Journal of Economics and Sociology, 58*(4), 865–883. https://doi.org/10.1111/j.1536-7150.1999.tb03398.x

Gomes, A. (2000). Going public without governance: managerial reputation effects. *The Journal of Finance, 55*(2), 615–646.

González, F. (2016). Creditor rights, bank competition, and corporate investment during the global financial crisis. *Journal of Corporate Finance, 37*, 249–270. https://doi.org/10.1016/j.jcorpfin.2016.01.001

González, F. (2018). Creditor rights, financial health, and corporate investment efficiency. *The North American Journal of Economics and Finance.* https://doi.org/10.1016/j.najef.2018.11.002

Gonzalez, M., Molina, C. A., Pablo, E., & Rosso, J. W. (2017). The effect of ownership concentration and composition on dividends: evidence from Latin America. *Emerging Markets Review, 30,* 1–18. https://doi.org/10.1016/j.ememar.2016.08.018

Gordon, M. J. (1959). Dividends, Earnings, and Stock Prices. *Review of Economics and Statistics, 41*(2), 99–105.

Gordon, M., & Lintner, J. (1956). Distribution of income of corporations among dividend, retained earning and taxes. *The American Economic Review, 46*(2), 97–113.

Gordon, M. B. (2017). Bribery and corruption in public service delivery: experience from the Ghana Judicial Service. Available at SSRN 2922519.

Gould, D. J. (2001). Administrative corruption: incidence, causes, and remedial strategies. *Public Administration and Public Policy, 94,* 761–774.

Graeff, P., & Mehlkop, G. (2003). The impact of economic freedom on corruption: different patterns for rich and poor countries. *European Journal of Political Economy, 19*(3), 605–620. https://doi.org/10.1016/S0176-2680(03)00015-6

Graham, J. R. (2000). How big are the tax benefits of debt? *The Journal of Finance, 55*(5), 1901–1941.

Graham, J. R., & Harvey, C. R. (2001). The theory and practice of corporate finance: evidence from the field. *Journal of Financial Economics, 60*(2–3), 187–243. http://dx.doi.org/10.1016/S0304-405X(01)00044-7

Granado-Peiró, N., & López-Gracia, J. (2017). Corporate governance and capital structure: a Spanish study. *European Management Review, 14*(1), 33–45. https://doi.org/10.1111/emre.12088

Greif, A. (1994). Cultural beliefs and the organization of society: a historical and theoretical reflection on collectivist and individualist societies. *Journal of Political Economy, 102*(5), 912–950.

Greusard, O. (2018). The impact of prosecution on corporate investment: evidence from the anti-bribery enforcement actions. Available at SSRN 3200407.

Grullon, G., Michaely, R., & Swaminathan, B. (2002). Are dividend changes a sign of firm maturity? *Journal of Business, 75*(3), 387–424.

Gründler, K., & Potrafke, N. (2019). Corruption and economic growth: new empirical evidence. *European Journal of Political Economy, 60*, 101810. https://doi.org/10.1016/j.ejpoleco.2019.08.001

Guermazi, A. (2014). Financial liberalization, credit constraints and collateral: the case of manufacturing industry in Tunisia. *Procedia Economics and Finance, 13*, 82–100.

Gugler, K. (2003). Corporate governance, dividend payout policy, and the interrelation between dividends, R&D, and capital investment. *Journal of Banking and Finance, 27*(7), 1297–1321. doi:10.1016/S0378-4266(02)00258-3

Gugler, K., Mueller, D. C., & Yurtoglu, B. B. (2008). Insider ownership, ownership concentration and investment performance: an international comparison. *Journal of Corporate Finance, 14*(5), 688–705. http://dx.doi.org/10.1016/j.jcorpfin.2008.09.007

Guiso, L., Sapienza, P., & Zingales, L. (2003). People's opium? Religion and economic attitudes. *Journal of Monetary Economics, 50*(1), 225–282. https://doi.org/10.1016/S0304-3932(02)00202-7

Guizani, M., & Abdalkrim, G. (2022). Board gender diversity, financial decisions and free cash flow: empirical evidence from Malaysia. *Management Research Review, 45*(2), 198–216. doi:10.1108/MRR-03-2021-0246

Gul, F. A., Srinidhi, B., & Ng, A. C. (2011). Does board gender diversity improve the informativeness of stock prices? *Journal of Accounting and Economics, 51*(3), 314–338. https://doi.org/10.1016/j.jacceco.2011.01.005

Gulen, H., & Ion, M. (2015). Policy uncertainty and corporate investment. *The Review of Financial Studies, 29*(3), 523–564. doi:10.1093/rfs/hhv050

Gungoraydinoglu, A., & Öztekin, Ö. (2011). Firm- and country-level determinants of corporate leverage: some new international evidence. *Journal of Corporate Finance, 17*(5), 1457–1474. http://dx.doi.org/10.1016/j.jcorpfin.2011.08.004

Guo, Y., & Li, S. (2015). Anti-corruption measures in China: suggestions for reforms. *Asian Education and Development Studies*, *4*(1), 7–23. doi:10.1108/AEDS-10-2014-0048

Gupta, G. (2022). CEO's educational background, economic policy uncertainty and investment-cash flow sensitivity: evidence from India. *Applied Economics*, *54*(5), 568–579. doi:10.1080/00036846.2021.1967279

Gupta, G., & Mahakud, J. (2018). Business group affiliation and corporate investment. *Journal of Management Research*, *18*(1), 56–67.

Gupta, G., Mahakud, J., & Verma, V. (2020). CEO's education and investment–cash flow sensitivity: an empirical investigation. *International Journal of Managerial Finance*.

Gupta, M. S., & Tiongson, E. (2000). *Corruption and the Provision of Health Care and Education Services*. International Monetary Fund.

Gupta, S., Davoodi, H., & Alonso-Terme, R. (2002). Does corruption affect income inequality and poverty? *Economics of Governance*, *3*(1), 23–45. doi:10.1007/s101010100039

Gurgur, T., & Shah, A. (2005). *Localization and Corruption: Panacea or Pandora's Box?* (Vol. 3486). World Bank Publications.

Gurunlu, M., & Gursoy, G. (2010). The influence of foreign ownership on capital structure of non-financial firms: evidence from Istanbul stock exchange. *IUP Journal of Corporate Governance*, *9*(4), 21–29.

Gwartney, J. D., Lawson, R., & Block, W. (1996). *Economic Freedom of the World, 1975–1995*. Fraser Institute.

Gyapong, E., Ahmed, A., Ntim, C. G., & Nadeem, M. (2021). Board gender diversity and dividend policy in Australian listed firms: the effect of ownership concentration. *Asia Pacific Journal of Management*, *38*(2), 603–643. doi:10.1007/s10490-019-09672-2

Gyimah-Brempong, K. (2002). Corruption, economic growth, and income inequality in Africa. *Economics of Governance*, *3*(3), 183–209. doi:10.1007/s101010200045

Gyimah-Brempong, K., & de Gyimah-Brempong, S. M. (2006). Corruption, growth, and income distribution: are there regional differences? *Economics of Governance*, *7*(3), 245–269. doi:10.1007/s10101-005-0008-2

Habib, M., & Zurawicki, L. (2002). Corruption and foreign direct investment. *Journal of International Business Studies*, *33*(2), 291–307. doi:10.1057/palgrave.jibs.8491017

Habib, S., Abdelmonen, S., & Khaled, M. (2020). The effect of corruption on the environmental quality in African countries: a panel quantile regression analysis. *Journal of the Knowledge Economy*, *11*(2), 788–804. doi:10.1007/s13132-018-0571-8

Habibov, N. (2016). Effect of corruption on healthcare satisfaction in post-soviet nations: a cross-country instrumental variable analysis of twelve countries. *Social Science & Medicine*, *152*, 119–124.

Hachten, W. A. (1989). Media development without press freedom: Lee Kuan Yew's Singapore. *Journalism Quarterly*, *66*(4), 822–827. doi:10.1177/107769908906600407

Hackbarth, D. (2008). Managerial traits and capital structure decisions. *Journal of Financial and Quantitative Analysis*, *43*(4), 843–881. doi:10.1017/S002210900001437X

Hagen, I. (1992). Democratic communication: media and social participation. *Democratic Communications in the Information Age*, 16–27.

Hakhverdian, A., & Mayne, Q. (2012). Institutional trust, education, and corruption: a micro-macro interactive approach. *The Journal of Politics*, *74*(3), 739–750.

Halkos, G., & Tzeremes, N. (2011). Investigating the cultural patterns of corruption: a nonparametric analysis. *Munich Personal RePEc Archive*. https://mpra.ub.uni-muenchen.de/32546/1/MPRA_paper_32546.pdf

Hall, G. C., Hutchinson, P. J., & Michaelas, N. (2004). Determinants of the capital structures of European SMEs. *Journal of Business Finance & Accounting*, *31*(5–6), 711–728. https://doi.org/10.1111/j.0306-686X.2004.00554.x

Hamada, B. I., Abdel-Salam, A.-S. G., & Elkilany, E. A. (2019). Press freedom and corruption: an examination of the relationship. *Global Media and Communication*, *15*(3), 303–321. doi:10.1177/1742766519871676

Hao, Y., Wei, W., & Chang, C.-P. (2018). Are women more likely than men to oppose corruption in China? Not yet. *Applied Economics Letters, 25*(3), 152–157. doi:10.1080/13504851.2017. 1305072

Haque, F., Arun, T. G., & Kirkpatrick, C. (2011). Corporate governance and capital structure in developing countries: a case study of Bangladesh. *Applied Economics, 43*(6), 673–681. doi:10.1080/00036840802599909

Harada, K., & Nguyen, P. (2011). Ownership concentration and dividend policy in Japan. *Managerial Finance, 37*(4), 362–379. doi:10.1108/03074351111115313

Harford, J., Klasa, S., & Maxwell, W. F. (2014). Refinancing risk and cash holdings. *The Journal of Finance, 69*(3), 975–1012.

Haron, R. (2016). Do Indonesian firms practice target capital structure? A dynamic approach. *Journal of Asia Business Studies, 10*(3), 318–334. doi:10.1108/JABS-07-2015-0100

Harrison, D. A., Price, K. H., & Bell, M. P. (1998). Beyond relational demography: time and the effects of surface-and deep-level diversity on work group cohesion. *Academy of Management Journal, 41*(1), 96–107.

Harstad, B., & Svensson, J. (2011). Bribes, lobbying, and development. *American Political Science Review, 105*(1), 46–63. doi:10.1017/S0003055410000523

Hart, N. (2009). Expert highlights importance of engaging citizens in anti-corruption process. Retrieved from www.ammancity100. gov.jo/en/content/news-and-media/expert-highlights-import ance-engaging-citizens-anti-corruption-process

Hassaballa, H. (2015). The effect of corruption on carbon dioxide emissions in the MENA region. *European Journal of Sustainable Development, 4*(2), 301–301.

Hau, H. (2001). Geographic patterns of trading profitability in Xetra. *European Economic Review, 45*(4-6), 757–769.

Haugen, R. A., & Senbet, L. W. (1986). Corporate finance and taxes: a review. *Financial Management, 15*(3), 5–21.

Hauser, R. (2013). Did dividend policy change during the financial crisis? *Managerial Finance, 39*(6), 584–606. doi:10.1108/ 03074351311322861

Hayashi, F. (1982). Tobin's marginal q and average q: a neoclassical interpretation. *Econometrica: Journal of the Econometric Society*, 213–224.

He, Y., Chen, C., & Hu, Y. (2019). Managerial overconfidence, internal financing, and investment efficiency: evidence from China. *Research in International Business and Finance, 47*, 501–510. https://doi.org/10.1016/j.ribaf.2018.09.010

Heaton, J. B. (2002). Managerial optimism and corporate finance. *Financial Management, 31*(2), 33–45.

Heinkel, R. (1978). *Dividend Policy as a Signal of Firm Value in Essays on Financial Markets with Imperfect Information* (Ph.D). University of California, Berkeley.

Heo, Y., Hou, F., & Park, S. G. (2021). Does corruption grease or sand the wheels of investment or innovation? Different effects in advanced and emerging economies. *Applied Economics, 53*(1), 35–60. doi:10.1080/00036846.2020.1791313

Herzfeld, T., & Weiss, C. (2003). Corruption and legal (in)effectiveness: an empirical investigation. *European Journal of Political Economy, 19*(3), 621–632. https://doi.org/10.1016/S0176-2680(03)00018-1

Hetherington, M. J. (1998). The political relevance of political trust. *American Political Science Review, 92*(4), 791–808. doi:10.2307/2586304

Hewa Wellalage, N., & Locke, S. (2015). Impact of ownership structure on capital structure of New Zealand unlisted firms. *Journal of Small Business and Enterprise Development, 22*(1), 127–142. doi:10.1108/JSBED-09-2011-0004

Heyneman, S. P. (2002). Defining the influence of education on social cohesion. *International Journal of Educational Policy, Research and Practice, 3*(4), 73–97.

Higgins, R. C. (1972). The corporate dividend-saving decision. *Journal of Financial & Quantitative Analysis, 7*(2), 1527–1541.

Hills, G., Fiske, L., & Mahmud, A. (2009). Anti-corruption as strategic CSR: a call to action for corporations. *FSG Social Impact Advisors*, 1–52.

Hirshleifer, D., & Thakor, A. V. (1992). Managerial conservatism, project choice, and debt. *The Review of Financial Studies, 5*(3), 437–470.

Ho, H. (2003). Dividend policies in Australia and Japan. *International Advances in Economic Research*, *9*(2), 91–99. Retrieved from http://www.scopus.com/inward/record.url?eid=2-s2.0-33748540245&partnerID=40&md5=104f6e07510a9c07630a061a51ae5676

Hofstede, G. (1984). *Culture's Consequences: International Differences in Work-related Values* (Vol. 5). Sage.

Hofstede, G. (1990). *Cultures and Organizations: Software of the Mind.* New York: McGraw-Hill.

Hofstede, G. (2001). *Culture's Consequences: Comparing values, Behaviors, Institutions and Organizations Across Nations.* Sage Publications.

Hofstede, G. (2011). Dimensionalizing cultures: the Hofstede model in context. *Online Readings in Psychology and Culture*, *2*(1), 1–26.

Hofstede, G., Hofstede, G. J., & Minkov, M. (1991). *Cultures and Organizations: Intercultural Cooperation and its Importance for Survival.* New York: McGraw-Hill.

Hofstede, G., Hofstede, G. J., & Minkov, M. (2010). *Cultures and Organizations: Software of the Mind* (3rd edn.). Citeseer.

Holder, M. E., Langrehr, F. W., & Hexter, J. L. (1998). Dividend policy determinants: an investigation of the influences of stakeholder theory. *FM: The Journal of the Financial Management Association*, *27*(3), 73.

Hollyer, J. R., Rosendorff, B. P., & Vreeland, J. R. (2011). Democracy and transparency. *The Journal of Politics*, *73*(4), 1191–1205.

Holman, M. R. (2014). Sex and the city: female leaders and spending on social welfare programs in U.S. municipalities. *Journal of Urban Affairs*, *36*(4), 701–715. doi:10.1111/juaf.12066

Holmstrom, B., & Costa, J. R. i. (1986). Managerial incentives and capital management. *The Quarterly Journal of Economics*, *101*(4), 835–860. doi:10.2307/1884180

Hope, O.-K., & Thomas, W. B. (2008). Managerial empire building and firm disclosure. *Journal of Accounting Research*, *46*(3), 591–626. doi:10.1111/j.1475-679X.2008.00289.x

Horsewood, N., & Voicu, A. M. (2012). Does corruption hinder trade for the new EU members? *Economics*, *6*(1). doi:10.5018/economics-ejournal.ja.2012-47

Hoshi, T., Kashyap, A., & Scharfstein, D. (1991). Corporate Structure, liquidity, and investment: evidence from Japanese industrial groups. *The Quarterly Journal of Economics, 106*(1), 33-60. doi:10.2307/2937905

Hossain, A. T., Hossain, T., & Kryzanowski, L. (2021). Political corruption and corporate payouts. *Journal of Banking & Finance, 123*, 106016. https://doi.org/10.1016/j.jbankfin.2020.106016

House, R., Javidan, M., Hanges, P., & Dorfman, P. (2002). Understanding cultures and implicit leadership theories across the globe: an introduction to project GLOBE. *Journal of World Business, 37*(1), 3–10. https://doi.org/10.1016/S1090-9516(01)00069-4

House, R. J., Hanges, P. J., Javidan, M., Dorfman, P. W., & Gupta, V. (2004). *Culture, Leadership, and Organizations: The GLOBE Study of 62 Societies.* Sage Publications.

Hovakimian, A., Hovakimian, G., & Tehranian, H. (2004). Determinants of target capital structure: the case of dual debt and equity issues. *Journal of Financial Economics, 71*(3), 517–540. https://doi.org/10.1016/S0304-405X(03)00181-8

Howatt, B., Zuber, R. A., Gandar, J. M., & Lamb, R. P. (2009). Dividends, earnings volatility and information. *Applied Financial Economics, 19*(7), 551–562. doi:10.1080/09603100802345397

Hsiao, A., Vogt, V., & Quentin, W. (2019). Effect of corruption on perceived difficulties in healthcare access in sub-Saharan Africa. *PLOS ONE, 14*(8), e0220583. doi:10.1371/journal.pone.0220583

Hu, C., & Liu, Y.-J. (2015). Valuing diversity: CEOs' career experiences and corporate investment. *Journal of Corporate Finance, 30*(0), 11–31. http://dx.doi.org/10.1016/j.jcorpfin.2014.08.001

Hu, Y., & Xu, M. (2019). China's anti-corruption campaign, political connections and private firms' debt financing. *China Finance Review International, 9*(4), 521–553. doi:10.1108/CFRI-09-2018-0132

Huang, B.-Y., Lin, C.-M., & Huang, C.-M. (2011). The influences of ownership structure: evidence from China. *The Journal of Developing Areas, 45*, 209–227. Retrieved from http://www.jstor.org/stable/23215271

Huang, G., & Song, F. M. (2006). The determinants of capital structure: evidence from China. *China Economic Review, 17*(1), 14–36. http://dx.doi.org/10.1016/j.chieco.2005.02.007

Huang, Q., & Yuan, T. (2021). Does political corruption impede firm innovation? Evidence from the United States. *Journal of Financial and Quantitative Analysis, 56*(1), 213–248. doi:10.1017/S0022109019000966

Huang, T., Wu, F., Yu, J., & Zhang, B. (2015). Political risk and dividend policy: evidence from international political crises. *Journal of International Business Studies, 46*(5), 574–595. doi:10.1057/jibs.2015.2

Huang, W., Jiang, F., Liu, Z., & Zhang, M. (2011). Agency cost, top executives' overconfidence, and investment-cash flow sensitivity — evidence from listed companies in China. *Pacific-Basin Finance Journal, 19*(3), 261–277. http://dx.doi.org/10.1016/j.pacfin.2010.12.001

Huang, W., & Peng, Y. (2021). Anti-corruption and corporate investment: evidence from financial disclosure laws.

Huňady, J., & Orviská, M. (2015). The effect of corruption on tax revenue in OECD and Latin America countries. *Theoretical and Practical Aspects of Public Finance, 1*(1), 80.

Hunt, J., & Laszlo, S. (2012). Is bribery really regressive? Bribery's costs, benefits, and mechanisms. *World Development, 40*(2), 355–372. https://doi.org/10.1016/j.worlddev.2011.06.001

Hussain, H. I., Ali, M., Hassan, M. K., & El-Khatib, R. (2020). Asymmetric capital structure speed of adjustment, equity mispricing and Shari'ah compliance of Malaysian firms. *International Review of Economics & Finance.* https://doi.org/10.1016/j.iref.2020.10.017

Husted, B. W. (1999). Wealth, culture, and corruption. *Journal of International Business Studies, 30*(2), 339–359. doi:10.1057/palgrave.jibs.8490073

Huther, J., & Shah, A. (1998). *Applying a Simple Measure of Good Governance to the Debate on Fiscal Decentralization* (Vol. 1894). World Bank Publications.

Huynh, K. P., & Petrunia, R. J. (2010). Age effects, leverage and firm growth. *Journal of Economic Dynamics and Control, 34*(5), 1003–1013. https://doi.org/10.1016/j.jedc.2010.01.007

Hwang, J. (2002). A note on the relationship between corruption and government revenue. *Journal of Economic Development, 27*(2), 161–176.

Imam, P. A., & Jacobs, D. (2014). Effect of corruption on tax revenues in the middle east. *Review of Middle East Economics and Finance, 10*(1), 1–24. doi:doi:10.1515/rmeef-2014-0001

Inglehart, R. (1997). *Modernization and Postmodernization in 43 Societies.* Princeton University Press.

Inglehart, R., & Baker, W. E. (2000). Modernization, cultural change, and the persistence of traditional values. *American Sociological Review,* 19–51.

International, T. (2012). Putting corruption out of business. Retrieved from https://www.transparency.org/en/news/putting-corruption-out-of-business

International, T. (2013). Press freedom: too many attacks go unpunished. Retrieved from https://www.transparency.org/en/news/too-many-attacks-on-journalists-and-press-freedom-go-unpunished

Ittonen, K., Miettinen, J., & Vähämaa, S. (2010). Does female representation on audit committees affect audit fees? *Quarterly Journal of Finance and Accounting, 49*(3/4), 113–139. Retrieved from http://www.jstor.org/stable/23074633

Ivanova, K. (2011). Corruption and air pollution in Europe. *Oxford Economic Papers, 63*(1), 49–70. doi:10.1093/oep/gpq017

Ivanyna, M., Moumouras, A., & Rangazas, P. (2010). The culture of corruption, tax evasion, and optimal tax policy. *Economic Inquiry, 54,* 520–542.

Ivanyna, M., & Shah, A. (2011). Decentralization and corruption: new cross-country evidence. *Environment and Planning C: Government and Policy, 29*(2), 344–362. doi:10.1068/c1081r

Jabbouri, I. (2016). Determinants of corporate dividend policy in emerging markets: evidence from MENA stock markets. *Research in International Business and Finance, 37,* 283–298. https://doi.org/10.1016/j.ribaf.2016.01.018

Jacob, C., & Jijo Lukose, P. J. (2018). Institutional ownership and dividend payout in emerging markets: evidence from India. *Journal of Emerging Market Finance, 17*(1_suppl), S54–S82. doi:10.1177/0972652717751538

Jagger, P., & Shively, G. (2015). Taxes and Bribes in Uganda. *The Journal of Development Studies, 51*(1), 66–79. doi:10.1080/00220388.2014.947278

Jain, A. K. (2001). Corruption: a review. *Journal of economic surveys, 15*(1), 71–121.

Jain, P. K., Kuvvet, E., & Pagano, M. S. (2017). Corruption's impact on foreign portfolio investment. *International Business Review, 26*(1), 23–35. https://doi.org/10.1016/j.ibusrev.2016.05.004

Jalan, B. (1982). *Problems and Policies in Small Economies,* London: Taylor & Francis.

Jaslowitzer, P., Megginson, W. L., & Rapp, M. S. (2018). State ownership and corporate investment. Available at SSRN 2735698.

Javidan, M. (2004). Performance orientation. *Culture, Leadership, and Organizations: The GLOBE Study of, 62,* 239–281.

Javidan, M., & House, R. (2001). Culture acumen for the GLOBE manager: lessons from project GLOBE. *Organizational Dynamics, 29,* 289–305.

Javorcik, B. S., & Wei, S.-J. (2009). Corruption and cross-border investment in emerging markets: firm-level evidence. *Journal of International Money and Finance, 28*(4), 605–624. https://doi.org/10.1016/j.jimonfin.2009.01.003

Jens, C. E. (2017). Political uncertainty and investment: causal evidence from U.S. gubernatorial elections. *Journal of Financial Economics, 124*(3), 563–579. https://doi.org/10.1016/j.jfineco.2016.01.034

Jensen, G. R., Solberg, D. P., & Zorn, T. S. (1992). Simultaneous determination of insider ownership, debt, and dividend policies. *Journal of Financial & Quantitative Analysis, 27*(2), 247–263.

Jensen, M. C. (1986). Agency costs of free cash flow, corporate finance, and takeovers. *American Economic Review, 76*(2), 323.

Jensen, M. C. (1993). The modern industrial revolution, exit, and the failure of internal control systems. *Journal of Finance, 48*(3), 831–880.

Jensen, M. C., & Meckling, W. H. (1976). Theory of the firm: managerial behavior, agency costs and ownership structure. *Journal of Financial Economics, 3*(4), 305–360. http://dx.doi.org/10.1016/0304-405X(76)90026-X

Jensen, N. M., & Malesky, E. J. (2018). Nonstate actors and compliance with international agreements: an empirical analysis of the OECD Anti-Bribery Convention. *International Organization*, *72*(1), 33–69.

Jeon, J. Q., Lee, C., & Moffett, C. M. (2011). Effects of foreign ownership on payout policy: evidence from the Korean market. *Journal of Financial Markets*, *14*(2), 344–375. http://dx.doi.org/10.1016/j.finmar.2010.08.001

Jetter, M., Agudelo, A. M., & Hassan, A. R. (2015). The effect of democracy on corruption: income is key. *World Development*, *74*, 286–304. https://doi.org/10.1016/j.worlddev.2015.05.016

Jha, C., & Panda, B. (2017). Individualism and corruption: a cross-country analysis. *Economic Papers: A Journal of Applied Economics and Policy*, *36*(1), 60–74. doi:10.1111/1759-3441.12163

Jha, C. K., & Sarangi, S. (2017). Does social media reduce corruption? *Information Economics and Policy*, *39*, 60–71. https://doi.org/10.1016/j.infoecopol.2017.04.001

Ji, A. E. (2016). The impact of board size on firm-level capital investment efficiency. *International Journal of Economics and Finance*, *8*(10), 110–120.

Jia, F., Li, G., Lu, X., & Xie, S. (2021). CEO given names and corporate green investment. *Emerging Markets Review*, *48*, 100808. https://doi.org/10.1016/j.ememar.2021.100808

Jiraporn, P. (2006). Share repurchases, shareholder rights, and corporate governance provisions. *The North American Journal of Economics and Finance*, *17*(1), 35–47. http://dx.doi.org/10.1016/j.najef.2005.03.003

Jiraporn, P., Chatjuthamard, P., Tong, S., & Kim, Y. S. (2015). Does corporate governance influence corporate risk-taking? Evidence from the institutional shareholders services (ISS). *Finance Research Letters*, *13*, 105–112. https://doi.org/10.1016/j.frl.2015.02.007

Jiraporn, P., Kim, J. C., & Kim, Y. S. (2011). Dividend payouts and corporate governance quality: an empirical investigation. *Financial Review*, *46*(2), 251–279. doi:10.1111/j.1540-6288.2011.00299.x

Jõeveer, K. (2013). Firm, country and macroeconomic determinants of capital structure: evidence from transition economies. *Journal of Comparative Economics*, *41*(1), 294–308. http://dx.doi.org/10.1016/j.jce.2012.05.001

John, K., Litov, L., & Yeung, B. (2008). Corporate governance and risk-taking. *The Journal of Finance, 63*(4), 1679–1728. doi:10.1111/j.1540-6261.2008.01372.x

John, K., & Williams, J. (1985). Dividends, dilution, and taxes: a signalling equilibrium. *Journal of Finance, 40*(4), 1053–1070.

John, S. F., & Muthusamy, K. (2010). Leverage, growth and profitability as determinants of dividend payout ratio-evidence from Indian paper industry. *Asian Journal of Business Management Studies, 1*(1), 26–30.

Johnson, S., La Porta, R., Lopez-de-Silanes, F., & Shleifer, A. (2000). Tunneling. *American Economic Review, 90*(2), 22–27.

Jones, T. M., & Gautschi, F. H. (1988). Will the ethics of business change? A survey of future executives. *Journal of Business Ethics, 7*(4), 231–248. doi:10.1007/BF00381827

Jordan, J., Lowe, J., & Taylor, P. (1998). Strategy and financial policy in UK small firms. *Journal of Business Finance & Accounting, 25*(1–2), 1–27.

Jorgenson, D. W. (1963). Capital theory and investment behaviour.

Judge, W. Q., McNatt, D. B., & Xu, W. (2011). The antecedents and effects of national corruption: a meta-analysis. *Journal of World Business, 46*(1), 93–103. https://doi.org/10.1016/j.jwb.2010.05.021

Julio, B., & Yook, Y. (2012). Political uncertainty and corporate investment cycles. *The Journal of Finance, 67*(1), 45–83. doi:10.1111/j.1540-6261.2011.01707.x

Junankar, P. N. (1972). *Investment: Theories and Evidence.* London: Macmillan International Higher Education.

Kabasakal, H., & Bodur, M. (2004). Humane orientation in societies, organizations, and leader attributes. *Culture, Leadership, and Organizations: The GLOBE Study, 62*, 564–601.

Kadapakkam, P.-R., Kumar, P. C., & Riddick, L. A. (1998). The impact of cash flows and firm size on investment: the international evidence. *Journal of Banking & Finance, 22*(3), 293–320. https://doi.org/10.1016/S0378-4266(97)00059-9

Kaffenberger, M. (2012). *The effect of Educational Attainment on Corruption Participation in Sub-Saharan Africa.* https://etd.library.vanderbilt.edu/etd-03222012-205534

Kale, J. R., & Noe, T. H. (1990). Dividends, uncertainty and underwriting costs under asymmetric information. *Journal of Financial Research, 13*(4), 265.

Kalenborn, C., & Lessmann, C. (2013). The impact of democracy and press freedom on corruption: conditionality matters. *Journal of Policy Modeling, 35*(6), 857–886. https://doi.org/10.1016/j.jpolmod.2013.02.009

Kang, W., Lee, K., & Ratti, R. A. (2014). Economic policy uncertainty and firm-level investment. *Journal of Macroeconomics, 39*, 42–53. https://doi.org/10.1016/j.jmacro.2013.10.006

Kaplan, S. N., & Minton, B. A. (1994). Appointments of outsiders to Japanese boards: determinants and implications for managers. *Journal of Financial Economics, 36*(2), 225–258. http://dx.doi.org/10.1016/0304-405X(94)90025-6

Kaplan, S. N., & Reishus, D. (1990). Outside directorships and corporate performance. *Journal of Financial Economics, 27*(2), 389–410. http://dx.doi.org/10.1016/0304-405X(90)90061-4

Kashefi-Pour, E., Amini, S., Uddin, M., & Duxbury, D. (2020). Does cultural difference affect investment–cash flow sensitivity? Evidence from OECD countries. *British Journal of Management, 31*(3), 636–658.

Kashyap, A. K., Lamont, O. A., & Stein, J. C. (1994). Credit conditions and the cyclical behavior of inventories. *The Quarterly Journal of Economics, 109*(3), 565–592.

Katsios, S. (2006). The shadow economy and corruption in Greece. *South-Eastern Europe Journal of Economics, 1*, 61–80.

Kaufmann, D., Kraay, A., & Mastruzzi, M. (2003). *Governance Matters: Governance Indicators for 1996–2002. III* (Vol. 3106). World Bank.

Kayhan, A., & Titman, S. (2007). Firms' histories and their capital structures. *Journal of Financial Economics, 83*(1), 1–32. https://doi.org/10.1016/j.jfineco.2005.10.007

Khaghaghordyan, A. (2014). International anti-corruption normative framework: the state of the art. *Anti-corruption Policies Revisited. Work Package: Wp1. Social, Legal, Anthropological and Political Approaches to Theory of Corruption* (pp. 145–162).

Khan, M. (2006). Determinants of corruption in developing countries: the limits of conventional economic analysis. *International Handbook on the Economics of Corruption,* (pp. 216–244).

Khan, W. A., & Vieito, J. P. (2013). Ceo gender and firm performance. *Journal of Economics and Business, 67*, 55–66. http://dx.doi.org/10.1016/j.jeconbus.2013.01.003

Khaw, K. L.-H., Zainudin, R., & Rashid, R. M. (2019). Cost of debt financing: does political connection matter? *Emerging Markets Review*, 100632.

Khémiri, W., & Noubbigh, H. (2018). Determinants of capital structure: evidence from sub-Saharan African firms. *The Quarterly Review of Economics and Finance, 70*, 150–159. https://doi.org/10.1016/j.qref.2018.04.010

Khémiri, W., & Noubbigh, H. (2020). Does sub-Saharan Africa overinvest? Evidence from a panel of non-financial firms. *The Quarterly Review of Economics and Finance, 77*, 118–130. https://doi.org/10.1016/j.qref.2019.11.005

Khlif, H., & Amara, I. (2019). Political connections, corruption and tax evasion: a cross-country investigation. *Journal of Financial Crime, 26*(2), 401–411. doi:10.1108/JFC-01-2018-0004

Khoo, J., & Cheung, A. (2021). Does geopolitical uncertainty affect corporate financing? Evidence from MIDAS regression. *Global Finance Journal, 47*, 100519. https://doi.org/10.1016/j.gfj.2020.100519

Khwaja, A. I., & Mian, A. (2005). Do lenders favor politically connected firms? Rent provision in an emerging financial market. *The Quarterly Journal of Economics, 120*(4), 1371–1411. doi:10.1162/003355305775097524

Kiel, G. C., & Nicholson, G. J. (2003). Board composition and corporate performance: how the Australian experience informs contrasting theories of corporate governance. *Corporate Governance: An International Review, 11*(3), 189–205.

Kilincarslan, E. (2021). The influence of board independence on dividend policy in controlling agency problems in family firms. *International Journal of Accounting & Information Management, 29*(4), 552–582. doi:10.1108/IJAIM-03-2021-0056

Kilincarslan, E., & Demiralay, S. (2021). Dividend policies of travel and leisure firms in the UK. *International Journal of Accounting & Information Management, 29*(2), 324–344. doi:10.1108/IJAIM-09-2020-0144

Kim, H., Heshmati, A., & Aoun, D. (2006). Dynamics of capital structure: the case of Korean listed manufacturing companies. *Asian Economic Journal, 20*(3), 275–302.

Kim, W. S., Kiymaz, H., & Oh, S. (2020). Do country-level legal, corporate governance, and cultural characteristics influence the relationship between insider ownership and dividend policy? *Pacific-Basin Finance Journal, 64*, 101457. https://doi.org/10.1016/j.pacfin.2020.101457

Kittova, Z., & Stienhauser, D. (2018). Influence of culture on corruption within the OECD countries. *Ad Alta: Journal of Interdisciplinary Research, 8*(1), 121–126.

Kizilkaya, O. (2017). Effect of Corruption on FDI in transition economies: evidence from causality analysis. *Uluslararasıİktisadi ve İdari İncelemeler Dergisi* (19), 25–42.

Klasa, S., Maxwell, W. F., & Ortiz-Molina, H. (2009). The strategic use of corporate cash holdings in collective bargaining with labor unions. *Journal of Financial Economics, 92*(3), 421–442. http://dx.doi.org/10.1016/j.jfineco.2008.07.003

Klein, A. (2002). Audit committee, board of director characteristics, and earnings management. *Journal of Accounting Economics Letters, 33*(3), 375–400.

Klemenčič, G., & Stusek, J. (2008). Specialised anti-corruption institutions: review of models, Paris: OECD.

Klitgaard, R. (1988). *Controlling Corruption.* Berkeley: University of California Press.

Knack, S., & Azfar, O. (2003). Trade intensity, country size and corruption. *Economics of Governance, 4*(1), 1–18. doi:10.1007/s101010200051

Knyazeva, A., Knyazeva, D., & Masulis, R. W. (2013). The supply of corporate directors and board independence. *The Review of Financial Studies, 26*(6), 1561–1605.

Ko, K., & Moon, S.-G. (2014). The relationship between religion and corruption: are the proposed causal links empirically valid? *International Review of Public Administration, 19*(1), 44–62. doi:10.1080/12294659.2014.887353

Koirala, S., Marshall, A., Neupane, S., & Thapa, C. (2020). Corporate governance reform and risk-taking: evidence from a quasi-natural experiment in an emerging market. *Journal of Corporate Finance, 61*, 101396. https://doi.org/10.1016/j.jcorpfin.2018.08.007

Köksal, B., & Orman, C. (2015). Determinants of capital structure: evidence from a major developing economy. *Small Business Economics, 44*(2), 255–282. doi:10.1007/s11187-014-9597-x

Kolstad, I., & Wiig, A. (2016). Does democracy reduce corruption? *Democratization, 23*(7), 1198–1215. doi:10.1080/13510347.2015.1071797

Kong, D., Tao, Y., & Wang, Y. (2020). China's anti-corruption campaign and firm productivity: evidence from a quasi-natural experiment. *China Economic Review, 63*, 101535. https://doi.org/10.1016/j.chieco.2020.101535

Koo, D. S., Ramalingegowda, S., & Yu, Y. (2017). The effect of financial reporting quality on corporate dividend policy. *Review of Accounting Studies, 22*(2), 753–790. doi:10.1007/s11142-017-9393-3

Kornai, J. (1979). Resource-constrained versus demand-constrained systems. *Econometrica: Journal of the Econometric Society,* 801–819.

Kotera, G., Okada, K., & Samreth, S. (2012). Government size, democracy, and corruption: an empirical investigation. *Economic Modelling, 29*(6), 2340–2348. https://doi.org/10.1016/j.econmod.2012.06.022

Kowalewski, O., Stetsyuk, I., & Talavera, O. (2007). Corporate governance and dividend policy in Poland. *Working Papers — Financial Institutions Center at the Wharton School,* 1–35.

Koyck, L. M. (1954). *Distributed Lags and Investment Analysis* (Vol. 4). North-Holland Publishing Company.

Koyuncu, C., Ozturkler, H., & Yilmaz, R. (2010). Privatization and corruption in transition economies: a panel study. *Journal of Economic Policy Reform, 13*(3), 277–284. doi:10.1080/17487870.2010.503099

Kraus, A., & Litzenberger, R. H. (1973). A state-preference model of optimal financial leverage. *The Journal of Finance, 28*(4), 911–922.

Kroeze, R., Vitória, A., & Geltner, G. (2018). *Anticorruption in History: From Antiquity to the Modern Era.* Oxford: Oxford University Press.

Kumar, S., Colombage, S., & Rao, P. (2017). Research on capital structure determinants: a review and future directions. *International Journal of Managerial Finance, 13*(2), 106–132. doi:10.1108/IJMF-09-2014-0135

Kuncoro, A. (2006). Corruption and business uncertainty in Indonesia. *ASEAN Economic Bulletin, 23*(1), 11–30. Retrieved from http://www.jstor.org/stable/41316941

Kunicova, J., & Rose-Ackerman, S. (2005). Electoral rules and constitutional structures as constraints on corruption. *British Journal of Political Science, 35*(4), 573–606. doi:10.1017/S0007123405000311

Kusnadi, Y., Yang, Z., & Zhou, Y. (2015). Institutional development, state ownership, and corporate cash holdings: evidence from China. *Journal of Business Research, 68*(2), 351–359. https://doi.org/10.1016/j.jbusres.2014.06.023

La Porta, R., Lopez-de-Silanes, F., Shleifer, A., & Vishny, R. (1998). Law and finance. *Journal of Political Economy, 106*, 42.

La Porta, R., Lopez-de-Silanes, F., Shleifer, A., & Vishny, R. (1999). The quality of government. *The Journal of Law, Economics, and Organization, 15*(1), 222–279. doi:10.1093/jleo/15.1.222

La Porta, R., Lopez-De-Silanes, F., Shleifer, A., & Vishny, R. W. (2000). Agency problems and dividend policies around the world. *Journal of Finance, 55*(1), 1–33.

La Porter, R., Lopez-De-Silanes, F., Shleifer, A., & Vishny, R. W. (1997). Trust in large organizations. *American Economic Review, 87*(2), 333–338.

La Rocca, M., La Rocca, T., & Cariola, A. (2011). Capital structure decisions during a firm's life cycle. *Small Business Economics, 37*(1), 107–130. doi:10.1007/s11187-009-9229-z

Labhane, N. B. (2018). Dividend policy decisions in India: standalone versus business group-affiliated firms. *Global Business Review, 20*(1), 133–150. doi:10.1177/0972150918803990

Labhane, N. B., & Mahakud, J. (2016). Determinants of dividend policy of Indian companies: a panel data analysis. *Paradigm, 20*(1), 36–55. doi:10.1177/0971890716637698

Laffont, J.-J., & Tirole, J. (1993). *A Theory of Incentives In Procurement and Regulation.* MIT Press.

Lalountas, D. A., Manolas, G. A., & Vavouras, I. S. (2011). Corruption, globalization and development: how are these three phenomena related? *Journal of Policy Modeling, 33*(4), 636–648. https://doi.org/10.1016/j.jpolmod.2011.02.001

Lam, K. C. K., Sami, H., & Zhou, H. (2012). The role of cross-listing, foreign ownership and state ownership in dividend policy in an emerging market. *China Journal of Accounting Research, 5*(3), 199–216. http://dx.doi.org/10.1016/j.cjar.2012.06.001

Lambsdorff, J. G. (1999). Corruption in empirical research: a review. *Transparency International, Processed, 6.*

Lambsdorff, J. G. (2007a). Causes and consequences of corruption: what do we know from a cross-section of countries? *International Handbook on the Economics of Corruption, 1.*

Lambsdorff, J. G. (2007b). *The Institutional Economics of Corruption and Reform: Theory, Evidence and Policy.* Cambridge: Cambridge University Press.

Lambsdorff, J. G., & Cornelius, P. (2000). Corruption, foreign investment and growth. *The Africa Competitiveness Report, 2001,* 70–78.

Lamont, O. (1997). Cash flow and investment: evidence from internal capital markets. *The Journal of Finance, 52*(1), 83–109.

Lang, L., Ofek, E., & Stulz, R. (1996). Leverage, investment, and firm growth. *Journal of Financial Economics, 40*(1), 3–29. http://dx.doi.org/10.1016/0304-405X(95)00842-3

Lang, L. H. P., & Litzenberger, R. H. (1989). Dividend announcements: cash flow signalling vs. free cash flow hypothesis? *Journal of Financial Economics, 24*(1), 181–191. http://dx.doi.org/10.1016/0304-405X(89)90077-9

Langer, E. J. (1975). The illusion of control. *Journal of Personality and Social Psychology, 32*(2), 311.

Larwood, L., & Whittaker, W. (1977). Managerial myopia: self-serving biases in organizational planning. *Journal of Applied Psychology, 62*(2), 194.

Le, Q. V., & Rishi, M. (2006). Corruption and capital flight: an empirical assessment. *International Economic Journal, 20*(4), 523–540. doi:10.1080/10168730601027161

Le, T. P. V., & Tannous, K. (2016). Ownership structure and capital structure: a study of Vietnamese listed firms. *Australian Economic Papers, 55*(4), 319–344. doi:10.1111/1467-8454.12089

Leary, M. T., & Roberts, M. R. (2005). Do firms rebalance their capital structures? *The Journal of Finance, 60*(6), 2575–2619. https://doi.org/10.1111/j.1540-6261.2005.00811.x

Lederman, D., Loayza, N. V., & Soares, R. R. (2005). Accountability and corruption: political institutions matter. *Economics & Politics, 17*(1), 1–35. https://doi.org/10.1111/j.1468-0343.2005.00145.x

Leff, N. H. (1964). Economic development through bureaucratic corruption. *American Behavioral Scientist, 8*(3), 8–14.

Lei, G., Wang, W., & Liu, M. (2015). Political uncertainty, dividend policy adjustments and market effects. *China Journal of Accounting Studies, 3*(1), 49–83. doi:10.1080/21697213.2015.1015370

Leite, M. C., & Weidmann, J. (1999). *Does Mother Nature Corrupt? Natural Resources, Corruption, and Economic Growth*. International Monetary Fund.

Leland, H. E., & Pyle, D. H. (1977). Informational asymmetries, financial structure, and financial intermediation. *The Journal of Finance, 32*(2), 371–387. doi:10.2307/2326770

Lemma, T. T. (2015). Corruption, debt financing and corporate ownership. *Journal of Economic Studies, 42*(3), 433–461. doi:10.1108/JES-02-2013-0029

Lemmon, M. L., & Zender, J. F. (2010). Debt capacity and tests of capital structure theories. *Journal of Financial and Quantitative Analysis, 45*(5), 1161–1187. doi:10.1017/S0022109010000499

Levine, R. (1999). *Bank-Based and Market-Based Financial Systems: Cross-country Comparisons* (Vol. 2143). World Bank Publications.

Lewellen, W. G., Stanley, K. L., Lease, R. C., & Schlarbaum, G. G. (1978). Some direct evidence on the dividend clientele phenomenon. *The Journal of Finance, 33*(5), 1385–1399. doi:10.1111/j.1540-6261.1978.tb03427.x

Leys, C. (1965). What is the problem about corruption? *The Journal of Modern African Studies, 3*(2), 215–230. doi:10.1017/S0022278X00023636

Li, H., Wang, T., Cao, Y., Song, L., Hou, Y., & Wang, Y. (2021). Culture, thinking styles and investment decision. *Psychological Reports*, 0033294121997778. doi:10.1177/0033294121 997778

Li, J., & Tang, Y. (2010). CEO hubris and firm risk taking in China: the moderating role of managerial discretion. *Academy of Management Journal, 53*(1), 45–68.

Li, K., Griffin, D., Yue, H., & Zhao, L. (2011). National culture and capital structure decisions: evidence from foreign joint ventures in China. *Journal of International Business Studies, 42*(4), 477–503. doi:10.1057/jibs.2011.7

Li, K., Griffin, D., Yue, H., & Zhao, L. (2013). How does culture influence corporate risk-taking? *Journal of Corporate Finance, 23*(0), 1–22. http://dx.doi.org/10.1016/j.jcorpfin.2013.07.008

Li, K., Xia, B., Chen, Y., Ding, N., & Wang, J. (2021). Environmental uncertainty, financing constraints and corporate investment: evidence from China. *Pacific-Basin Finance Journal, 70*, 101665. https://doi.org/10.1016/j.pacfin.2021.101665

Li, K., Yue, H., & Zhao, L. (2009). Ownership, institutions, and capital structure: evidence from China. *Journal of Comparative Economics, 37*(3), 471–490. https://doi.org/10.1016/j.jce.2009.07.001

Li, L., & Islam, S. Z. (2019). Firm and industry specific determinants of capital structure: evidence from the Australian market. *International Review of Economics & Finance, 59*, 425–437. https://doi.org/10.1016/j.iref.2018.10.007

Li, W., & Lie, E. (2006). Dividend changes and catering incentives. *Journal of Financial Economics, 80*(2), 293–308. http://dx.doi.org/10.1016/j.jfineco.2005.03.005

Li, X.-M., & Qiu, M. (2021). The joint effects of economic policy uncertainty and firm characteristics on capital structure: evidence from US firms. *Journal of International Money and Finance, 110*, 102279. https://doi.org/10.1016/j.jimonfin.2020.102279

Liang, C. C., Liu, Y., Troy, C., & Chen, W. W. (2020). Firm Characteristics and capital structure: evidence from ASEAN-4 economies. In C. F. Lee & M.-T. Yu (eds), *Advances in Pacific Basin Business, Economics and Finance* (Vol. 8, pp. 149–162). Emerald Publishing Limited.

Licht, A. N., Goldschmidt, C., & Schwartz, S. H. (2007). Culture rules: the foundations of the rule of law and other norms of governance. *Journal of Comparative Economics, 35*(4), 659–688. https://doi.org/10.1016/j.jce.2007.09.001

Linde, J., & Erlingsson, G. Ó. (2013). The eroding effect of corruption on system support in Sweden. *Governance, 26*(4), 585–603.

Lins, K. V. (2003). Equity ownership and firm value in emerging markets. *Journal of Financial and Quantitative Analysis, 38*(1), 159–184. doi:10.2307/4126768

Lintner, J. (1956). Distribution of incomes of corporations among dividends, retained earnings, and taxes. *American Economic Review, 46*(2), 97–113.

Lio, M.-C., Liu, M.-C., & Ou, Y.-P. (2011). Can the internet reduce corruption? A cross-country study based on dynamic panel data models. *Government Information Quarterly, 28*(1), 47–53. https://doi.org/10.1016/j.giq.2010.01.005

Lipset, S. M., & Lenz, G. S. (2000). Corruption, culture, and markets. *Culture Matters: How Values Shape Human Progress, 112*, 112.

Lipset, S. M., & Man, P. (1960). *The Social Bases of Politics*. Baltimore: The Johns Hopkins University Press.

Lipset, S. M., & Raab, E. (1973). *The Politics of Unreason: Right-Wing Extremism in America, 1790–1970* (Vol. 5). San Francisco: Harper & Row.

Lipton, M., & Lorsch, J. W. (1992). A modest proposal for improved corporate governance. *The Business Lawyer, 48*(1), 59–77.

Litzenberger, R. H., & Ramaswamy, K. (1979). The effect of personal taxes and dividends on capital asset prices: theory and empirical evidence. *Journal of Financial Economics, 7*(2), 163–195. http://dx.doi.org/10.1016/0304-405X(79)90012-6

Liu, C., Chen, Y., Li, S., Sun, L., & Yang, M. (2021). Local political corruption and M&As. *China Economic Review, 69*, 101677. https://doi.org/10.1016/j.chieco.2021.101677

Liu, G., & Zhang, C. (2019). Economic policy uncertainty and firms' investment and financing decisions in China. *China Economic Review, 63*, 101279. https://doi.org/10.1016/j.chieco.2019.02.007

Liu, Q., Lu, R., & Ma, X. (2015). Corruption, financial resources and exports. *Review of International Economics, 23*(5), 1023–1043. https://doi.org/10.1111/roie.12194

Liu, Q., Tian, G., & Wang, X. (2011). The effect of ownership structure on leverage decision: new evidence from Chinese listed firms. *Journal of the Asia Pacific Economy, 16*(2), 254–276. doi:10.1080/13547860.2011.564755

Liu, X. (2016). Corruption culture and corporate misconduct. *Journal of Financial Economics, 122*(2), 307–327. http://dx.doi.org/10.1016/j.jfineco.2016.06.005

Liu, X., Latif, Z., Danish, Latif, S., & Mahmood, N. (2021). The corruption-emissions nexus: do information and communication technologies make a difference? *Utilities Policy, 72*, 101244. https://doi.org/10.1016/j.jup.2021.101244

Liu, Y., Gan, H., & Karim, K. (2020). Corporate risk-taking after adoption of compensation clawback provisions. *Review of Quantitative Finance and Accounting, 54*(2), 617–649. doi:10.1007/s11156-019-00801-y

Liu, Y., Neely, P., & Karim, K. (2022). The impact of CFO gender on corporate overinvestment. *Advances in Accounting, 57*, 100599. https://doi.org/10.1016/j.adiac.2022.100599

Low, P. Y., & Chen, K. H. (2004). Diversification and capital structure: some international evidence. *Review of Quantitative Finance and Accounting, 23*(1), 55–71. doi:10.1023/B:REQU.0000037064.15144.04

Lowenstein, R. L. (1970). Press freedom as a political indicator. *International Communication, Media, Channels, Functions,* 129–142.

Lu, J., & Wang, W. (2015). Board independence and corporate investments. *Review of Financial Economics, 24*, 52–64. https://doi.org/10.1016/j.rfe.2015.01.001

Lu, Q., & Zhang, Y. (2020, 4–6 Dec.). Corruption, process of marketization and cash dividend policies. Paper presented at the 2020 *16th Dahe Fortune China Forum and Chinese High-educational Management Annual Academic Conference (DFHMC).*

Lui, F. T. (1985). An equilibrium queuing model of bribery. *Journal of Political Economy, 93*(4), 760–781.

Lv, M., & Bai, M. (2019). Political uncertainty and corporate debt financing: empirical evidence from China. *Applied Economics*, *51*(13), 1433–1449. doi:10.1080/00036846.2018.1527455

Mac an Bhaird, C., & Lucey, B. (2014). Culture's influences: an investigation of inter-country differences in capital structure. *Borsa Istanbul Review*, *14*(1), 1–9. https://doi.org/10.1016/j.bir.2013.10.004

MacDonald, R., & Majeed, M. T. (2011). *Causes of Corruption in European Countries: History, Law, and Political Stability*. Glasgow: University of Glasgow.

Macdonell, R., & Pesic, M. (2006). The role of the media in curbing corruption. *The Role of Parliament in Curbing Corruption*, 111–128.

MacKie-Mason, J. K. (1990). Do taxes affect corporate financing decisions? *The Journal of Finance*, *45*(5), 1471–1493. https://doi.org/10.1111/j.1540-6261.1990.tb03724.x

Macrae, J. (1982). Underdevelopment and the economics of corruption: a game theory approach. *World Development*, *10*(8), 677–687. https://doi.org/10.1016/0305-750X(82)90093-6

Malmendier, U., & Tate, G. (2005). CEO overconfidence and corporate investment. *The Journal of Finance*, *60*(6), 2661–2700.

Malmendier, U., Tate, G., & Yan, J. (2011). Overconfidence and early-life experiences: the effect of managerial traits on corporate financial policies. *The Journal of Finance*, *66*(5), 1687–1733.

Mande, V., Park, Y. K., & Son, M. (2012). Equity or debt financing: does good corporate governance matter? *Corporate Governance: An International Review*, *20*(2), 195–211. https://doi.org/10.1111/j.1467-8683.2011.00897.x

Manos, R. (2001). *Capital Structure and Dividend Policy: Evidence from Emerging Markets* (Ph.D). University of Birmingham.

Manzetti, L., & Wilson, C. J. (2007). Why do corrupt governments maintain public support? *Comparative Political Studies*, *40*(8), 949–970. doi:10.1177/0010414005285759

Marcel, J. J., Barr, P. S., & Duhaime, I. M. (2011). The influence of executive cognition on competitive dynamics. *Strategic Management Journal*, *32*(2), 115–138.

March, J. G., & Shapira, Z. (1987). Managerial perspectives on risk and risk taking. *Management Science*, *33*(11), 1404–1418.

Marciukaityte, D. (2019). Labor laws and corporate investment. *Journal of Financial Research, 42*(2), 413–444.

Margaritis, D., & Psillaki, M. (2007). Capital structure and firm efficiency. *Journal of Business Finance & Accounting, 34*(9–10), 1447–1469.

Margaritis, D., & Psillaki, M. (2010). Capital structure, equity ownership and firm performance. *Journal of Banking & Finance, 34*(3), 621–632. https://doi.org/10.1016/j.jbankfin.2009.08.023

Maria, N. S. B., Susilowati, I., Fathoni, S., & Mafruhah, I. (2021). The effect of education and macroeconomic variables on corruption index in G20 member countries. *Economies, 9*(1). doi:10.3390/economies9010023

Markus, H. R., & Kitayama, S. (1991). Culture and the self: implications for cognition, emotion, and motivation. *Psychological review, 98*(2), 224.

Marquette, H., & Peiffer, C. (2015). Corruption and collective action. *DLP Research Paper*. Retrieved from http://publications.dlprog.org/CorruptionandCollectiveAction.pdf

Marsh, P. (1995). The choice between debt and equity: an empirical study. *Journal of Finance, 37*(1), 121–144.

Masron, T. A., & Subramaniam, Y. (2018). The environmental Kuznets curve in the presence of corruption in developing countries. *Environmental Science and Pollution Research, 25*(13), 12491–12506. doi:10.1007/s11356-018-1473-9

Matemilola, B. T., Bany-Ariffin, A. N., Azman-Saini, W. N. W., & Nassir, A. M. (2018). Does top managers' experience affect firms' capital structure? *Research in International Business and Finance, 45*, 488–498. https://doi.org/10.1016/j.ribaf.2017.07.184

Matsa, D. A. (2010). Capital structure as a strategic variable: evidence from collective bargaining. *The Journal of Finance, 65*(3), 1197–1232. https://doi.org/10.1111/j.1540-6261.2010.01565.x

Matsueda, R. L. (1988). The current state of differential association theory. *Crime & Delinquency, 34*(3), 277–306. doi:10.1177/0011128788034003005

Mauro, P. (1995). Corruption and growth. *The Quarterly Journal of Economics, 110*(3), 681–712.

McCahery, J. A., Sautner, Z., & Starks, L. T. (2016). Behind the scenes: the corporate governance preferences of institutional investors. *The Journal of Finance, 71*(6), 2905–2932.

McChesney, F. S. (1987). Rent extraction and rent creation in the economic theory of regulation. *The Journal of Legal Studies, 16*(1), 101–118.

McConnell, J. J., & Servaes, H. (1990). Additional evidence on equity ownership and corporate value. *Journal of Financial Economics, 27*(2), 595–612. https://doi.org/10.1016/0304-405X(90)90069-C

McCusker, R. (2007). Review of anti-corruption strategies. Australian Institute of Criminology.

McDonald, R. L., & Soderstrom, N. (1986). *Dividend and Share Changes: Is There a Financing Hierarchy?* Cambridge, MA: National Bureau of Economic Research.

McLean, R. D., Zhang, T., & Zhao, M. (2012). Why does the law matter? Investor protection and its effects on investment, finance, and growth. *The Journal of Finance, 67*(1), 313–350.

McQuail, D. (2010). *McQuail's Mass Communication Theory.* Sage Publications.

Means, D. B., Charoenwong, C., & Kang, Y. K. (1992). Changing dividend policies caused by the Tax Reform Act of 1986: an empirical analysis. *Journal of Economics and Finance, 16*(3), 153–160. doi:10.1007/BF02920317

Med bechir, C., & Jouirou, M. (2021). Investment efficiency and corporate governance: evidence from Asian listed firms. *Journal of Sustainable Finance & Investment,* 1–23.

Megginson, W. L., Nash, R. C., & Van Randenborgh, M. (1994). The financial and operating performance of newly privatized firms: an international empirical analysis. *The Journal of Finance, 49*(2), 403–452.

Megginson, W. L., Ullah, B., & Wei, Z. (2014). State ownership, soft-budget constraints, and cash holdings: evidence from China's privatized firms. *Journal of Banking & Finance, 48*(0), 276–291. http://dx.doi.org/10.1016/j.jbankfin.2014.06.011

Mehdi, M., Sahut, J.-M., & Teulon, F. (2017). Do corporate governance and ownership structure impact dividend policy in emerging market during financial crisis? *Journal of Applied*

*Accounting Research, 18*(3), 274–297. doi:10.1108/JAAR-07-2014-0079

Meng, Q. (2013). *Corporate Investment, Financing and Payout Decisions: Evidence from UK Listed Companies.* University of Birmingham.

Menocal, R. A., Taxell, N., Johnsøn, J. S., Schmaljohann, M., Montero, A. G., De Simone, F., Tobias, J. (2015). Why corruption matters: understanding causes, effects and how to address them. *Evidence Paper on Corruption, Department for International Development*, London.

Mensah, Y. M. (2014). An analysis of the effect of culture and religion on perceived corruption in a global context. *Journal of Business Ethics, 121*(2), 255–282. doi:10.1007/s10551-013-1696-0

Méon, P.-G., & Sekkat, K. (2005). Does corruption grease or sand the wheels of growth? *Public Choice, 122*(1), 69–97. doi:10.1007/s11127-005-3988-0

Méon, P.-G., & Weill, L. (2010). Is corruption an efficient grease? *World Development, 38*(3), 244–259. https://doi.org/10.1016/j.worlddev.2009.06.004

Meyer, J. R., & Kuh, E. (1957). *The Investment Decision: An Empirical Study.* Cambridge, MA: Harvard University Press.

Midavaine, J., Dolfsma, W., & Aalbers, R. (2016). Board diversity and R & D investment. *Management Decision, 54*(3), 558–569.

Miljkovic, D., & Rimal, A. (2008). The impact of socio-economic factors on political instability: a cross-country analysis. *The Journal of Socio-Economics, 37*(6), 2454–2463. https://doi.org/10.1016/j.socec.2008.04.007

Miller, A., & Listhaug, O. (1999). Political performance and institutional trust. *Critical Citizens: Global Support for Democratic Government*, 204–216.

Miller, A. H., & Listhaug, O. (1990). Political parties and confidence in government: a comparison of Norway, Sweden and the United States. *British Journal of Political Science, 20*(3), 357–386. doi:10.1017/S0007123400005883

Miller, M. H., & Modigliani, F. (1961). Dividend policy, growth, and the valuation of shares. In H. R. Vane, C. Mulhearn, Harry M. Markowitz, Merton H. Miller, William F. Sharpe, Robert

C. Merton and Myrin S. Scholes (eds), *Elgar Reference Collection. Pioneering Papers of the Nobel Memorial Laureates in Economics*, (Vol. 2, pp. 113–135). Cheltenham, U.K. and Northampton, MA: Edward Elgar.

Miller, M. H., & Rock, K. (1985). Dividend policy under asymmetric information. *Journal of Finance, 40*(4), 1031–1051.

Miller, M. H., & Scholes, M. S. (1982). Dividend and taxes: some empirical evidence. *Journal of Political Economy, 90*(6), 23.

Milliken, F. J., & Martins, L. L. (1996). Searching for common threads: understanding the multiple effects of diversity in organizational groups. *Academy of Management Review, 21*(2), 402–433.

Mills, K., Morling, S., & Tease, W. (1995). The influence of financial factors on corporate investment. *Australian Economic Review, 28*(2), 50–64. https://doi.org/10.1111/j.1467-8462.1995.tb00889.x

Ministry for Europe and Foreign Affairs. (2021). *France's Anti-Corruption Strategy in Its Cooperation Action 2021–2030.* Retrieved from https://www.diplomatie.gouv.fr/IMG/pdf/strategie_anticorruption_de_la_fce_ds_son_aciton_de_coop_en_cle81dc7d.pdf

Mishra, C. S., & McConaughy, D. L. (1999). Founding family control and capital structure: the risk of loss of control and the aversion to debt. *Entrepreneurship Theory and Practice, 23*(4), 53–64. doi:10.1177/104225879902300404

Mocan, N. (2008). What determines corruption? International evidence from microdata. *Economic Inquiry, 46*(4), 493–510. https://doi.org/10.1111/j.1465-7295.2007.00107.x

Modigliani, F., & Miller, M. H. (1958). The cost of capital, corporation finance and the theory of investment. *The American, 1*, 3.

Mohamed, M. R., Kaliappan, S. R., Ismail, N. W., & Azman-Saini, W. N. W. (2015). Effect of foreign aid on corruption: evidence from sub-Saharan African countries. *International Journal of Social Economics, 42*(1), 47–63. doi:10.1108/IJSE-04-2013-0089

Mohtadi, H., & Roe, T. L. (2003). Democracy, rent seeking, public spending and growth. *Journal of Public Economics, 87*(3), 445–466. https://doi.org/10.1016/S0047-2727(01)00135-9

Moidfar, S., & Ahmadi, H. (2011). Political Corruption and political stability.

Mollah, A. S. (2001). *Dividend policy and behaviour, and security price reaction to the announcement of dividends in an emergency market: a study of companies listed on the Dhaka stock exchange* (Thesis Ph.D.). University of Leeds (Business School), Leeds. Retrieved from http://etheses.whiterose.ac.uk/700/

Moradi, A., & Paulet, E. (2019). The firm-specific determinants of capital structure: an empirical analysis of firms before and during the Euro Crisis. *Research in International Business and Finance, 47*, 150–161. https://doi.org/10.1016/j.ribaf.2018.07.007

Morais, F., Serrasqueiro, Z., & Ramalho, J. J. (2022). Capital structure speed of adjustment heterogeneity across zero leverage and leveraged European firms. *Research in International Business and Finance, 62*, 101682.

Morck, R., Shleifer, A., & Vishny, R. W. (1988). Management ownership and market valuation: an empirical analysis. *Journal of Financial Economics, 20*, 293–315.

Morck, R., Yeung, B., & Yu, W. (2000). The information content of stock markets: why do emerging markets have synchronous stock price movements? *Journal of Financial Economics, 58*(1), 215–260. https://doi.org/10.1016/S0304-405X(00)00071-4

Morris, S. D., & Klesner, J. L. (2010). Corruption and trust: theoretical considerations and evidence from Mexico. *Comparative Political Studies, 43*(10), 1258–1285. doi:10.1177/0010414010369072

Muhammad, H., Migliori, S., & Consorti, A. (2022). Corporate governance and R&D investment: does firm size matter? *Technology Analysis & Strategic Management*, 1–15. doi:10.1080/09537325.2022.2042508

Mulier, K., Schoors, K., & Merlevede, B. (2016). Investment-cash flow sensitivity and financial constraints: evidence from unquoted European SMEs. *Journal of Banking & Finance, 73*, 182–197. https://doi.org/10.1016/j.jbankfin.2016.09.002

Mundi, H. S., & Kaur, P. (2022). CEO overconfidence and capital structure decisions: evidence from India. *Vikalpa, 47*(1), 19–37. doi:10.1177/02560909221079270

Murdoch, A. (2009). How much culture is there in corruption? Some thoughts on transformation-cum-collective culture shock in post-communist Poland. *Journal of Intercultural Management, 1*(1), 42–63.

Murphy, K. M., Shleifer, A., & Vishny, R. W. (1993). Why is rent-seeking so costly to growth? *The American economic review, 83*(2), 409–414. Retrieved from www.jstor.org/stable/2117699

Musallam, S. R., & Lin, C. C. P. (2019). An ownership structures and dividend policy: evidence from listed plantation companies in Malaysia. *Management & Accounting Review (MAR), 18*(2), 21–46.

Musila, J. W., & Sigué, S. P. (2010). Corruption and international trade: an empirical investigation of African countries. *World Economy, 33*(1), 129–146.

Myers, S. C. (1977). Determinants of corporate borrowing. *Journal of Financial Economics, 5*(2), 147–175. http://dx.doi.org/10.1016/0304-405X(77)90015-0

Myers, S. C. (1984). *Capital Structure Puzzle*. Cambridge, MA: National Bureau of Economic Research.

Myers, S. C., & Majluf, N. S. (1984). Corporate financing and investment decisions when firms have information that investors do not have. *Journal of Financial Economics, 13*(2), 187–221. http://dx.doi.org/10.1016/0304-405X(84)90023-0

Myers, S. C., & Majluf, N. S. (1984). Stock issues and investment policy when firms have information that investors do not have. *Journal of Financial Economics* (13), 24. http://hdl.handle.net/1721.1/2002

Myers, S. C., & Rajan, R. G. (1998). The paradox of liquidity. *The Quarterly Journal of Economics, 113*(3), 733–771. doi:10.1162/003355398555739

Myerson, R. B. (1993). Effectiveness of electoral systems for reducing government corruption: a game-theoretic analysis. *Games and Economic Behavior, 5*(1), 118–132. https://doi.org/10.1006/game.1993.1006

Myles, G. D., & Yousefi, H. (2015). Corruption and seigniorage. *Journal of Public Economic Theory, 17*(4), 480–503.

Naeem, M., & Khurram, S. (2020). Does a CEO's culture affect dividend policy? *Finance Research Letters, 35*, 101302. https://doi.org/10.1016/j.frl.2019.09.017

Nam, V. H., Nguyen, M. N., Nguyen, D. A., & Luu, H. N. (2020). The impact of corruption on the performance of newly established enterprises: empirical evidence from a transition economy. *Borsa Istanbul Review.* https://doi.org/10.1016/j.bir.2020. 05.006

Neudorfer, B., & Neudorfer, N. S. (2014). Decentralization and political corruption: disaggregating regional authority. *Publius: The Journal of Federalism, 45*(1), 24–50. doi:10.1093/publius/ pju035

Neudorfer, N. S., & Theuerkauf, U. G. (2014). Buying war not peace: the influence of corruption on the risk of ethnic war. *Comparative Political Studies, 47*(13), 1856–1886. doi:10.1177/ 0010414013516919

Newton, L. H., Hodges, L., & Keith, S. (2004). Accountability in the professions: accountability in journalism. *Journal of Mass Media Ethics, 19*(3-4), 166–190. doi:10.1080/08900523.2004. 9679687

Nguyen, L. T., Nguyen, H. T., & Pham, M. H. (2021). Bribe or die: gender differences in entrepreneurship in emerging markets. *Applied Economics, 53*(19), 2170–2191. doi:10.1080/00036846.2020.1856325

Nguyen, N. H., Phan, H. V., & Lee, E. (2020). Shareholder litigation rights and capital structure decisions. *Journal of Corporate Finance, 62*, 101601. https://doi.org/10.1016/j.jcorpfin. 2020.101601

Nguyen, T. T., & Van Dijk, M. A. (2012). Corruption, growth, and governance: private vs. state-owned firms in Vietnam. *Journal of Banking & Finance, 36*(11), 2935–2948

Nguyen, T. V., Bach, T. N., Le, T. Q., & Le, C. Q. (2017). Local governance, corruption, and public service quality: evidence from a national survey in Vietnam. *International Journal of Public Sector Management, 30*(2), 137–153. doi:10.1108/IJPSM-08-2016-0128

Nguyen, X. M., & Tran, Q. T. (2022). Corruption and corporate investment efficiency around the world. *European Journal of Management and Business Economics, 31*(4), 425–438. doi:10.1108/EJMBE-11-2020-0321

Nidar, S., & Sugianti, I. (2020). The effect of life cycle stages on leverage in Indonesian listed companies. *Advances in Business, Management and Entrepreneurship* (pp. 251–255). CRC Press.

Nielsen, S., & Huse, M. (2010). The contribution of women on boards of directors: going beyond the surface. *Corporate Governance: An International Review, 18*(2), 136–148.

Nikoloski, Z., & Mossialos, E. (2013). Corruption, inequality and population perception of healthcare quality in Europe. *BMC Health Services Research, 13*(1), 472. doi:10.1186/1472-6963-13-472

Nishikawa, Y., Hashemi Joo, M., & Parhizgari, A. M. (2021). Languages and dividend policy. *Journal of Behavioral Finance,* 1–19. doi:10.1080/15427560.2021.1913158

Nissim, D., & Ziv, A. (2001). Dividend changes and future profitability. *Journal of Finance, 56*(6), 2111–2133.

Nivorozhkin, E. (2005). Financing choices of firms in EU accession countries. *Emerging Markets Review, 6*(2), 138–169. https://doi.org/10.1016/j.ememar.2004.10.002

Noonan, J. T. (1984). *Bribes: The Intellectual History of a Moral Idea.* Berkeley: The University of California Press and Macmillan Publishing Company.

Nordhaus, W. D. (1975). The political business cycle. *The Review of Economic Studies, 42*(2), 169–190. doi:10.2307/2296528

Norris, P. (2009). *Public Sentinel: News Media and Governance Reform.* World Bank Publications.

North, C. M., Orman, W. H., & Gwin, C. R. (2013). Religion, corruption, and the rule of law. *Journal of Money, Credit and Banking, 45*(5), 757–779. https://doi.org/10.1111/jmcb.12024

O'Toole, C. M., & Tarp, F. (2014). Corruption and the efficiency of capital investment in developing countries. *Journal of International Development, 26*(5), 567–597.

Obydenkova, A. V., & Arpino, B. (2018). Corruption and trust in the European Union and national institutions: changes over the great recession across European states. *JCMS: Journal of Common Market Studies, 56*(3), 594–611.

Oliva, P. (2015). Environmental regulations and corruption: automobile emissions in Mexico city. *Journal of Political Economy, 123*(3), 686–724. doi:10.1086/680936

Olivelle, P. (2012). *King, Governance, and Law in Ancient India: Kautilya's Arthasastra*. Oxford: Oxford University Press.

Onali, E., Galiakhmetova, R., Molyneux, P., & Torluccio, G. (2016). CEO power, government monitoring, and bank dividends. *Journal of Financial Intermediation*, *27*, 89–117. http://dx.doi.org/10.1016/j.jfi.2015.08.001

Ones, D. S., & Viswesvaran, C. (1998). Gender, age, and race differences on overt integrity tests: results across four large-scale job applicant datasets. *Journal of Applied Psychology*, *83*(1), 35.

Opler, T., Pinkowitz, L., Stulz, R., & Williamson, R. (1999). The determinants and implications of corporate cash holdings. *Journal of Financial Economics*, *52*(1), 3–46.

Osei-Assibey, E., Domfeh, K. O., & Danquah, M. (2018). Corruption, institutions and capital flight: evidence from sub-Saharan Africa. *Journal of Economic Studies*, *45*(1), 59–76. doi:10.1108/JES-10-2016-0212

Osma, B. G. (2008). Board independence and real earnings management: the case of R&D expenditure. *Corporate Governance: An International Review*, *16*(2), 116–131. https://doi.org/10.1111/j.1467-8683.2008.00672.x

Ozkan, A. (2001). Determinants of capital structure and adjustment to long run target: evidence from UK company panel data. *Journal of Business Finance & Accounting*, *28*(1–2), 175–198. https://doi.org/10.1111/1468-5957.00370

Özşahin, Ş., & Üçler, G. (2017). The consequences of corruption on inflation in developing countries: evidence from panel cointegration and causality tests. *Economies*, *5*(4), 49.

Paldam, M. (2001). Corruption and religion adding to the economic model. *Kyklos*, *54*(2–3), 383–413. https://doi.org/10.1111/1467-6435.00160

Paldam, M. (2002). The cross-country pattern of corruption: economics, culture and the seesaw dynamics. *European Journal of Political Economy*, *18*(2), 215–240. https://doi.org/10.1016/S0176-2680(02)00078-2

Palvia, A., Vähämaa, E., & Vähämaa, S. (2015). Are female CEOs and chairwomen more conservative and risk averse? Evidence from the banking industry during the financial crisis. *Journal of Business Ethics*, *131*(3), 577–594. doi:10.1007/s10551-014-2288-3

Pan, X., & Tian, G. G. (2020). Political connections and corporate investments: evidence from the recent anti-corruption campaign in China. *Journal of Banking & Finance, 119*, 105108. https://doi.org/10.1016/j.jbankfin.2017.03.005

Pangle, T. L. (1988). *The Laws of Plato.* Chicago: University of Chicago Press.

Papaioannou, G. J., & Savarese, C. M. (1994). Corporate dividend policy response to the Tax Reform Act of 1986. *Financial Management, 23*(1), 56–63. doi:10.2307/3666056

Park, H. (2003). Determinants of corruption: a cross-national analysis. *Multinational Business Review, 11*(2), 29–48. doi:10.1108/1525383X200300010

Pathak, R. D., Naz, R., Rahman, M. H., Smith, R. F. I., & Nayan Agarwal, K. (2009). E-governance to cut corruption in public service delivery: a case study of Fiji. *International Journal of Public Administration, 32*(5), 415–437. doi:10.1080/01900690902799482

Paulo Esperança, J., Matias Gama, A. P., & Azzim Gulamhussen, M. (2003). Corporate debt policy of small firms: an empirical (re)examination. *Journal of Small Business and Enterprise Development, 10*(1), 62–80. doi:10.1108/14626000310461213

Pawlina, G., & Renneboog, L. (2005). Is investment-cash flow sensitivity caused by agency costs or asymmetric information? Evidence from the UK. *European Financial Management, 11*(4), 483–513. https://doi.org/10.1111/j.1354-7798.2005.00294.x

Payne, J. E., & Saunoris, J. W. (2020). Corruption and firm tax evasion in transition economies: results from censored quantile instrumental variables estimation. *Atlantic Economic Journal, 48*(2), 195–206. doi:10.1007/s11293-020-09666-2

Pei, Y., Zhu, Y., & Wang, N. (2021). How do corruption and energy efficiency affect the carbon emission performance of China's industrial sectors? *Environmental Science and Pollution Research, 28*(24), 31403–31420. doi:10.1007/s11356-021-13032-3

Pellegrini, L., & Gerlagh, R. (2004). Corruption's effect on growth and its transmission channels. *Kyklos, 57*(3), 429–456. https://doi.org/10.1111/j.0023-5962.2004.00261.x

Persson, A., Rothstein, B., & Teorell, J. (2013). Why anticorruption reforms fail — systemic corruption as a collective action problem. *Governance, 26*(3), 449–471. https://doi.org/10.1111/j.1468-0491.2012.01604.x

Persson, T., Tabellini, G., & Trebbi, F. (2003). Electoral rules and corruption. *Journal of the European Economic Association, 1*(4), 958–989. doi:10.1162/154247603322493203

Persson, T., & Tabellini, G. E. (2005). *The Economic Effects of Constitutions.* MIT Press.

Peter Smith, G. (2010). What are the capital structure determinants for tax-exempt organizations? *Financial Review, 45*(3), 845–872. https://doi.org/10.1111/j.1540-6288.2010.00274.x

Petersen, M. A., & Rajan, R. G. (1994). The benefits of lending relationships: evidence from small business data. *The Journal of Finance, 49*(1), 3–37. https://doi.org/10.1111/j.1540-6261.1994.tb04418.x

Pettit, R. R. (1977). Taxes, transactions costs and the clientele effect of dividends. *Journal of Financial Economics, 5*(3), 419–436. http://dx.doi.org/10.1016/0304-405X(77)90046-0

Pfaffermayr, M., Stöckl, M., & Winner, H. (2013). Capital structure, corporate taxation and firm age. *Fiscal Studies, 34*(1), 109–135. https://doi.org/10.1111/j.1475-5890.2013.00179.x

Pfeffer, J., & Salancik, G. R. (2003). *The External Control of Organizations: A Resource Dependence Perspective.* Stanford University Press.

Phan, D. H. B., Tran, V. T., & Nguyen, D. T. (2019). Crude oil price uncertainty and corporate investment: new global evidence. *Energy Economics, 77*, 54–65. https://doi.org/10.1016/j.eneco.2018.08.016

Phan, M. H., & Archer, L. (2020). Corruption and SME financing structure: the case of Vietnamese manufacturing. *Journal of Economics and Development, 22*(2), 265–279. doi:10.1108/JED-12-2019-0074

Phung, D. N., & Le, T. P. V. (2013). Foreign ownership, capital structure and firm performance: empirical evidence from Vietnamese listed firms. *IUP Journal of Corporate Governance, 12*(2), 40–58.

Picard, R. G. (1985). *The Press and the Decline of Democracy: The Democratic Socialist Response in Public Policy* (Vol. 4). Greenwood Publishing Group.

Picur, R. D., & Riahi-Belkaoui, A. (2006). The impact of bureaucracy, corruption and tax compliance. *Review of Accounting and Finance, 5*(2), 174–180. doi:10.1108/14757700610668985

Pieroni, L., & d'Agostino, G. (2013). Corruption and the effects of economic freedom. *European Journal of Political Economy, 29*, 54–72. https://doi.org/10.1016/j.ejpoleco.2012.08.002

Pindado, J., & De la Torre, C. (2006). The role of investment, financing and dividend decisions in explaining corporate ownership structure: empirical evidence from Spain. *European Financial Management, 12*(5), 661–687.

Pindado, J., Requejo, I., & de la Torre, C. (2011). Family control and investment–cash flow sensitivity: empirical evidence from the Euro zone. *Journal of Corporate Finance, 17*(5), 1389–1409. https://doi.org/10.1016/j.jcorpfin.2011.07.003

Pindado, J., Requejo, I., & de la Torre, C. (2012). Do family firms use dividend policy as a governance mechanism? Evidence from the Euro zone. *Corporate Governance (Oxford), 20*(5), 413–431. doi:10.1111/j.1467-8683.2012.00921.x

Piplica, D. (2011). Corruption and inflation in transition EU member countries. *Ekonomska misao i praksa*, (2), 469–506.

Podobnik, B., Shao, J., Njavro, D., Ivanov, P. C., & Stanley, H. E. (2008). Influence of corruption on economic growth rate and foreign investment. *The European Physical Journal B, 63*(4), 547–550. doi:10.1140/epjb/e2008-00210-2

Policardo, L., & Carrera, E. J. S. (2018). Corruption causes inequality, or is it the other way around? An empirical investigation for a panel of countries. *Economic Analysis and Policy, 59*, 92–102. https://doi.org/10.1016/j.eap.2018.05.001

Pope, J. (2000). *The Elements of a National Integrity System.* Germany: Transparency International.

Poprawe, M. (2015). On the relationship between corruption and migration: empirical evidence from a gravity model of migration. *Public Choice, 163*(3), 337–354. doi:10.1007/s11127-015-0255-x

Portes, R., & Rey, H. (2005). The determinants of cross-border equity flows. *Journal of International Economics, 65*(2), 269–296. https://doi.org/10.1016/j.jinteco.2004.05.002

Poterba, J. M., & Summers, L. H. (1984). New evidence that taxes affect the valuation of dividends. *Journal of Finance, 39*(5), 1397–1415.

Pucheta-Martínez, M. C., & Bel-Oms, I. (2016). The board of directors and dividend policy: the effect of gender diversity. *Industrial and Corporate Change, 25*(3), 523–547. doi: 10.1093/icc/dtv040

Putnam, R., & Leonardi, R. (1993). *Making Democracy Work: Civic Traditions in Modern Italy.* Princeton, NJ: Princeton University Press.

Pyman, M., Eastwood, S., Hungerford, J., & Elliott, J. (2017). Research comparing 41 national anti-corruption strategies: insights and guidance for leaders. *London: Norton Rose Fulbright, 48,* 5–18.

Pyman, M., Eastwood, S., Hungerford, J., & Elliott, J. (2018). Analysing the anti-corruption approaches of the 26 top-ranked countries: an opportunity for a new generation of strategies. *The Institute for Statecraft.*

Qi, D., Wu, W., & Zhang, H. (2000). Shareholding structure and corporate performance of partially privatized firms: evidence from listed Chinese companies. *Pacific-Basin Finance Journal, 8*(5), 587–610. https://doi.org/10.1016/S0927-538X(00)00013-5

Qian, X., & Sandoval-Hernandez, J. (2016). Corruption distance and foreign direct investment. *Emerging Markets Finance and Trade, 52*(2), 400–419. doi:10.1080/1540496X.2015.1047301

Qing, Y. (2018). *Political Connections and Corporate Dividend Payout: Evidence from the Recent Anti-Corruption Campaign in China.* https://core.ac.uk/display/33573173?source=2

Quah, J. (2017). Anti-corruption agencies in Asia Pacific countries: an evaluation of their performance and challenges. *Transparency International.*

Rahmani, T., Komijani, A., & Fallahi, S. (2012). An examination of the relationship between corruption and inflation tax: a cross-country study. *Journal of Tax Research, 20*(13), 45–70.

Rajan, R. G., & Zingales, L. (1995). What do we know about capital structure? Some evidence from international data. *Journal of Finance, 50*(5), 1421–1460.

Rajesh Kumar, B., & Sujit, K. S. (2018). Determinants of dividends among Indian firms — an empirical study. *Cogent Economics & Finance, 6*(1), 1423895. doi:10.1080/23322039.2018.1423895

Ramjee, A., & Gwatidzo, T. (2012). Dynamics in capital structure determinants in South Africa. *Meditari Accountancy Research, 20*(1), 52–67.

Ramli, N. A., Latan, H., & Solovida, G. T. (2019). Determinants of capital structure and firm financial performance — a PLS-SEM approach: evidence from Malaysia and Indonesia. *The Quarterly Review of Economics and Finance, 71*, 148–160. https://doi.org/10.1016/j.qref.2018.07.001

Rao, S. (2008). Accountability, democracy, and globalization: a study of broadcast journalism in India. *Asian Journal of Communication, 18*(3), 193–206. doi:10.1080/01292980802207041

Rauch, J. E., & Evans, P. B. (2000). Bureaucratic structure and bureaucratic performance in less developed countries. *Journal of Public Economics, 75*(1), 49–71. https://doi.org/10.1016/S0047-2727(99)00044-4

Razafindrakoto, M., & Roubaud, F. (2010). Are international databases on corruption reliable? A comparison of expert opinion surveys and household surveys in sub-Saharan Africa. *World Development, 38*(8), 1057–1069. https://doi.org/10.1016/j.worlddev.2010.02.004

Reinhard, L., & Li, S. (2010). A note on capital structure target adjustment–Indonesian evidence. *International Journal of Managerial Finance.*

Reiss, M. C., & Mitra, K. (1998). The effects of individual difference factors on the acceptability of ethical and unethical workplace behaviors. *Journal of Business Ethics, 17*(14), 1581–1593. doi:10.1023/A:1005742408725

Ren, Y.-S., Ma, C.-Q., Apergis, N., & Sharp, B. (2021). Responses of carbon emissions to corruption across Chinese provinces. *Energy Economics, 98*, 105241. https://doi.org/10.1016/j.eneco.2021.105241

Richardson, S. A. (2003). *Corporate Governance and the Over-Investment of Surplus Cash.* University of Michigan.

Riedel, N., Fuest, C., & Maffini, G. (2010). How does corruption in developing countries affect corporate investment and tax compliance?, Beiträge zur Jahrestagung des Vereins für Socialpolitik 2010: Ökonomie der Familie – Session: Corporate Taxation, No. A17-V1, Verein für Socialpolitik, Frankfurt a. M.

Rijckeghem, C. V., & Weder, B. (1997). Corruption and the rate of temptation: do low wages in the civil service cause corruption? *Journal Issue, 1997,* 73, Washington, D.C.: International Monetary Fund.

Rivas, M. F. (2013). An experiment on corruption and gender. *Bulletin of Economic Research, 65*(1), 10–42. https://doi.org/10.1111/j.1467-8586.2012.00450.x

Robertson, C. J., & Watson, A. (2004). Corruption and change: the impact of foreign direct investment. *Strategic Management Journal, 25*(4), 385–396. https://doi.org/10.1002/smj.382

Rock, M. T. (2009). Corruption and democracy. *The Journal of Development Studies, 45*(1), 55–75. doi:10.1080/00220380802468579

Rock, M. T., & Bonnett, H. (2004). The comparative politics of corruption: accounting for the East Asian paradox in empirical studies of corruption, growth and investment. *World Development, 32*(6), 999–1017. https://doi.org/10.1016/j.worlddev.2003.12.002

Root, H. (1999). The importance of being small. *Center for International Studies Working Paper* (pp. 99–13).

Rose-Ackerman, S. (1997). The political economy of corruption. *Corruption and the Global Economy, 31*(60), 54.

Rose-Ackerman, S. (1999). *Corruption and Government: Causes, Consequences and Reform.* New York: Cambridge University Press.

Rose-Ackerman, S. (2012). International actors and the promises and pitfalls of anti-corruption reform. *U. Pa. J. Int'l L., 34,* 447.

Rose-Ackerman, S., & Palifka, B. J. (2016). *Corruption and Government: Causes, Consequences, and Reform*: Cambridge University Press, New York.

Ross, S. A. (1977). The determination of financial structure: the incentive-signalling approach. *The Bell Journal of Economics*, 23–40.

Roubini, N. (2007). Current market turmoil: non-priceable Knightian 'uncertainty' rather than priceable market 'risk'. *RGE Monitor, 15.*

Roy, A. (2015). Dividend policy, ownership structure and corporate governance: an empirical analysis of Indian firms. *Indian Journal of Corporate Governance, 8*(1), 1–33. doi:10.1177/0974686215574422

Rozeff, M. S. (1982). Growth, beta and agency costs as determinants of dividend payout ratios. *Journal of Financial Research, 5*(3), 249.

Ruegger, D., & King, E. W. (1992). A study of the effect of age and gender upon student business ethics. *Journal of Business Ethics, 11*(3), 179–186. doi:10.1007/BF00871965

Saadi, S., & Chkir, I. (2008). Taxation and dividend policy: new empirical evidence. *Journal of Corporate Ownership and Control, 5*(4), 266–273.

Saha, S., & Ben Ali, M. S. (2017). Corruption and economic development: new evidence from the Middle Eastern and North African countries. *Economic Analysis and Policy, 54*, 83–95. https://doi.org/10.1016/j.eap.2017.02.001

Saha, S., & Gounder, R. (2013). Corruption and economic development nexus: variations across income levels in a non-linear framework. *Economic Modelling, 31*, 70–79. https://doi.org/10.1016/j.econmod.2012.11.012

Saha, S., Gounder, R., & Su, J.-J. (2009). The interaction effect of economic freedom and democracy on corruption: a panel cross-country analysis. *Economics Letters, 105*(2), 173–176. https://doi.org/10.1016/j.econlet.2009.07.010

Saha, S., & Su, J.-J. (2012). Investigating the interaction effect of democracy and economic freedom on corruption: a cross-country quantile regression analysis. *Economic Analysis and Policy, 42*(3), 389–396.

Saif-Alyousfi, A. Y. H., Md-Rus, R., Taufil-Mohd, K. N., Mohd Taib, H., & Shahar, H. K. (2020). Determinants of capital structure:

evidence from Malaysian firms. *Asia-Pacific Journal of Business Administration, 12*(3/4), 283–326. doi:10.1108/APJBA-09-2019-0202

Samimi, A. J., & Abedini, M. (2012). Control of corruption and inflation tax: new evidence from selected developing countries. *Procedia — Social and Behavioral Sciences, 62,* 441–445. https://doi.org/10.1016/j.sbspro.2012.09.072

Samimi, A. J., Abedini, M., & Abdollahi, M. (2012). Corruption and inflation tax in selected developing countries. *Middle-East Journal of Scientific Research, 11*(3), 391–395.

Sanders, D. (1981). *Patterns of Political Instability.* New York: Macmillan.

Sandholtz, W., & Gray, M. M. (2003). International integration and national corruption. *International Organization, 57*(4), 761–800. doi:10.1017/S0020818303574045

Sandholtz, W., & Koetzle, W. (2000). Accounting for corruption: economic structure, democracy, and trade. *International Studies Quarterly, 44*(1), 31–50. doi:10.1111/0020-8833.00147

Sandholtz, W., & Taagepera, R. (2005). Corruption, culture, and communism. *International Review of Sociology, 15*(1), 109–131. doi:10.1080/03906700500038678

Sanjian, A. S. (1994). *The Social Construction of Deviance and the Transition from Communist Rule* (pp. 111–129). New York: Woodrow Wilson Center Press.

Santos, M. S., Moreira, A. C., & Vieira, E. S. (2014). Ownership concentration, contestability, family firms, and capital structure. *Journal of Management & Governance, 18*(4), 1063–1107. doi:10.1007/s10997-013-9272-7

Sardar, Z. (1995). Can small countries survive the future? *Futures, 27*(8), 883–889. https://doi.org/10.1016/0016-3287(95)00052-X

Sarwar, B., & Hassan, M. (2021). Impact of economic policy uncertainty on dividend decision: a moderating role of board financial expertise. *Journal of Public Affairs, 21*(3), e2613. https://doi.org/10.1002/pa.2613

Sawicki, J. (2009). Corporate governance and dividend policy in Southeast Asia pre- and post-crisis. *European Journal of Finance, 15*(2), 211–230. doi:10.1080/13518470802604440

Schellenger, M. H., Wood, D. D., & Tashakori, A. (1989). Board of director composition, shareholder wealth, and dividend policy. *Journal of Management, 15*(3), 457.

Schneider, F. (2015). Does corruption promote emigration?. *IZA World of Labor, 192.* doi: 10.15185/izawol.192

Schneider, F., Hofreither, M. F., & Neck, R. (1989). The consequences of a changing shadow economy for the "official" economy: some empirical results for austria. Paper presented at the *The Political Economy of Progressive Taxation*. Berlin: Heidelberg.

Schöberlein, J. (2020). Anti-corruption agencies in Europe. https:// knowledgehub.transparency.org/assets/uploads/helpdesk/ Overview-of-Anti-Corruption-Agencies-in-Europe_2020_PR. pdf

Schopf, J. C. (2011). Following the money to determine the effects of democracy on corruption: the case of Korea. *Journal of East Asian Studies, 11*(1), 1–39. doi:10.1017/S1598240800006937

Schrand, C. M., & Zechman, S. L. C. (2012). Executive overconfidence and the slippery slope to financial misreporting. *Journal of Accounting and Economics, 53*(1), 311–329. https://doi.org/ 10.1016/j.jacceco.2011.09.001

Schwartz, S. H. (1992). Universals in the content and structure of values: theoretical advances and empirical tests in 20 countries. In M. P. Zanna (ed), *Advances in Experimental Social Psychology* (Vol. 25, pp. 1–65). Academic Press.

Schwartz, S. H. (1994). Are there universal aspects in the structure and contents of human values? *Journal of Social Issues, 50*(4), 19–45.

Schwindt-Bayer, L. A., & Mishler, W. (2005). An integrated model of women's representation. *The Journal of Politics, 67*(2), 407–428.

Scott, W. R. (1995). *Institutions and Organizations* (Vol. 2). Thousand Oaks, CA: Sage.

Sekely, W. S., & Collins, J. M. (1988). Cultural influences on international capital structure. *Journal of International Business Studies, 19*(1), 87–100. doi:10.1057/palgrave.jibs.8490376

Seldadyo, H., & De Haan, J. (2005). The determinants of corruption. *The Economist, 66*, 1–60.

Seleim, A., & Bontis, N. (2009). The relationship between culture and corruption: a cross-national study. *Journal of Intellectual Capital, 10*(1), 165–184. doi:10.1108/14691930910922978

Seligson, M. A. (2002). The impact of corruption on regime legitimacy: a comparative study of four Latin American countries. *The Journal of Politics, 64*(2), 408–433. doi:10.1111/1468-2508.00132

Serfling, M. (2016). Firing costs and capital structure decisions. *The Journal of Finance, 71*(5), 2239–2286. https://doi.org/10.1111/jofi.12403

Serra, D. (2006). Empirical determinants of corruption: a sensitivity analysis. *Public Choice, 126*(1), 225–256. doi:10.1007/s11127-006-0286-4

Setia-Atmaja, L. (2010). Dividend and debt policies of family controlled firms: the impact of board independence. *International Journal of Managerial Finance, 6*(2), 128–142. doi:10.1108/17439131011032059

Setia-Atmaja, L. Y. (2009). Governance mechanisms and firm value: the impact of ownership concentration and dividends. *Corporate Governance, 17*(6), 694–709. doi:10.1111/j.1467-8683.2009.00768.x

Setiawan, D., Bandi, B., Kee Phua, L., & Trinugroho, I. (2016). Ownership structure and dividend policy in Indonesia. *Journal of Asia Business Studies, 10*(3), 230–252. doi:10.1108/JABS-05-2015-0053

Shabbir, G., & Anwar, M. (2007). Determinants of corruption in developing countries. *The Pakistan Development Review, 46*(4), 751–764. Retrieved from http://www.jstor.org/stable/41261194

Shah, A. (2006). Corruption and decentralized public governance. *Handbook of Fiscal Federalism* (p. 478).

Shahab, M. R., Pajooyan, J., & Ghaffari, F. (2015). The effect of corruption on shadow economy: an empirical analysis based on panel data. *International Journal of Business and Development Studies, 7*(1), 85–100. doi:10.22111/ijbds.2015.2202

Shailer, G., & Wang, K. (2015). Government ownership and the cost of debt for Chinese listed corporations. *Emerging Markets Review, 22*, 1–17. http://dx.doi.org/10.1016/j.ememar.2014.11.002

Shao, L., Kwok, C. C. Y., & Guedhami, O. (2010). National culture and dividend policy. *Journal of International Business Studies, 41*(8), 1391–1414. doi:10.1057/jibs.2009.74

Shao, L., Kwok, C. C. Y., & Guedhami, O. (2013). Dividend policy: balancing shareholders' and creditors' interests. *Journal of Financial Research, 36*(1), 43–66. doi:10.1111/j.1475-6803.2013.12002.x

Shao, L., Kwok, C. C. Y., & Zhang, R. (2013). National culture and corporate investment. *Journal of International Business Studies, 44*(7), 745–763. doi:10.1057/jibs.2013.26

Shapira, Z. (1995). *Risk Taking: A Managerial Perspective.* Russell Sage Foundation.

Sharma, C., & Mitra, A. (2015). Corruption, governance and firm performance: evidence from Indian enterprises. *Journal of Policy Modeling, 37*(5), 835–851. https://doi.org/10.1016/j.jpolmod.2015.05.001

Sheel, A. (1994). Determinants of Capital structure choice and empirics on leverage behavior: a comparative analysis of hotel and manufacturing firms. *Hospitality Research Journal, 17*(3), 1–16. doi:10.1177/109634809401700302

Shehu, S. (2016). The hard road of Albania in fighting corruption. Paper presented at the *The Ninth International Congress on Social Sciences and Humanities.*

Sheila, H. (1985). Small is dangerous. *Micro States in a Macro World.* London: Francis Pinter.

Shen, C., & Williamson, J. B. (2005). Corruption, democracy, economic freedom, and state strength: a cross-national analysis. *International Journal of Comparative Sociology, 46*(4), 327–345. doi:10.1177/0020715205059206

Shen, J., Firth, M., & Poon, W. P. H. (2016). Credit expansion, corporate finance and overinvestment: recent evidence from China. *Pacific-Basin Finance Journal, 39*, 16–27. https://doi.org/10.1016/j.pacfin.2016.05.004

Shen, W., & Lin, C. (2009). Firm profitability, state ownership, and top management turnover at the listed firms in China: a behavioral perspective. *Corporate Governance: An International Review, 17*(4), 443–456.

Shin, M., Zhang, B., Zhong, M., & Lee, D. J. (2018). Measuring international uncertainty: the case of Korea. *Economics Letters*, *162*, 22–26.

Shirazi, H. (2012). The effect of corruption on trade volume of selected countries in the Middle East and Latin America (2002–2008). *Quarterly Journal of Quantitative Economics*, *8*(4), 31.

Shleifer, A., & Vishny, R. W. (1986). Large shareholders and corporate control. *Journal of Political Economy*, *94*(3, Part 1), 461–488.

Shleifer, A., & Vishny, R. W. (1993). Corruption. *The Quarterly Journal of Economics*, *108*(3), 599–617. doi:10.2307/2118402

Shleifer, A., & Vishny, R. W. (1997). A survey of corporate governance. *The Journal of Finance*, *52*(2), 737–783.

Short, H., Keasey, K., & Duxbury, D. (2002). Capital structure, management ownership and large external shareholders: a UK analysis. *International Journal of the Economics of Business*, *9*(3), 375–399. doi:10.1080/1357151021000010382

Short, H., Zhang, H., & Keasey, K. (2002). The link between dividend policy and institutional ownership. *Journal of Corporate Finance*, *8*(2), 105–122. http://dx.doi.org/10.1016/S0929-1199(01)00030-X

Shumetie, A., & Watabaji, M. D. (2019). Effect of corruption and political instability on enterprises' innovativeness in Ethiopia: pooled data based. *Journal of Innovation and Entrepreneurship*, *8*(1), 11. doi:10.1186/s13731-019-0107-x

Siermann, C. L. (1998). *Politics, Institutions and The Economic Performance of Nations*. Edward Elgar Publishing.

Sikalidis, A., Bozos, K., Chantziaras, A., & Grose, C. (2022). Influences of family ownership on dividend policy under mandatory dividend rules. *Review of Quantitative Finance and Accounting*, *59*(3), 939–967. doi:10.1007/s11156-022-01064-w

Simintzi, E., Vig, V., & Volpin, P. (2015). Labor protection and leverage. *The Review of Financial Studies*, *28*(2), 561–591. doi:10.1093/rfs/hhu053

Simon, M., & Houghton, S. M. (2003). The relationship between overconfidence and the introduction of risky products: evidence from a field study. *Academy of Management Journal*, *46*(2), 139–149.

Smith, J. D. (2016). US political corruption and firm financial policies. *Journal of Financial Economics, 121*(2), 350–367. https://doi.org/10.1016/j.jfineco.2015.08.021

Sogorb-Mira, F. (2005). How SME uniqueness affects capital structure: evidence from a 1994–1998 Spanish data panel. *Small Business Economics, 25*(5), 447–457. Retrieved from http://www.jstor.org/stable/40229446

Solé-Ollé, A., & Sorribas-Navarro, P. (2014). Does corruption erode trust in government. *Evidence from a Recent Surge of Local Scandals in Spain, Document de Treball de l'IEB, 26.*

Sommer, U., Bloom, P. B.-N., & Arikan, G. (2013). Does faith limit immorality? The politics of religion and corruption. *Democratization, 20*(2), 287–309. doi:10.1080/13510347.2011.650914

Sousa, L. D. (2010). Anti-corruption agencies: between empowerment and irrelevance. *Crime, Law and Social Change, 53*(1), 5–22. doi:10.1007/s10611-009-9211-3

Spitsin, V., Vukovic, D. B., Spitsina, L., & Özer, M. (2022). The impact of high-tech companies' performance and growth on capital structure. *Competitiveness Review: An International Business Journal incorporating Journal of Global Competitiveness* (Vol. 32, pp. 975–994). Emerald Group Publishing Limited. doi:10.1108/CR-03-2021-0042

Srinivasan, T. N. (1986). The costs and benefits of being a small, remote, island, landlocked, or mini-state economy. *The World Bank Research Observer, 1*(2), 205–218. doi:10.1093/wbro/1.2.205

Stensöta, H., Wängnerud, L., & Svensson, R. (2015). Gender and corruption: the mediating power of institutional logics. *Governance, 28*(4), 475–496. https://doi.org/10.1111/gove.12120

Stephen P. Ferris, Nilanjan Sen, & Ho Pei Yui. (2006). God save the queen and her dividends: corporate payouts in the United Kingdom. *The Journal of Business, 79*(3), 1149–1173. doi:10.1086/500672

Stiglitz, J. E. (1985). Credit markets and the control of capital. *Journal of Money, Credit and Banking, 17*(2), 133–152.

Stiglitz, J. E., & Weiss, A. (1981). Credit rationing in markets with imperfect information. *The American Economic Review, 71*(3), 393–410.

Stoke, D. (1962). Popular evaluations of government. *Ethics and Bigness.* New York: Harper.

Strebulaev, I. A. (2007). Do tests of capital structure theory mean what they say? *The Journal of Finance, 62*(4), 1747–1787. https://doi.org/10.1111/j.1540-6261.2007.01256.x

Stulz, R. (1990). Managerial discretion and optimal financing policies. *Journal of Financial Economics, 26*(1), 3–27. http://dx.doi.org/10.1016/0304-405X(90)90011-N

Stulz, R. M. (2005). The limits of financial globalization. *The Journal of Finance, 60*(4), 1595–1638.

Su, L. D. (2010). Ownership structure, corporate diversification and capital structure. *Management Decision, 48*(2), 314–339. doi:10.1108/00251741011022644

Subramaniam, V., Tang, T. T., Yue, H., & Zhou, X. (2011). Firm structure and corporate cash holdings. *Journal of Corporate Finance, 17*(3), 759–773. https://doi.org/10.1016/j.jcorpfin.2010.06.002

Sulemana, I., & Kpienbaareh, D. (2020). Corruption and air pollution: a comparative study of African and OECD countries. *Air Quality, Atmosphere & Health, 13*(12), 1421–1429. doi:10.1007/s11869-020-00896-6

Sulitzeanu-Kenan, R., Tepe, M., & Yair, O. (2021). Public sector honesty and corruption: field evidence from 40 countries. *Journal of Public Administration Research and Theory.* doi:10.1093/jopart/muab033

Sun, J., Ding, L., Guo, J. M., & Li, Y. (2016). Ownership, capital structure and financing decision: evidence from the UK. *The British Accounting Review, 48*(4), 448–463. https://doi.org/10.1016/j.bar.2015.04.001

Sung, H.-E. (2003). Fairer sex or fairer system? Gender and corruption revisited. *Social Forces, 82*(2), 703–723. doi:10.1353/sof.2004.0028

Sung, H. E. (2004). Democracy and political corruption: a cross-national comparison. *Crime, Law and Social Change, 41*(2), 179–193. doi:10.1023/B:CRIS.0000016225.75792.02

Suryadarma, D. (2012). How corruption diminishes the effectiveness of public spending on education in Indonesia. *Bulletin of Indonesian Economic Studies, 48*(1), 85–100. doi:10.1080/00074918.2012.654485

Sutherland, E. H., Cressey, D. R., & Luckenbill, D. F. (1992). *Principles of Criminology*. Altamira Press.

Svensson, J. (2003). Who must pay bribes and how much? evidence from a cross-section of firms. *Quarterly Journal of Economics, 118*.

Svensson, J. (2005). Eight questions about corruption. *Journal of Economic Perspectives, 19*(3), 19–42. doi:10.1257/0895330057 74357860

Swaleheen, M. U. (2007). Corruption and investment choices: a panel data study. *Kyklos, 60*(4), 601–616. https://doi.org/10.1111/j. 1467-6435.2007.00387.x

Swamy, A., Knack, S., Lee, Y., & Azfar, O. (2001). Gender and corruption. *Journal of Development Economics, 64*(1), 25–55. https://doi.org/10.1016/S0304-3878(00)00123-1

Tahir, M., Ibrahim, H., Zulkafli, A. H., & Mushtaq, M. (2020). Corruption, national culture, law and dividend repatriation policy. *Journal of Multinational Financial Management, 57–58*, 100658. https://doi.org/10.1016/j.mulfin.2020.100658

Tanzi, M. V. (1994). *Corruption, Governmental Activities, and Markets*. International Monetary Fund.

Tanzi, V. (1998). Corruption around the world: causes, consequences, scope, and cures. *Staff Papers, 45*(4), 559–594. doi:10.2307/3867585

Tanzi, V., & Davoodi, H. (1998). Corruption, public investment, and growth. Paper presented at the *The Welfare State, Public Investment, and Growth*, Tokyo.

Tarus, D. K., & Ayabei, E. (2016). Board composition and capital structure: evidence from Kenya. *Management Research Review, 39*(9), 1056–1079. doi:10.1108/MRR-01-2015-0019

Tavares, J. (2003). Does foreign aid corrupt? *Economics Letters, 79*(1), 99–106. https://doi.org/10.1016/S0165-1765(02) 00293-8

Tekeş, B., Üzümcüoğlu, Y., Hoe, C., & Özkan, T. (2019). The relationship between Hofstede's cultural dimensions, Schwartz's cultural values, and obesity. *Psychological Reports, 122*(3), 968–987.

Terracino, J. B. (2012). *The International Legal Framework Against Corruption: States' Obligations to Prevent and Repress Corruption.* Intersentia.

Thakur, B. P. S., & Kannadhasan, M. (2019). Corruption and cash holdings: evidence from emerging market economies. *Emerging Markets Review, 38*, 1–17. https://doi.org/10.1016/j.ememar.2018.11.008

Thanatawee, Y. (2011). Life-Cycle theory and free cash flow hypothesis: evidence from dividend policy in Thailand. *International Journal of Financial Research, 2*(2). doi:10.5430/ijfr.v2n2p52

The White House (2021). *United States Strategy on Countering Corruption.* Retrieved from Washington.

Thede, S., & Gustafson, N. Å. (2012). The multifaceted impact of corruption on international trade. *The World Economy, 35*(5), 651–666.

Thompson, E. K., & Adasi Manu, S. (2021). The impact of board composition on the dividend policy of US firms. *Corporate Governance: The International Journal of Business in Society, 21*(5), 737–753. doi:10.1108/CG-05-2020-0182

Thomsen, S., & Pedersen, T. (2000). Ownership structure and economic performance in the largest European companies. *Strategic Management Journal, 21*(6), 689–705. https://doi.org/10.1002/(SICI)1097-0266(200006)21:6<689::AID-SMJ115>3.0.CO;2-Y

Titman, S., & Wessels, R. (1988). The determinants of capital structure choice. *Journal of Finance, 43*(1), 1–19.

Tobin, J. (1969). A general equilibrium approach to monetary theory. *Journal of Money, Credit and Banking, 1*(1), 15–29.

Tong, W. (2014). Analysis of corruption from sociocultural perspectives. *International Journal of Business and Social Science, 5*(11).

Topchii, V., Zadereiko, S., Didkivska, G., Bodunova, O., & Shevchenko, D. (2021). International anti-corruption standards. *Baltic Journal of Economic Studies, 7*(5), 277–286.

Torgler, B., & Valev, N. T. (2006). Corruption and Age. *Journal of Bioeconomics, 8*(2), 133–145. doi:10.1007/s10818-006-9003-0

Tran, D. V. (2020). Economic policy uncertainty and bank dividend policy. *International Review of Economics, 67*(3), 339–361. doi:10.1007/s12232-020-00344-y

Tran, H. T. (2019). Institutional quality and market selection in the transition to market economy. *Journal of Business Venturing*, *34*(5), 105890. https://doi.org/10.1016/j.jbusvent.2018.07.001

Tran, Q. T. (2019a). Corporate cash holdings and financial crisis: new evidence from an emerging market. *Eurasian Business Review*, *10*(2), 271–285. doi:10.1007/s40821-019-00134-9

Tran, Q. T. (2019b). Corruption, agency costs and dividend policy: international evidence. *The Quarterly Review of Economics and Finance*, *76*, 325–334. https://doi.org/10.1016/j.qref.2019.09.010

Tran, Q. T. (2019c). Creditors and dividend policy: reputation building versus debt covenant. *European Research on Management and Business Economics*, *25*(3), 114–121. https://doi.org/10.1016/j.iedeen.2019.06.001

Tran, Q. T. (2019d). Economic policy uncertainty and corporate risk-taking: international evidence. *Journal of Multinational Financial Management*, *52–53*, 100605. https://doi.org/10.1016/j.mulfin.2019.100605

Tran, Q. T. (2019e). Independent directors and corporate investment: evidence from an emerging market. *Journal of Economics Development*, *21*(1), 30–41.

Tran, Q. T. (2020a). Corruption and corporate cash holdings: international evidence. *Journal of Multinational Financial Management*, *54*, 100611. https://doi.org/10.1016/j.mulfin.2019.100611

Tran, Q. T. (2020b). Creditor protection, shareholder protection and investment efficiency: new evidence. *The North American Journal of Economics and Finance*, *52*, 101170. https://doi.org/10.1016/j.najef.2020.101170

Tran, Q. T. (2020c). Foreign ownership and investment efficiency: new evidence from an emerging market. *International Journal of Emerging Markets*, *15*(6), 1185–1199. doi:10.1108/IJOEM-07-2019-0573

Tran, Q. T. (2021a). Economic policy uncertainty and cost of debt financing: international evidence. *The North American Journal of Economics and Finance*, *57*, 101419. https://doi.org/10.1016/j.najef.2021.101419

Tran, Q. T. (2021b). Local corruption and dividend policy: evidence from Vietnam. *Economic Analysis and Policy*, *70*, 195–205. https://doi.org/10.1016/j.eap.2021.02.011

Tran, Q. T. (2022). Corruption and corporate risk-taking: evidence from emerging markets. *International Journal of Emerging Markets, 17*(5), 1238–1255. doi:10.1108/IJOEM-08-2019-0602

Tran, Q. T., Alphonse, P., & Nguyen, X. M. (2017). Dividend policy: shareholder rights and creditor rights under the impact of the global financial crisis. *Economic Modelling, 64*, 502–512. https://doi.org/10.1016/j.econmod.2017.03.010

Transparency International (2011). *National Integrity System Background Rationale and Methodology.* Berlin.

Trantidis, A. (2016). Is government contestability an integral part of the definition of democracy? *Politics, 37*(1), 67–81. doi:10.1177/0263395715619635

Treisman, D. (2000). The causes of corruption: a cross-national study. *Journal of Public Economics, 76*(3), 399–457. https://doi.org/10.1016/S0047-2727(99)00092-4

Truex, R. (2011). Corruption, attitudes, and education: survey evidence from Nepal. *World Development, 39*(7), 1133–1142. https://doi.org/10.1016/j.worlddev.2010.11.003

Tucker, A. W. (1950). A two-person dilemma. *Prisoner's Dilemma.*

Tunali, C. B., & Weill, L. (2020). Is corruption a greater evil than sin? *Review of Business, 40*(2).

Ucar, E. (2019). Creative culture, risk-taking, and corporate financial decisions. *European Financial Management, 25*(3), 684–717. https://doi.org/10.1111/eufm.12198

UK Home Office (2017). *UK Anti-Corruption Strategy 2017 to 2022.* Retrieved from London.

Ullah, I., Fang, H.-X., Ur Rahman, M., & Iqbal, A. (2022). CEO military background and investment efficiency. *Emerging Markets Finance and Trade, 58*(4), 1089–1102. doi:10.1080/1540496X.2021.1937115

Ullah, I., Majeed, M. A., & Fang, H.-X. (2021). Female CEOs and corporate investment efficiency: evidence from China. *Borsa Istanbul Review, 21*(2), 161–174.

Ullah, I., Majeed, M. A., Fang, H.-X., & Khan, M. A. (2020). Female CEOs and investment efficiency: evidence from an emerging economy. *Pacific Accounting Review, 32*(4), 443–474. doi:10.1108/PAR-08-2019-0099

Ullah, I., Zeb, A., Khan, M. A., & Xiao, W. (2020). Board diversity and investment efficiency: evidence from China. *Corporate Governance: The International Journal of Business in Society, 20*(6), 1105–1134. doi:10.1108/CG-01-2020-0001

Ullah, M. A., & Ahmad, E. (2016). Inequality and corruption: evidence from panel data. *Forman Journal of Economic Studies, 12.*

Umutlu, M. (2010). Firm leverage and investment decisions in an emerging market. *Quality & Quantity, 44*(5), 1005–1013.

United Nations Pacific Regional Anti-Corruption. (2020). The role of non-state actors and citizens in corruption prevention in the pacific. Retrieved from https://www.unodc.org/documents/southeastasiaandpacific/pacific/2020/UN-PRAC_Paper_-_Role_of_non-State_Actors_and_Citizens_in_Corruption_Prevention_in_the_Pacific.pdf

UNODC (2021). University module series on anti-corruption. Retrieved from https://www.unodc.org/e4j/en/anti-corruption/module-4/index.html

Urch, E. J. (1929). The law code of Hammurabi. *ABAJ, 15*, 437.

Uslaner, E. M. (2010). Tax evasion, corruption, and the social contract in transition. *Developing Alternative Frameworks for Explaining Tax Compliance, 59*, 174.

Uslaner, E. M., & Rothstein, B. (2016). The historical roots of corruption: state building, economic inequality, and mass education. *Comparative Politics, 48*(2), 227–248.

Utami, S. R., & Inanga, E. L. (2011). Agency costs of free cash flow, dividend policy, and leverage of firms in Indonesia. *European Journal of Economics, Finance and Administrative Sciences*, (33), 7–24. Retrieved from http://www.scopus.com/inward/record.url?eid=2-s2.0-79959724695&partnerID=40&md5=83185818f68fcc36238ddf0b49511d9f

Vakilifard, H. R., Gerayli, M. S., Yanesari, A. M., & Ma'atoofi, A. R. (2011). Effect of corporate governance on capital structure: case of the Iranian listed firms. *European Journal of Economics, Finance and Administrative Sciences, 35*, 165–172.

Vian, T. (2020). Corruption and administration in healthcare. In *Handbook on Corruption, Ethics and Integrity in Public Administration* (pp. 115–128). MA: Edward Elgar Publishing.

Victor, B., & Cullen, J. B. (1988). The organizational bases of ethical work climates. *Administrative Science Quarterly*, 101–125.

Villoria, M., Van Ryzin, G. G., & Lavena, C. F. (2013). Social and political consequences of administrative corruption: a study of public perceptions in Spain. *Public Administration Review*, *73*(1), 85–94.

Virta, H. (2010). The linkage between corruption and shadow economy size: does geography matter? *International Journal of Development Issues*, *9*(1), 4–24. doi:10.1108/144689510 11033770

Vitell, S. J., Nwachukwu, S. L., & Barnes, J. H. (1993). The effects of culture on ethical decision-making: an application of Hofstede's typology. *Journal of Business Ethics*, *12*(10), 753–760. doi:10.1007/BF00881307

Vo, X. V. (2019). Leverage and corporate investment — evidence from Vietnam. *Finance Research Letters*, *28*, 1–5. https://doi.org/10.1016/j.frl.2018.03.005

von Eije, H., & Megginson, W. L. (2008). Dividends and share repurchases in the European Union. *Journal of Financial Economics*, *89*(2), 347–374. http://dx.doi.org/10.1016/j.jfineco.2007.11.002

Voyer, P. A., & Beamish, P. W. (2004). The effect of corruption on Japanese foreign direct investment. *Journal of Business Ethics*, *50*(3), 211–224. doi:10.1023/B:BUSI.0000024737.57926.bf

Waisman, M., Ye, P., & Zhu, Y. (2015). The effect of political uncertainty on the cost of corporate debt. *Journal of Financial Stability*, *16*, 106–117. https://doi.org/10.1016/j.jfs.2015.01.002

Wang, X., Manry, D., & Wandler, S. (2011). The impact of government ownership on dividend policy in China. *Advances in Accounting*, *27*(2), 366–372. http://dx.doi.org/10.1016/j.adiac.2011.08.003

Wang, Y., Chen, C. R., & Huang, Y. S. (2014). Economic policy uncertainty and corporate investment: evidence from China. *Pacific-Basin Finance Journal*, *26*, 227–243. https://doi.org/10.1016/j.pacfin.2013.12.008

Wang, Y., Wei, Y., & Song, F. M. (2017). Uncertainty and corporate R&D investment: evidence from Chinese listed firms. *International Review of Economics & Finance*, *47*, 176–200. https://doi.org/10.1016/j.iref.2016.10.004

Wang, Y., & You, J. (2012). Corruption and firm growth: evidence from China. *China Economic Review, 23*(2), 415–433.

Weaver, D. H. (1977). The press and government restriction: a cross-national study over time. *Gazette (Leiden, Netherlands), 23*(3), 152–169. doi:10.1177/001654927702300301

Wedeman, A. (2003). Development and corruption: the East Asian paradox. In *Political Business in East Asia* (pp. 50–77). Routledge.

Wei, F., & Kong, Y. (2017). Corruption, financial development and capital structure: evidence from China. *China Finance Review International, 7*(3), 295–322. doi:10.1108/CFRI-10-2016-0116

Wei, J. G., Zhang, W., & Xiao, J. Z. (2004). Dividend payment and ownership structure in China. *Advances in Financial Economics, 9*, 22. doi:10.1016/S1569-3732(04)09008-5

Wei, S.-J. (2000a). How taxing is corruption on international investors? *The Review of Economics and Statistics, 82*(1), 1–11. doi:10.1162/003465300558533

Wei, S.-J. (2000b). *Natural Openness and Good Government.* Cambridge, MA: National Bureau of Economic Research.

Wei, S.-J., & Kaufmann, D. (1999). *Does Grease Money Speed up the Wheels of Commerce?* The World Bank.

Weill, L. (2011). How corruption affects bank lending in Russia. *Economic Systems, 35*(2), 230–243. https://doi.org/10.1016/j.ecosys.2010.05.005

Wen, Y., Rwegasira, K., & Bilderbeek, J. (2002). Corporate governance and capital structure decisions of the Chinese listed firms. *Corporate Governance: An International Review, 10*(2), 75–83. https://doi.org/10.1111/1467-8683.00271

Weston, J. F., & Brigham, E. F. (1979). *Managerial Finance* (7th edn). Dryden Press.

Williams, K., & O'Reilly, C. (1998). The complexity of diversity: a review of forty years of research. *Research in Organizational Behavior, 21*, 77–140.

Williamson, O. E. (2000). The new institutional economics: taking stock, looking ahead. *Journal of Economic Literature, 38*(3), 595–613.

Wiwattanakantang, Y. (1999). An empirical study on the determinants of the capital structure of Thai firms. *Pacific-Basin Finance Journal*, *7*(3), 371–403. https://doi.org/10.1016/S0927-538X(99)00007-4

World Bank (1997). *Helping Countries Combat Corruption: The Role of the World Bank* (pp. 1–69). World Bank Washington, D.C.

Wu, H., Li, S., Ying, S. X., & Chen, X. (2018). Politically connected CEOs, firm performance, and CEO pay. *Journal of Business Research*, *91*, 169–180. https://doi.org/10.1016/j.jbusres.2018.06.003

Wu, K., & Liu, J. (2022). Purifying political ecology: how anti-corruption campaign affects capital structure decisions? Available at SSRN 4067819.

Wu, L., & Yue, H. (2009). Corporate tax, capital structure, and the accessibility of bank loans: evidence from China. *Journal of Banking & Finance*, *33*(1), 30–38. https://doi.org/10.1016/j.jbankfin.2006.10.030

Wu, S.-Y. (2006). Corruption and cross-border investment by multinational firms. *Journal of Comparative Economics*, *34*(4), 839–856. https://doi.org/10.1016/j.jce.2006.08.007

Xiao, G. (2013). Legal shareholder protection and corporate R&D investment. *Journal of Corporate Finance*, *23*, 240–266.

Xie, J., & Zhang, Y. (2020). Anti-corruption, government intervention, and corporate cash holdings: evidence from China. *Economic Systems*, *44*(1), 100745. https://doi.org/10.1016/j.ecosys.2020.100745

Xu, G., & Yano, G. (2017). How does anti-corruption affect corporate innovation? Evidence from recent anti-corruption efforts in China. *Journal of Comparative Economics*, *45*(3), 498–519. https://doi.org/10.1016/j.jce.2016.10.001

Xu, G., Zhang, D., & Yano, G. (2017). Can corruption really function as "protection money" and "grease money"? Evidence from Chinese firms. *Economic Systems*, *41*(4), 622–638.

Xu, X., & Li, Y. (2018). Local corruption and corporate cash holdings: sheltering assets or agency conflict? *China Journal of Accounting Research*, *11*(4), 307–324. https://doi.org/10.1016/j.cjar.2018.05.001

Xu, X., Li, Y., Liu, X., & Gan, W. (2017). Does religion matter to corruption? Evidence from China. *China Economic Review, 42,* 34–49. https://doi.org/10.1016/j.chieco.2016.11.005

Xu, X., & Wang, Y. (1997). *Ownership Structure, Corporate Governance, and Corporate Performance: The Case of Chinese Stock Companies* (Vol. 1794). World Bank Publications.

Yakubu, I. N., Kapusuzoglu, A., & Ceylan, N. B. (2021). Trade-off theory versus pecking order theory: the determinants of capital structure decisions for the ghanaian listed firms. In H. Dinçer & S. Yüksel (eds), *Strategic Outlook in Business and Finance Innovation: Multidimensional Policies for Emerging Economies* (pp. 111–122). Emerald Publishing Limited.

Yan, Y., Xu, X., & Lai, J. (2021). Does Confucian culture influence corporate R&D investment? Evidence from Chinese private firms. *Finance Research Letters, 40,* 101719. https://doi.org/10.1016/j.frl.2020.101719

Yang, Y., Yang, X., & Tang, D. (2020). The dynamic relationship between regional corruption and carbon emissions in China. *Clean Technologies and Environmental Policy.* doi:10.1007/s10098-020-01965-1

Yartey, C. A. (2009). The stock market and the financing of corporate growth in Africa: the case of Ghana. *Emerging Markets Finance and Trade, 45*(4), 53–68. doi:10.2753/REE1540-496X450404

Yeganeh, H. (2014). Culture and corruption: a concurrent application of Hofstede's, Schwartz's and Inglehart's frameworks. *International Journal of Development Issues, 13*(1), 2–24. doi:10.1108/IJDI-04-2013-0038

Yensu, J., & Adusei, C. (2016). Dividend policy decision across African countries. *International Journal of Economics and Finance, 8*(6), 63–77.

Yoon, K. H., & Ratti, R. A. (2011). Energy price uncertainty, energy intensity and firm investment. *Energy Economics, 33*(1), 67–78. https://doi.org/10.1016/j.eneco.2010.04.011

Yu, D. D., & Aquino, R. Q. (2009). Testing capital structure models on Philippine listed firms. *Applied Economics, 41*(15), 1973–1990. doi:10.1080/00036840601131805

Zacharias, N. A., Six, B., Schiereck, D., & Stock, R. M. (2015). CEO influences on firms' strategic actions: a comparison of

CEO-, firm-, and industry-level effects. *Journal of Business Research, 68*(11), 2338–2346. http://dx.doi.org/10.1016/j.jbusres.2015.03.045

Zakaria, M. (2009). Openness and corruption: a time-series analysis. *Zagreb International Review of Economics and Business, 12*(2), 1–14.

Zakharov, N. (2018). Does corruption hinder investment? Evidence from Russian regions. *European Journal of Political Economy, 56*, 39–61. https://doi.org/10.1016/j.ejpoleco.2018.06.005

Zeitun, R., & Goaied, M. (2021). The nonlinear effect of foreign ownership on capital structure in Japan: a panel threshold analysis. *Pacific-Basin Finance Journal, 68*, 101594. https://doi.org/10.1016/j.pacfin.2021.101594

Zelekha, Y., & Sharabi, E. (2012). Corruption, institutions and trade. *Economics of Governance, 13*(2), 169–192. doi:10.1007/s10101-012-0109-7

Zeng, S., & Wang, L. (2015). CEO gender and corporate cash holdings. Are female CEOs more conservative? *Asia-Pacific Journal of Accounting & Economics, 22*(4), 449–474. doi:10.1080/16081625.2014.1003568

Zhang, G., Han, J., Pan, Z., & Huang, H. (2015). Economic policy uncertainty and capital structure choice: evidence from China. *Economic Systems, 39*(3), 439–457. https://doi.org/10.1016/j.ecosys.2015.06.003

Zhang, H. (2008). Corporate governance and dividend policy: a comparison of Chinese firms listed in Hong Kong and in the Mainland. *China Economic Review, 19*(3), 437–459. http://dx.doi.org/10.1016/j.chieco.2008.01.001

Zhang, H., An, R., & Zhong, Q. (2019). Anti-corruption, government subsidies, and investment efficiency. *China Journal of Accounting Research, 12*(1), 113–133. https://doi.org/10.1016/j.cjar.2018.12.001

Zhang, M., Zhang, W., & Zhang, S. (2016). National culture and firm investment efficiency: international evidence. *Asia-Pacific Journal of Accounting & Economics, 23*(1), 1–21. doi:10.1080/16081625.2015.1027714

Zhang, Y., & Kim, M.-H. (2017). Do public corruption convictions influence citizens' trust in government? The answer might not be a simple yes or no. *The American Review of Public Administration, 48*(7), 685–698. doi:10.1177/0275074017728792

Zhang, Y.-J., Jin, Y.-L., Chevallier, J., & Shen, B. (2016). The effect of corruption on carbon dioxide emissions in APEC countries: a panel quantile regression analysis. *Technological Forecasting and Social Change, 112*, 220–227. https://doi.org/10.1016/j.techfore.2016.05.027

Zhao, J. H., Kim, S. H., & Du, J. (2003). The impact of corruption and transparency on foreign direct investment: an empirical analysis. *MIR: Management International Review, 43*(1), 41–62. Retrieved from http://www.jstor.org/stable/40835633

Zhao, X., & Xu, H. D. (2015). E-government and corruption: a longitudinal analysis of countries. *International Journal of Public Administration, 38*(6), 410–421. doi:10.1080/01900692.2014.942736

Zheng, B., & Xiao, J. (2020). Corruption and investment: theory and evidence from China. *Journal of Economic Behavior & Organization, 175*, 40–54. https://doi.org/10.1016/j.jebo.2020.03.018

Zheng, Y. (2016). The impact of E-participation on corruption: a cross-country analysis. *International Review of Public Administration, 21*(2), 91–103. doi:10.1080/12294659.2016.1186457

Zimmerman, J. L. (1983). Taxes and firm size. *Journal of Accounting and Economics, 5*, 119–149. https://doi.org/10.1016/0165-4101(83)90008-3

Zingales, L. (1995). What determines the value of corporate votes? *The Quarterly Journal of Economics, 110*(4), 1047–1073.

Zinn, J. O. (2009). *Social Theories of Risk and Uncertainty: An Introduction*. Malden: John Wiley & Sons.

Zou, H., & Xiao, J. Z. (2006). The financing behaviour of listed Chinese firms. *The British Accounting Review, 38*(3), 239–258. http://dx.doi.org/10.1016/j.bar.2006.04.008

Zúñiga, N. (2017). Harmful rents and rent-seeking. *U4 Helpdesk Answer, 12*.

# Index

Printed in the USA
CPSIA information can be obtained
at www.ICGtesting.com
JSHW012106301023
51026JS00003B/19